ACTA UNIVERSITATIS GOTHOBURGENSIS

GOTHENBURG STUDIES IN ENGLISH 36

JOYCE CARY'S "HARD CONCEPTUAL LABOUR"

A STRUCTURAL ANALYSIS OF TO BE A PILGRIM

BY
INGVAR SÖDERSKOG

ACTA UNIVERSITATIS GOTHOBURGENSIS
GÖTEBORG SWEDEN

© Ingvar Söderskog
ISBN 91-7346-032-X
ISSN 0072-503X

Distributors:
ACTA UNIVERSITATIS GOTHOBURGENSIS
Box 5096
S-402 22 Göteborg 5
Sweden

Printed in Sweden by Gotab, Kungälv 1977

CONTENTS

"General theme is form and content."

. . .

"Form only has value as expression and fortification
of content. But they are one."

Joyce Cary

(Excerpts from a working note-book on <u>To be a Pilgrim</u>)

PREFACE

Since Joyce Cary's death in 1957 his novels have attracted a great deal
of critical attention but still there are very few studies of his narrative technique. Thus, as late as 1971, Giles Mitchell pointed out:

> There is a growing body of Cary criticism but most of it does
> Cary the disservice of being enthusiastic without being care-
> fully analytical. Most of these works deal with Cary's ideas
> and his characters without reference to technical matters of
> language and structure. There are only four works in existence
> which attempt to deal with these matters in detail.[1]

Unfortunately Mitchell does not say what works he is thinking of. To my
knowledge no writer on Cary has examined his narrative technique on the
strictly formal lines laid down by Wayne C. Booth in The Rhetoric of
Fiction apart from Jack Wolkenfeld who, in Joyce Cary, The Developing
Style, examines both "manner" and "matter". In my view, however, Dr.
Wolkenfeld's survey of Cary's "style" has not been grounded in thorough
analysis of the individual novels and therefore suffers from generali-
zations that are too sweeping to do justice to the particularity of his
art. My motive behind writing a thesis on a single novel is the belief
that it might satisfy a need that, so far, has been left unsupplied. As
early as 1958 Marjorie Ryan called for an analysis of The Horse's Mouth,
in her view the "most ambitious" of Cary's "picaresque" novels, because
she thought that it might "show that Cary, though not a flawless novelist
and not an innovator, is more of a craftsman than the popular critics
would have us believe."[2] Although, undoubtedly, The Horse's Mouth is one
of the author's very best novels, I consider To be a Pilgrim more representative of his fiction. It is my belief that an analysis of the latter
novel will equally well support a view of Cary's craftsmanship that, as
far as I can see, Mrs. Ryan has been the first and, perhaps, the only
one to advance.

As in my analysis I have allowed no room for discussing the author's
ideas and critical opinion, I have tried to make up for these omissions
by supplying an introductory part. In chapter 1 of this part I discuss
his philosophy of life and art theory. In chapter 3 I consider some aspects
of To be a Pilgrim in the light of the criticism that it has been the
object of.

Like the other books of his first trilogy To be a Pilgrim is narrated
in the first person. My analysis therefore begins with an examination
of what is sometimes called the epic situation, i.e. the fictitious
speaker's position in time and space and other aspects in which the
verisimilitude of his autonomy should be considered. Throughout my
study this "situation" remains a crucial point because it is tied up
with the author's relation to his narrating "I".

I am indebted to many critics who have written about Cary. Particular
mention must be made of Professor Barbara Hardy of Birkbeck College,
University of London, who was appointed by the Faculty of Arts to
criticize my thesis when it was publicly discussed in the English
Department of the University of Göteborg. I wish to thank her very
sincerely for her criticism of my work and her suggestions for its
improvement.

I wish to thank Mrs. Winifred Davin, the literary executrix of the Joyce
Cary Estate, who allowed me to see the author's manuscripts and note-
books and who kindly answered my numerous questions about him. I am also
grateful to the staff of the Bodleian Library, Oxford, for the efficient
help they gave me while I was working there on the Cary papers.

I am also indebted to David Lister, Karin Möller, and Eleanor Wikborg
(all of the University of Göteborg) for their criticism. I owe special
thanks to Britt Andersson who typed the entire manuscript and to
Olga Dahlgren who typed some passages revised for the publication of
my thesis in Gothenburg Studies in English.

Professor Erik Frykman, University of Göteborg, awakened my interest in
literary criticism. Throughout my work on Cary I have been fortunate
to enjoy his supervision and guidance. I owe him a great debt of grati-
tude for his encouragement and generous help.

NOTE

All page references enclosed within parentheses in
the body of the text are to the Carfax edition of
To be a Pilgrim.

PART ONE

AN INTRODUCTION

CHAPTER 1   JOYCE CARY, THINKER AND ARTIST: AN INTRODUCTION

Joyce Cary's road to fame was long and discouraging. Although already at the age of twenty he was determined to make a literary career, it took him more than twenty years of studies, practice, and false starts before, in 1932, he had a novel published. It is true that from then on he produced an even flow of works until his death in 1957, but he remained an experimenter whose struggle for the mastery of form mirrors the constant challenge that his view of life meant to him as an artist.

BACKGROUND

Joyce Cary was born in 1888 and belonged to an old Devon family which came into the possession of Irish land in the reign of Elizabeth I. Early enough he had a most varied experience of life. After leaving school he was an art student in Paris and Edinburgh where, at the age of twenty, he gave up painting to read law at Oxford. There literary pursuits made him fritter away his days. As a student of law he failed disastrously and was given a fourth-class degree. Cary then tried his luck abroad by joining a British Red Cross unit in the Balkan War of 1912 - 1913. After that he entered the Colonial Service and was sent to Nigeria where for six years he acted as both soldier and civil servant until, in 1920, failing health made him resign and go back to Britain. He settled in Oxford with his wife and growing family. For the twelve following years Cary wrote a great deal but published very little. He was firmly resolved to become a novelist and although money to him and his wife meant some worry, he doggedly continued his self-education. About this period he wrote:[1]

> As soon as I had finished a book or even half finished it, I
> could not bear it. The truth was, as I see now, that I was
> still an imitative writer. I had a genuine desire to create,
> in writing, but I had not yet found an idea satisfying to
> myself. I was in short still educating myself, and this
> process in Oxford went on much more vigorously than in Africa.[2]

THE CRITICISM OF CARY AND THE EVALUATION OF HIS ACHIEVEMENT

In a way Cary remained an imitative writer throughout his life, and in their attempts to describe his style critics have stressed his affinity with an impressive number of great English novelists, ranging from some

well-known eighteenth-century names, such as Smollett and Sterne, to the
symbolists of his own day. Andrew Wright says that Cary's originality
does not lie "in his discovery of new mines, but in re-exploration of
the old ones",[3] and he ascribes the author's "great versatility" to his
"anxiety to achieve, in his novels, a marriage between intuition and
form".[4] Walter Allen views Cary in a similar broad perspective at the
same time as he is anxious to pinpoint his particularity:

> In classic English fiction for the most part - there are
> obvious exceptions, Richardson and Sterne the most conspicuous
> - the action of the novel is as it were completed before the
> reader picks up the book and reads. . . . With Joyce and
> Virginia Woolf, and in a different way with Lawrence, this is
> not so; their aim was precisely to break down the old barriers
> between reader and character.
> . . .
> We experience much the same thing when we read Cary, at any
> rate after his early novels: while reading we are at the
> cutting-edge of the present. Cary is incomparable among living
> novelists at pinning down the sense of life at the actual
> moment of being lived. He succeeds in capturing this even in
> his first-person novels, which, as fictitious autobiography,
> must be retrospective.[5]

Allen and Wright enjoyed the privilege of belonging to the author's close
acquaintances and they certainly knew that they pointed to what in Cary's
own opinion was the gist of his art, viz. the objectification of his
vision.[6] However, their sweeping comparisons hardly open a clear approach
to the author and I think that, on the whole, his reputation has suffered
from the generosity with which his critics have suggested pigeon-holes
over the history of the English novel. Although most of them discuss
his novels with the greatest interest and respect, they tend to shy at any
definite assessment of his achievement. This apparent uncertainty is in
my view due to the fact that Cary criticism offers no attempts at a
complete and strictly systematic analysis of his narrative technique.
Only through a detailed study of structure and the relation between
structure and theme do we stand a chance to understand, in full, what
the objectification of Cary's vision implies. Only then do we realize
that in Cary the conception of art and even the struggle with form make
a statement about a view of life. It is true that most critics seem to
be more or less aware of this but few, if any, have convincingly
demonstrated it.

CARY'S EPISTEMOLOGY AND POLITICAL THEORY

Joyce Cary was no abstract thinker.[7] At least he looked upon abstraction as foreign to life.[8] Therefore he considered his fiction the only perfect valid statement of his philosophy. Nevertheless a student of Cary can hardly do without Power in Men, his political treatise, which is a most helpful companion to his world.[9]

Cary's political theory is essentially liberal, and his treatise actually appeared under the auspices of the Liberal Book Club,[10] but he was never a member of the Party. It is true that the publication of what he himself had insisted on giving the less demagogic name of "Liberty and Freedom" won for him, in 1939, the offer of standing for a constituency but the book did not sell well enough to make him risk a fling at practical politics.[11]

In Cary's belief, every man is "condemned to freedom" because he has been born unique.[12] From this follows that truth to individual man can only be partial because his unique character and freedom are facts that imply that the world cannot be meaningful until he has learnt to read into its "chaos" an interpretation that best satisfies his private needs

> . . . actual life is not like that, it doesn't have a total meaning, it is simply a wild confusion of events from which we have to select what we think significant for ourselves. Look at any morning paper. It makes no sense at all - it means nothing but chaos. We read only what we think important; that is to say, we provide our own sense to the news.[14]

Man, therefore, is the creator of his own existence. What makes him assume this role is an indomitable urge that seems to equal what in psychoanalysis is called 'libido'. In Cary this force appears under various names, above all "spirit", "love", "creativity":

> The world loves its own creation, which is its life. Not merely the artist, but every man and woman, begins from childhood to create for himself a world to which, as creator, he is deeply attached. Each of these worlds is highly complex and extensive. One man, for instance, does not create for himself only a home, a business, a family, but a religion, a political idea, a nation, a world idea. He creates them in his imagination, and lives in them. Deprived of them, or even of any large part of them, he would wither and die.[15]

Throughout Cary's fiction there is a plea for freedom because in his view man's imagination, creativity, and "love" demand it:

> Liberty is creation in the act. It is therefore eternal and
> indestructible. Whether man recognizes it for what it is or
> calls it what it is not, it is always at work.[16]

Therefore, in Cary's works, all who listen to the voice of their own
creative demon are men of power. Often they have come down in the world
if by the world we mean established society. They suffer injustice and
misery, but, for all that, they remain celebrants of love and liberty.

In Cary's philosophy liberty does not, in the first place, imply "absence
from restraint" but rather an "opportunity" for the largest possible
number of people to make the best of their individual gifts.[17] Therefore,
in his use of the word, liberty demands both individual and government
responsibility or else one man's opportunity will equal another man's
burden. Thus he rejects the traditional view of liberty as a minimum of
state intervention and control. Contrary to Herbert Spencer who considered
all state action an evil since he ascribed welfare to the evolutionary
process, Cary advocates a political system that is rigid enough to ensure
the individual's security and pliable enough to allow of freedom and
change.[18] It is characteristic of Cary's mode of thought that his ideal
state implies a dualism and therefore demands that every citizen embrace
toleration as a basic virtue, or its "democratic pragmatism"[19] will come
to nothing. Therefore the following lines give an excellent epitome of
Cary's liberal creed.

> Toleration is the natural air of freedom. Without it there is
> full liberty only for one man, one opinion, one party, or one
> creed. Whatever means a state uses to repress or limit the free
> exchange of ideas are destructive of liberty. For as ideas
> demand action, a man who acquires no new ideas initiates
> nothing and adds nothing to the power, knowledge, and liberty
> of society.[20]

Cary's belief in his gospel of freedom was firm enough and, in his view,
nothing could check the advance of democracy. This does not imply,
however, that he took a particularly rose-coloured view of life itself.
For the Carfax edition of his collected works[21] he for some time entertained the idea of writing a general preface which was meant to be
called "The Comedy of Freedom". The title is interesting because it
implies an ironic undercutting of the author's belief in freedom. We
must, however, consider that what Cary calls "life in creation" equals
a paradox in so far as man's love of creation, which implies change, is
destined to turn into love of the world that he has created for himself
and which, in the course of time, he becomes increasingly anxious to

preserve. Life, therefore, is the stage of an incessant conflict between
creators calling for freedom and preservers who demand security. This
conflict is Cary's basic theme and is in evidence throughout his fiction
Wherever youth is opposed to age, present to past, dissent to conformity
liberalism to conservatism, imagination to reason, etc., we are faced
with what Malcolm Foster describes as a "freedom-versus-security conflic
It is a tug of war that does not only split his world into two opposing
camps. It also splits individual man and, in Cary's fiction, the individ
characters. In his view we are all "in a jam" and have to remain so beca
in this conflict he sees the dynamics of life:

> . . . for me all characters are in a jam, all of us are in a
> jam, a special and incurable difficulty from which there is no
> escape. It continues all our lives and affects every aspect of
> our existence - we are born to freedom in a world condemned to
> be free, for its own good, for its maintenance and for its own
> destruction.23

CARY'S ART THEORY AND USE SYMBOLIC FORM

In Art and Reality Cary discusses the creation of art in the light of
his basic beliefs.24 The book actually equals his aesthetic will because
its completion was a race with his approaching death.25 Owing to the
author's eloquence and disbelief in abstract argument it is nevertheless
a most readable statement of his art theory.

Those who expect Art and Reality to apply in the first place to the
composition of his own novels are sure to experience some disappointment
In this book there is hardly any discussion of his own professional
problems. On this point, as we shall see, he may have acted wisely. On
the other hand it is to be regretted that, with equal consistency, he
avoids commenting on the obvious influence that his reading of William
Blake had on his development. Throughout his life Cary seems to have
been a student of Blake even though, as Margie Averitt points out, it
seems impossible to establish this influence.26 The fact remains, howeve
that to the understanding of Cary some knowledge of the great visionary'
doctrines and art will be most helpful indeed.

Cary's view of art is truly Romantic in so far as it is based on an
idealistic epistomology which, like Blake's, believes in the creative
and revealing power of the imagination. As, according to Cary, all
creativity originates in inspiration, life and art amount to the same

thing.[27] Indeed, as René Wellek points out, this view of inspiration equals a justification of art and the necessity of myth and symbol to act as its vehicle.[28]

In Cary's view, too, art cannot do without the symbol[29] and by subscribing to Keats's famous dictum that "Beauty is truth, truth beauty" he professes his symbolist creed:

> Has this statement any basis? I suggest, with all diffidence, that it does mean something of importance; that when we recognize beauty in any ordered form of art, we are actually discovering new formal relations, in a reality which is permanent and objective to ourselves, which is part of that real that includes both human nature and its reactions to colour, line, mass and sound, and the material consistencies which maintain them. That is, we are recognizing aesthetic meaning in the character of the universe, and this aesthetic order of meaning gives us the same sense of belonging to a rational and spiritual whole of character as does the moral truth of a Dante or Tolstoy.[30]

According to Cary the touchstone of truth, beauty, and art lies in its ability to give us an experience of the transcendental unity that, to Blake, equalled God.[31] In Cary's view as well as in Blake's, man's reason severs him from this unity. At the same time, however, man's fallen state, his disunity, necessitates a restoration of the divine unity. As disunity means life in "chaos" and solitude it alerts in him a need of communication and communion. Cary describes man's situation thus:

> We are not alone in feeling, in sympathy, but we are alone in mind, and so we are compelled, each of us, to form our own ideas of things, and if we want to convey these ideas and our feelings about them, we have to use art. Only art can convey both the fact and the feeling about the fact, for it works in the medium of common sympathies, common feeling, universal reaction to colour, sound, form. It is the bridge between souls, meaning by that not only men's minds but their character and feeling. And it carries almost all the traffic.[32]

If man wants to shed his loneliness and win understanding and sympathy, he must use art, i.e. learn to speak in symbolic language:

> All art uses the symbol. There is no other means by which one individual mind can express itself in material form and so communicate with another.[33]

This communication implies that man has to realize that facts hold no real truth unless they also hold some valuation. Like Tolstoy, whom Cary admired, he consequently emphasizes the emotional truth of art.

As we have seen, a restoration of Blakean unity demands that we bridge the gap between what Cary calls "the individual idea" and "the universal real of emotion".[34] It should, however, be observed that this gap is not only between the individual and his outer world. It also separates man's reason, his conscious ego, from the subconscious, his soul, which, at least in part, is supposed to be integral to the "universal real".

It is true that, like so much else in Cary, his psychology of art can be ascribed to Blakean influence even though there is actually no need to trace its origin further back than to C.G. Jung. In fact, it hardly seems unfair to describe it as a somewhat heavy-handed paraphrase of the latter symbol theory. Thus, what Cary considers a communication between man's isolated mind and "the universal real of emotion" well agrees with what in Jungian psychology is a cooperation between the conscious and the unconscious, the latter of which is defined as "that part of the mind which includes both the personal factor (the individual unconscious) and the disposition inherited from ancestors (the collective unconscious)".[35]

On the whole, some knowledge of Jung's theory will help us to understand, in full, what Cary's idea of art implies. We must, therefore, consider that what the author describes as "a rational and spiritual whole of character" equals, in Jung, man's heritage of "countless typical experiences" handed down through ages.[36] These experiences are, according to Jung, to be found in dreams, myth, and literature as recurrent themes or "archetypes" on the truth of which, in his view, all men subconsciously agree and which, in Cary, serve as bearers of "real" truth.[37]

It is true that Cary's view of art evidences less originality than its lack of references to similar theories may make us believe. Nevertheless Art and Reality is interesting enough because of the author's preoccupati with the serious dilemma that in his professional experience artistic creation implies.

Cary's account of this dilemma offers us a new aspect of man's eternal freedom-vs-security conflict. All artists are in a "jam" because the communication of art always demands fresh symbols, i.e. unique means of expression that convey not only "facts" but also "feeling about the fact" whereas the writer's obsession with his message makes it a great temptati for him to seize upon established means, e.g. the well-defined word or phrase, the well-known metaphor, the worn-out symbol, or, in short, concepts.[38] As "facts" and "feeling" imply tension, the force of an art symbol rests with its form. It is true that Cary's idea of symbolic form is, at bottom, a commonplace but for all that it remains interesting enough because in his philosophy it applies to all creation and consequently makes a restatement of his Blakean view of life as a complex of dualities, such as the material and the immaterial, the conscious and the unconscious, the partial of mind and the complete of character, the individual and the divine, i.e. various forms of disunity and unity, and in the last the complex unity that carries the "tremendous meaning" of Blake's "Tiger" or Keats's "Urn".[39]

In Cary form is thus tantamount to meaning. This means that although art originates from non-logical inspiration, its expression demands the conception of an apposite form that can only be achieved through "hard conceptual labour".[40] The artist's problem, Cary says, "is to translate his intuition into concept and his concept back into a vehicle which conveys the intuition".[41] Therefore he objects to Croce's strictly monistic epistemology which does not allow of any gap between intuition and expression as it would divide what the latter describes as "the seamless robe of the world".[42] Apart from the fact that Cary's Blakean world, unlike Croce's, implies a dualism he may as a "professional" have taken some offence at the latter's unwillingness to give the artist, the intermediary between intuition and expression, his proper due.[43]

What, then, does the artist's "hard conceptual labour" amount to? As Cary gives us to understand, the conception of a whole novel is "the result of a long and complex process of exploration, as well as construction".[44] However great a novelist's skill may be, he has to "proceed by trial and error"[45] which, to put it the other way, means that experimentation, i.e. the casting about for felicitous form, does not preclude the necessity of a creative principle. As I hope will be apparent from my analysis of To be a Pilgrim, the author's use of form tells of his dependence on such a formula. Then we will also realize that in his critical works he had every reason not to offer his reader such a pointer because a dissection of his novels in conceptual terms would have done the power of his art irreparable harm. It would have meant the dissolution of the "total symbol" that in Cary's view each work of true art amounts to.[46]

According to Blake "that which is not too explicit is fittest for
instruction, because it rouses the faculties to act".[47] Blake's dictum
is worthy of note because it has the character of a precept that well
applies to Cary's conception of form. Although, as far as I can see, he
never commented on the implicitness of his narration, it is in my view
one of the author's chief characteristics. This implicitness results from
his use of tacit cross-references, i.e. his coupling of words, utterances,
images, scenes, etc. which evidence both similarity and contrast or, as
Blake certainly would have had it, common identity.[48] No doubt, the force
of Cary's symbolism depends on the reader's experience of an identity
that transcends its ambivalence. In the concluding chapter of Art and
Reality he writes:

> . . . such education of the whole man again can be carried
> out only by means of the charged symbol, at once concept and
> experience. It is the ambivalence of the symbol that enables
> the artist, as teacher or expositor, as creator of meanings,
> to bridge the gap between the individual idea and the universal
> real of emotion, forming by art a personality which unites them
> both in a single active and rational will.[49]

In principle Cary's view of the reader's "instruction" agrees with Blake'
but even though for once he uses so unusually exact a term as "ambivalenc
his statement testifies to his characteristic unwillingness to offer any
useful rules.[50]

Cary's idea of symbolic form is in evidence throughout his fiction. His
narration abounds in what the Greek noun 'symbolon' suggests, i.e. the
union of two worlds.[51] It has a texture of comparisons implying polarity
and unifying identity. In principle each novel equals a system of lesser
and greater unities, a hierarchy of identities, or, in short, a "total
symbol". Cary writes:

> . . . the form of a book, page by page, is not the book, the
> work of art. All these separate pages and chapters, like the
> movements of a symphony, do not have a complete significance
> until the whole work is known. They are, so to speak, partly
> in suspension, until at the end of the last movement, the
> last chapter, they suddenly fall into their place. This is
> only to say again that the separate forms do not possess their
> whole content until the work is complete. That's why I call
> the book a total symbol. It is both richer than its parts and
> actually different from them.[52]

It seems that, so far, Cary's critics have failed to realize the consistency and complexity of his form-making. This is above all due to the fact
that, as far as I can see, no critic has been observant enough of the

author's use of irony. Thus it is by ironic undercutting of the explicit
narration that a great deal of implied comparison has been achieved.[53]

Furthermore, Cary's use of ambivalent form seems to be a crux criticorum
to those who have become so conscious of it that they fail to experience
any unity of vision in the author. Robert Bloom, in particular, has
objected to the "inclusiveness" of his narration because it results in
"ambiguity" and "contradiction" and makes "moral ideas appear impotent".[54]
This is how he sums up his point:

> . . . . I define the view of reality which both generates and
> impairs Cary's novels as indeterminateness - a species of
> captivating but disquieting moral largesse. . . . We find
> him driven to a kind of intellectual reluctance because he
> is so loath to slight the infinite variety and multiplicity
> of reality.[55]

Bloom is a man of moral principle and a rationalist and therefore he is
unable to identify himself with the author's unifying sensibility.[56]
Most probably Cary and, behind him, Blake would have considered the
critic's attack indicative of man's fallen state. However true it may
be that Bloom's conscious discrimination disqualifies him for the enjoyment of Cary's art and that many critics have stood up in the latter's
defence, his criticism is nevertheless valuable in so far as, ultimately,
it points to the preponderance of the author's concern with form.

Barbara Hardy describes Cary's form-making as "conspicuous" and it is
tempting to ascribe, as she does, this indisputable fact to the influence
of his professional experience of painting.[57] Anyhow, what makes his use
of form so "conspicuous" is, in my opinion, his strict reliance on a
creative formula that is well and, perhaps, too well founded in theory.
There, as we have seen, unlike Croce he considers form divorced from
vision and, as a consequence, he regards the artist's labour as "conceptual". As Cary's conception of form sometimes tends to seem "conceptual"
enough, there is no reason to reject Bloom's criticism as completely
unjustified. Above all, it indicates that the maximum enjoyment of Cary,
in fact, demands an ideal reader. Being the god of his own unified world,
the author was undoubtedly aware of this. Thus he comments on this point
in Art and Reality:

> For the first duty of a writer is to compose a form of meaning
> which shall be coherent to the reader even if that reader be
> himself.[58]

> For a reader must never be left in doubt about the meaning of
> a story. I mean, of course, the ideal reader; in the first
> place, the writer himself.[59]

In fact, throughout his career Cary seems to have been worried by the
misunderstanding that his books met with. In 1951 when at long last he
had become a writer of repute, he wrote these desperate words to Mark
Schorer, an expert on Blake, in answer to his review of Mister Johnson,
Cary's best-known African novel:[60]

> Ought I to go on as I am doing, presenting the books as yarns
> and letting a few people here and there find out by their own
> penetration what I am trying to do? Creating a homogenous
> picture of the world as it is, as perpetual creation of the
> free soul with all its complex results in art and religion
> and its politics, its special tragedy and special morality.
> . . . Or ought I to write a general preface to the whole series
> under the head (which I once thought of using) "The Comedy of
> Freedom?" But what worries me is not the reviews of Mr. John
> [sic] but that such theses on my work as I have seen, even a
> very good job that came to me this week from a Norwegian
> scholar - are just as much at sea as most of the newspaper
> notices.
>
> This man has discovered or sensed that the books are all part
> of one related scheme but he has no inkling of its nature.
> Perhaps such words as creation, freedom are so utterly worn
> out by fanatics and cranks, that they no longer carry any of
> their tremendous meaning.[61]

Cary's despair draws our attention to the final phase of the artistic
communication process, viz. the recipient's response to the art stimulus.
In his theory, reading is no passive process but calls for inspired
re-creation:

> The reader may believe that he is completely receptive and
> uncritical, he may and should attempt to expose himself to
> an experience without prejudice, but in fact he is performing
> a highly active and complex creative act. The reason he does
> not notice it is because most of it takes place in the sub-
> conscious.[62]

This view of the reader's function is in perfect agreement with Cary's
Jungian psychology of art. It implies that the reader's subconscious
participation rests with the author's ability to sustain his "emotional
satisfaction".[63] This means, as we learnt from Blake, that the narration
must not be "too explicit". Cary's theory demands that the reader is given
an experience of objective truth that, as it were, dawns on him from
outside as it once did upon the author himself:

> It stands over against him [the writer], like Housman's
> cherry tree, a piece of the real whose whole force is in

> its objectivity and universal truth. And he, as subject, has
> to use his brains to translate the effect of this real into
> a symbolic form which gives the same effect to another person.[64]

The artist's objectification of his own subjectivity is hardly digestible
to reason as, in theory, it demands that man, so to speak, turn his mind
inside out. Cary holds, however, that man in his virtual experience of
himself is not only creator but at the same time part of his creation.
Therefore, the subject-object dichotomy means in practice no insoluble
problem to the imaginative artist:

> It is impossible for us ever to think ourselves out of the
> universe, any more than a deep-sea fish can think itself out
> of the sea. But within this realm of being, we do recognize
> the distinction of the individual self from what is outside
> that self, and so I am writing of the individual as both
> separate from reality as creator and part of it as created.[65]

As has already been pointed out the hall-mark of Cary's art is to be
found in the objectification of his vision. We must, however, consider
that vision implies subjectivity and that objectification is only a
means to divert the reader's attention from this fact. It can therefore
never equal virtual objectivity. Perhaps it is fair to say that in his
novels Cary travels on the border-line between subjectivity and objectivity
even though such a description hardly does full justice to the solidity
of his art because it tends to imply the compromise of a neither-nor.
Thus whether we become observant of Cary's "propaganda" or not, depends
rather on the length of the reader's conscious vision than on the author's
ability to maintain a straight line of demarcation between idea and his
art.

Rather than describe Cary's narration as a balancing-act between subjectivity and objectivity it therefore seems more appropriate to suggest that
the full appreciation of his art demands from his reader a response that
is both emotional and intellectual, subconscious as well as conscious.
In this respect, to judge from Cary criticism in general, his fiction
complies well with the demands of his theory. Thus Walter Allen and
Charles G. Hoffman demonstrate willing "suspension of disbelief" although
both are perfectly aware of the real nature of his created world.[66] Hoffman
praises the author's "negative capability" as evidenced in his first trilogy:

> Each novel of the trilogy is a full portrait of a character,
> narrated in the first person from the view of the protagonist;

each portrait is different because of Cary's ability to enter
into the character portrayed.67

Allen takes a similar view of Cary's fiction in its entirety. Describing
the author as "the one Proteus of the English novel today" he makes an
interesting attempt to define what, in his view, makes Cary so decidedly
differ from his contemporaries:

> In a famous passage in the Biographia Literaria, Coleridge
> isolates two opposed modes of the creative activity in their
> purest and most comprehensive expression. 'While Shakespeare',
> he says, 'darts himself forth, and passes into all forms of
> character and passion, the one Proteus of the fire and flood,
> Milton attracts all forms and things to himself, into unity
> of his own ideal. All things and modes of action shape them-
> selves anew in the being of Milton; while Shakespeare becomes
> all things, yet for ever remaining himself.' Coleridge is not
> making a value-judgement; he is contrasting the objective
> imagination with the subjective, we might say the extrovert
> as artist with the introvert.
>
> Few poets and novelists are so completely of their type as
> Shakespeare and Milton; between the two extremes are infinite
> gradations. Yet if one looks at English fiction during the
> past thirty years in the light of Coleridge's distinction, it
> is apparent that it has been predominantly Miltonic, subjective,
> introvert; so much so that the Shakespearean, objective, extro-
> verted writer stands out with the novelty of the exceptional.
> He appears old-fashioned, or at least out of step with his
> time. The neat generalizations we evolve to sum up contemporary
> writing do not seem to apply to him. And this, perhaps, is the
> first thing that strikes us when we contemplate the novelist
> Joyce Cary against the background of his contemporaries. We are
> immediately aware of his d i f f e r e n c e , and the first
> difference is that pre-eminently he is 'the one Proteus' of
> the English novel to-day. Like the poet as seen by Keats, he
> appears to have 'no identity - he is continually in for and
> filling some other Body'.68

Allen's judgment makes no valid statement of Cary's art because it does
not allow for the author's ambiguous function which, besides, Coleridge's
distinction helps us to clarify. Although, of course, all justice should
be done to Cary's indisputable ability to "enter into the character
portrayed", a critical statement must not deny the fact that, at the
same time, his fiction evidences "unity of his own ideal". It is true
that this wedding of subjectivity and objectivity may seem unappeasable
to reason, but nevertheless this paradoxical inclusiveness is in perfect
agreement with the author's mode of thought. Therefore we are wise to
compare Allen's verdict with the ambivalent view on this point that,
discussing allegory, Cary takes in Art and Reality:

> Allegory is false because it lays down categorical imperatives
> for conduct in a world of particular and unique events. It
> treats the world as a mechanism whereas it is a world of free
> souls. And it is in this world of persons that the novelist
> must develop his meanings. He must show his meaning by creating
> persons who have the character of actual persons, in a world
> that could be actual but displays a moral order that does not
> present itself in life. It is an ideal order which remains an
> object of attainment for that writer in the world as he knows
> it in fact.[69]

Cary's view of allegory is interesting because it gives an instance of
the confusion that is bound to follow on his disbelief in exact definitions.[70] In his use, "allegory" seems rather to be a symbolist criterion
of failure than a strictly technical term. This, at least, is what the
reader is given to understand from the fact that, for all his unqualified
rejection of allegory, he is anxious not to put Bunyan on a par with the
"monkish author" of Everyman and equally zealous moralizers of his day:

> At first sight, the failure of Everyman is a defect of
> characterization. How are we to take any interest in such
> lay figures as Good Deeds and Kindred? But we don't object
> to Christian and Faithful, Byends or Giant Sloth in Pilgrim's
> Progress, or to Sir Wilfull by Congreve. These are like real
> people subject to mood and whims, but the characters of
> Everyman are mere conceptions, entirely abstract. What is
> more, the meaning is given in the form of a general precept,
> equally abstract. No real problem is proposed or answered.
> The whole matter could be equally well expressed in a copy-
> book maxim. And we do not believe, really believe, copybook
> maxims.[71]

However, if we subscribe to C.S. Lewis's view that "allegory . . . belongs
not to medieval man but to man, or even to mind, in general" and that "it
is of the very nature of thought and language to represent what is immaterial in picturable terms",[72] then, beyond doubt, Cary is an allegorist
even though his vision of the world as subject to continuous change makes
his meaning so radically different from the dry precepts of the morality
plays.

In Cary's contempt of allegory, however, there certainly lies a great
deal of fear that, in him, the idealist will get the better of the artist.
He admits that "allegory is an immense temptation to the writer, especially
the great, the obsessed writer":[73]

> Just because of this clearness, this definition of meaning,
> allegory is a standing temptation to the great writers. What's
> more, their greatest triumphs are achieved in that narrow
> space between allegory and the dramatic scene.[74]

Nevertheless the fact remains that Cary's view of a "unity-disunity"
pattern in life implies an allegorical interpretation. By necessity the
world of his fiction is "a metaphysical construction" as he admits in
his desperate letter to Mark Schorer:[75]

> . . . like others (like Blake again) obsessed with a view of
> the world which seems to me so obvious, but to other people
> apparently so dark, I am very anxious to make my world under-
> stood and felt.
>
> That's why, unlike Blake who invented his own mythology, to
> avoid the cliché of worn out definition, I use a quite differ-
> ent method of approach. I do not want to frighten people at
> the beginning by difficulties or by the idea of instruction.
> I do not want to start by saying "this novel is a metaphysical
> construction based on a comprehensive idea of life" or they
> will stop entering into my character's lives and instead treat
> the book, if they tackle it at all, as a kind of crossword-
> puzzle, asking what does this character stand for, - or that,
> - they will imagine an allegory. And I detest allegory - my
> people are real in a real world or they are nothing.[76]

In a letter of somewhat earlier date to his American publishers he gives
a more balanced view of his dilemma:

> The problem of construction, then, is to design a book in
> which all the characters and incidents form parts of one
> coherent experience for the judgment, and at the same to
> give it the vitality of a narrative from actual life - which
> in itself, of course, has no meaning, or such a confusion of
> meanings that it adds up to nonsense.
>
> And this is really the most difficult and troublesome part of
> the work because there is no end to it. When a critic wrote
> lately that I had no form, but plenty of life, in a book which
> had been under construction for several years, I was highly
> complimented. I would much rather be accused of wanting form -
> that is, meaning - than life; I suppose because I am so
> strongly aware of my own meaning.[77]

If we are to understand what makes Cary go so far as to "detest" allegory
we must realize that his strong "obsession" with his own meaning makes
his use of form so consistent that his world will undoubtedly afford the
reader the pastime of a crossword-puzzle if the allegorist in the author
should be found out. However, it must in justice be admitted that in
Cary's fiction allegory is so deeply submerged in verisimilitude that
it certainly takes more than one reading of a novel for the average
reader to experience the transparency of his world. Then, however, we
are liable to realize that, for all the variety the author is equal to,
it is Blake's pantheon that re-appears in novel after novel. Thus, in
Cary, too, we find a Urizen and a Los who in varying guises fight their

versions of the eternal war between, on the one hand, constancy, order,
and reason, and, on the other, change, freedom, and imagination. Between
them there is, in Cary, too, an Eve, a manifestation of the eternal
feminine who is constantly stirring the fire of the combatants by minister-
ing now to one, now to the other. Therefore a study of the author's
conception of character will greatly help us to understand his difficult
position in "the narrow space between allegory and the dramatic scene".
It will also help us to understand why his critics have arrived at such
different views of him as an impersonator. Thus Professor Hardy has given
a statement that signally differs from Allen's:

> Cary's power of spawning character has often been praised,
> rather oddly, for there is not a great deal of variety in his
> persons, either within single novels or in his work considered
> as a whole.[78]

In fact a complete view of Cary's achievement has, like Andrew Wright's
verdict below, to allow of both standpoints:

> But, although as a novelist Cary is rich - indeed a prodigious
> - inventor, his range is severely limited. He is often compared
> to Dickens, but Dickens draws a whole gallery of individuals
> because for him idiosyncrasy is the defining aspect of man;
> Cary portrays again and again the same three people because
> for him it is the commonness of the human dilemma which is
> compelling. The man who must create, the man who would pre-
> serve, and the woman who as female resembles both the one and
> the other but also differs from either - these are the types
> to which Cary mainly confines himself because, for all their
> singularities, they constitute in Cary's world the defining
> limits of human possibility.[79]

Cary's conception of character is illustrated by the varying use which
he puts this word to in his discursive writings. Thus he writes about
the composition of his first novel where the well-organized scene of an
ambivalent Africa in change had to be convincingly epitomized in the sole
and central character of his half-pagan heroine:

> My first published novel was called Aissa Saved. It came out
> in 1932. It deals with the life and death of a Negro girl
> converted by a mission. Actually her religion is a mixture
> of Christian and pagan ideas, and this is the case with all
> the converts. The general plot is of a drought and the efforts
> of both pagans and Christians to bring rain - the pagans by
> sacrifice, the Christians by prayer. At the end of the book
> Aissa herself is sacrificed.
> . . .
> The reason why the book took a long time to write was just
> because . . . it raised problems that I had not faced; . . .
> There is all the difference in the world between thinking that
> you have the answers to a question and trying to write those

answers down, or rather to illustrate them in a story, that
is, to find the characters whose story will reveal a situation
in depth, that is to say, in character.[80]

When, in the preface to Herself Surprised, the initial book of his first
trilogy, Cary writes that while working at it he had all along stuck to
the rule "character first", the word 'character' evidences an ambivalenc
of meaning that matches the title of the novel. As in the comment on
Aissa Saved the author actually dramatizes his creative dilemma by letti
'character' imply now particularity, now generality:

> The centre of the plan was character; the characters of my
> three leading persons in relation to, or in conflict with,
> other characters and the character of their times; (and
> beyond that, of course, with 'final' character, I mean the
> shape of things and feelings which are 'given', and which
> have to be so or nothing would exist at all) - the books
> had to be soaked in character.[81]

However "soaked in character" the author's novels may seem, we should no
be blind to the fact that at the same time they are, paradoxically enoug
"soaked" in Cary. It is unfortunate that, rather than describe allegory
as the opposite and ruin of the symbol and the representation of "charac
Cary did not try to level the distinction and bring his view into align-
ment with what seems to be a tendency in modern criticism.[82] It is true
that his disdain of allegory helps him to dramatize his vision of all
creation as disunity but as in his view this division ultimately suggest
unity, he should, in reason, have taken greater pains to define as far
as possible "the narrow space between allegory and the dramatic scene".

Ironically enough, Cary commits himself so strongly to the conflict
between concept or allegory and symbol that he apparently forgets that,
in accordance with his theory, their divergence actually implies con-
vergence and that, therefore, it ought to be possible to define a point
of intersection where concept and symbol amount to the same thing. It
should, in other words, be possible to achieve an unambiguous definition
of ultimate truth that appeals to both Urizen and Los.

In literary criticism "myth" is a concept that helps us to define this
agreement.[83] No doubt Cary was familiar with the term, although, as
below, his allegiance to his theory and due suspicion of abstractions
make him prefer to "educate"[84] his reader in words of his own:

At a certain primitive level, all men agree. The Australian
blackfellow and the university professor still find a common
good in morality. Courage, duty, affection, loyalty, self-
discipline, truth, these are fundamental values for both of
them. They differ only about their relative importance.

This moral constant is of course the reason not only why the
most foreign and ancient works of art from the paleolithic
cave-drawings to negro carving have a meaning for us but why
we can enter into the moral atmosphere of societies quite
strange to our own experience. For all exist and must exist
within a universal moral real.[85]

Thus what Cary describes as a "moral constant" or "a universal moral
real" is what critics usually mean by 'myth'. We should bear in mind
that this concept is the cope-stone of Jung's psychology of art. Therefore it is by no means an original idea that, in the concluding sentence
of Art and Reality, the author gives his eloquence full play to vitalize:

This is the only real truth that we can know, and art is the
only means by which we can achieve it. It is only in great art
and the logic of the subconscious where judgment has become
part of the individual emotional character that we move freely
in a world which is at once concept and feeling, rational order
and common emotion, in a dream which is truer than actual life
and a reality which is only there made actual, complete and
purposeful to our experience.[86]

What in my view mars Cary's discussion of art and, as we have seen, is
also in evidence in his conception of form, is the paradoxical obstinacy
with which he sticks to his theory and which makes him rather liable to
trust his conceptual thinking than depend on his own intuition or what
he calls "the logic of the subconscious" in the passage above. It is to
be regretted that the author's prejudice against abstractions forbade
him to use the concept of 'myth'. Admittedly, as René Wellek, among others,
points out, 'myth' has nowadays "so wide a range of meanings that it has
become difficult to argue about it with any clarity of reference".[87] When
it comes to the study of poets, such as Blake or Yeats, where we are
faced with "a system of archetypes" or "a scheme of metaphors, symbols,
and gods", however, Wellek holds that the term may prove to be of value.[88]
If, in Art and Reality, Cary had used the term as defined by Mark Schorer
in William Blake, he would have saved himself a good deal of, to a Urizenic
mind, circular argument and left the reader both much wiser and more
convinced. In Schorer's definition 'myth' is "a large controlling image
that gives philosophic meaning to the facts of ordinary life".[89] It is
such an image that controls the world of Cary's fiction as well as his
conception of form. Whether we describe this image as the result of an

allegorist's "conceptual labour" or a symbolist artist's intuition is, in my view, immaterial as long as we respond to it as something irrevocably meaningful.

Blake defined "the most sublime poetry" as "Allegory addressed to the Intellectual powers while it is altogether hidden from the Corporeal Understanding".[90] For all Cary's distrust of established definitions, the fact remains that these words make an excellent statement of both his ideal and his dilemma.

In this chapter I have discussed Cary's art theory at length because it gives the best approach to his myth. Remarkably enough, the very same myth seems embedded in the story of the young man who wanted to become a painter and a man of law but who became neither because reality had destined him for the precarious course of what, in his art, he describes as a "pilgrim".

CHAPTER 2   A SUMMARY OF THE FICTION

To be a Pilgrim can be described as a book of fictitious memoirs narrated
within what is hinted at as the speaker's journal written over a period
of three years which apparently are to be his last. The novel follows no
continuous story but equals a series of flash-backs experienced by the
ailing and rapidly aging Thomas Wilcher, a lawyer of some description.
He is the owner of Tolbrook, the ancient Wilcher family estate. Throughout his life he has been an eccentric bachelor and the victim of a racking
strain between attachment to the past and the present demands of his
exigent self. Agonized he has been clutching at religion but swerved into
miserliness and exhibitionism. He is suspicious, proud, and shrewd. He
is irritable and at times even irascible. A heart complaint makes him
liable to fainting fits. Since his family put an end to his liaison with
Sara Monday, his cook, and his ensuing despair possibly made him set his
London house on fire, his mental health seems uncertain. He himself,
anyhow, is doubtful of his sanity and his diary writing is actually a
desperate attempt by him to break his isolation and come to terms with
truth.

THE FRAME STORY

The basic story, i.e. Wilcher's diary, begins at Tolbrook Manor where he
has been brought from London to recover from the severe crisis that
followed on his separation from Sara Monday. There he is under the care
of Ann, his niece, who is a somewhat unworldly though, at bottom, determined, young doctor. Wilcher entertains the suspicion that his family
want her to have him certified as insane. Over the years the master
of Tolbrook has been worrying his presumptive heirs by frequently changing
his will, but his indecision seems rather to have divided them than incited
them into a plot. In fact, there is another niece who is suspicious
of Ann's intentions particularly since it is apparently true that, now
and then, she keeps the restless old man locked up at night. However,
even if Wilcher's prejudice against his family is in perfect accord with
his anxious nature, the fact remains that his fears are not unjustified.
It appears, for example, that Ann is in secret communion with his nephew
Robert, a headstrong earthy character who after a time of farming failures
in Canada now suddenly turns up determined to turn the neglected estate

into a modern farm, i.e. change the old man's world past recognition.
The young people turn out to be in love, and their affair suddenly ends
in marriage when a child appears to be on the way.

During Ann's pregnancy there arises a growing intimacy between uncle an
niece who begins to share the values that tie Wilcher to the old Manor
and the past. As a consequence, her relation to her husband takes a bad
turn which reaches its climax when, after a boy is born, Wilcher wins
Ann to a name that the father opposes. After that they grow more and mo
alien to one another. While Ann gives her spare time to writing a book
on her father, a fascinating politician, Robert takes up with a young
farm pupil and finally the couple vanish from the scene. For some time
Ann lives alone with her uncle, but then it appears that Robert has lef
too great a void in her life, and suddenly she leaves Tolbrook to see
her husband. Wilcher now experiences a feeling of loss that inflames hi
by now dormant need to join Sara, and he rushes away to London. There
Sara turns out to have started a new life with a young widower who bundl
Wilcher out into the street. Neither is Sara willing to renew her liais
with her former master who has not stood the strain of his trip but has
to be looked after. As he makes renewed attempts to see her, she calls
for Ann and her husband and then she grants Wilcher a second visit only
to hand him over to his family. Realizing Sara's deceit he collapses an
in a sense, the story ends exactly where it started. Wilcher has, in
other words, irrevocably completed his cycle of life and consequently
reached a terminal out of which there is no way back.

THE MEMOIRS

Throughout the novel Wilcher is mainly concerned with his past. Not eve
the upsetting events during his London visit can make him refrain from
interpolating diverse memories with little bearing on his actual situat
On these occasions he seems suddenly brought back into the cosy comfort
of his Tolbrook parlour and suspended above the vicissitudes of the
present action. It must, however, be pointed out that the reader learns
very little about the narrator's epic whereabouts. When he happens to
visualize himself, he is hardly ever in a situation that makes narrat
plausible. Lying in bed, or restlessly haunting the rooms of the sleepir
house, or talking to Ann, Wilcher opens his past to the reader.

The narrator is always in the centre of his own experience, but then he is, in general, as concerned with his family as he is with himself, and on certain points, for instance his education, professional training and career, we learn virtually nothing at all. In fact, Wilcher's memoirs make up a family chronicle that extends into a panorama of religious and political life in the Britain of his day. Most of the characters who people his world have hardly the balanced make-up of ordinary mortals. Either they grow into striking personalities of powerful resource or they dissolve into unprofiled sketches of unaccountable listlessness. In fact, all the characters fall into either category. They are strong or weak, successful or unsuccessful, active or passive, independent or dependent, radical or conservative, dissenting or consenting, happy or unhappy. Whether they appear before or after the "or", depends on their ability to "maintain the vital spark" (p.75).

The narrator's gallery of characters is varied indeed. There is, for example, Brown, an itinerant preacher and head of a small sect, the Benjamites. He carries away Lucy, Wilcher's headstrong sister, and to the dismay of his family marries her. Wilcher despises Brown and his sermons but at heart he is not left untouched and throughout his life he carries with him the memory of the little congregation singing the Bunyan hymn from which the novel has its title.

Lucy is hard, proud, and self-willed. She has a powerful influence on her younger brother. She both loves and ridicules him. He, however, admires her without reserve because her presence imbues him with a passionate sense of life.

Bill, the next eldest of Wilcher's two brothers, is a soldier and a kind, modest, and stoutly honest character. Like Amy, his wife, he evidences an instinctive confidence in life itself that recommends them both to the diffident narrator.

Edward, the eldest brother and Ann's father, is a brilliant Liberal politician and wit whose couplets Wilcher quotes to comment on what he relates. Fascinated by the extraordinary ease with which Edward makes his way, he becomes his devoted follower. At their father's death Edward inherits Tolbrook. In his capacity of family solicitor Wilcher has to act as his business manager which gives him a good deal of worry as his

brother is a waster of money as well as women. Nevertheless he tidies
up his brother's affairs so well that he succeeds him to the estate and
his mistress. Now, however, Edward's career has come to an end.
Suddenly he leaves politics to marry a very young girl. It appears to
be a most unpremeditated step which, soon enough, is followed by separation. When Edward attempts a come-back, everybody seems to have lost
faith in him. In fact, he has lost his faith in himself. His zest of
life starts to give out. His health deteriorates, and life becomes an
increasing burden to him. When, at last, he senses the proximity of deat
there is a turn of the tide because he feels that his departure will
offer a new opening.

Julie, Wilcher's mistress, had once risen to fame as a brilliant actress
She is a woman of refined tastes and a Catholic. Before she became part
of the narrator's life, she was in love with Edward. When they were
forced to break their liaison, she lapsed into dependence on Wilcher and
apathy. John, the narrator's beloved and gifted nephew shares Julie's
listlessness to which the exuberance of Gladys, his carefree wife, gives
a splendid contrast.

Wilcher's parents possibly make an intermediate group of characters. It
is true that, in the prime of his life, Colonel Wilcher was a tower of
indisputable strength but in the narrator's perspective he is an aging
man of failing faculties. The narrator's picture of his mother shows a
sensitive and good-hearted city belle lost in her rustic setting. To
all appearances she is a weak character but, in the loving eyes of her
son, she never becomes as unprepossessing as Julie and John.

CHAPTER 3   AN INTRODUCTION TO THE STUDY OF TO BE A PILGRIM

Of Joyce Cary's sixteen published novels those of the first trilogy have
by most critics been hailed as his greatest achievement. <u>Herself Surprised</u>,
the first piece of the sequence, and <u>The Horse's Mouth</u>, the concluding
part, stand out as the author's by far best sellers whereas <u>To be a Pilgrim</u>
has not won the same popularity. This does not mean that it is a dull
book. It is, however, a work of great complexity, and although a vein of
humour runs through the narration, it is not so easily accessible and
boisterous as in the flanking novels. It is a work looked upon with
considerable respect in Cary criticism[1] and in my view it makes the best
and most comprehensive statement of the author's philosophy. Together the
three   novels give an integrated exposition of a continuously changing
world and a plea for the "creative freedom" without which, in Cary's
opinion, life is bound to stagnate. Each book is written in the first
person by three different narrators who all can, in a sense, be described
as imaginative artists and who throughout their lives have to fight and
suffer for their creative freedom in a world of prejudice, i.e. of conceptual thought.

According to my original plan, my analysis of Cary's narrative technique
was to comprise the entire trilogy because I was particularly interested
in the three-dimensional solidity of character that the author has achieved
without apparently jeopardizing the formal objectivity of his first-person
narration. Soon, however, I found that particularly in <u>To be a Pilgrim</u>
the author's relation to his speaker offered so interesting an approach
to both his craft and theme that I decided to give my whole attention to
this novel.

Although some critics consider <u>To be a Pilgrim</u> one of Cary's very best
novels none has, in my opinion, viewed it in its entire complexity of
structure and has therefore not been able to take in the full range of
the author's vision. On the whole critics evidence too much concern with
the fiction proper to become aware of the speaker's uncertain identity
and question the author's apparent self-effacement. Although the "suspension of disbelief"[2] that these critics are capable of speaks in favour
of Cary's art, the fact remains that we can hardly get the author's full
message unless we sense his presence and share his implicit response to

his own vision.

Most critics seem to be of opinion that each of Cary's two trilogies
equals a series of monologues. Andrew Wright describes them as "six
kinds of interior monologue",[3] whereas Margie Averitt shows more circumspection by saying that "each first-person narrator enacts a drama of
subjective reality without relying completely on interior monologue".[4]

What may seem to support these writers' view of the narration as an
interior monologue is the indisputable fact that, as Walter Allen points
out, "while reading we are at the cutting-edge of the present"[5] or, as
Hazard Adams makes still clearer, that the "reminiscences are not treated
in chronological order, but instead depend on the mind of Wilcher [the
speaker] in the continuous present of actual writing".[6]

As far as I can see, Wilcher's soliloquy does not equal an "interior
monologue" if, by this term, we mean an objective recording of this
speaker's "stream of consciousness".[7] He virtually seems to be in conscious charge of the narration although his "epic situation"[8] testifies
to as great uncertainty as his identity. In time the distance between
this "I"-narrator's experience and narration seems short but it should
be observed that it is subject to considerable variation, and only rarely
is there no distance at all. Last but not least, it must be pointed
out that the speaker's narration, more or less continuously, implies the
presence of a listening vis-à-vis even though, as in T.S. Eliot's "The
Love Song of J. Alfred Prufrock", the listener may be one half of the
speaker's dual self.[9] Therefore we are wise, like Richard Kraus, to
consider the novel a modified form of the dramatic monologue.[10] Thus it
has not, in my view, been unequivocally conceived to act as an impartial
reflector of Wilcher's mind. However true in a sense this may be, it
must not blind us to the fact that at the same time it serves as a fictitious screen devised to hide the author's, after all, indisputable presence.

In addition to this, Cary tries to give his speaker's authority some
oblique support by describing him as a diarist and inviting the reader to
imagine that the book equals a private record. As I hope to show,[11]
this diary is an objectifying device that solely belongs to the fiction

and, contrary to his soliloquizing, in no way affects the character of
the narration. Nevertheless some critics find no difficulty in accepting
the speaker in the role of a diarist. Thus Walter Allen voices his
credulity:

> . . . as we see him in the journal he is writing - and the
> novel is really his journal - he is a little cracked, an old
> man on the verge of senility;[12]

Although a major part of To be a Pilgrim consists of the speaker's
memoirs, i.e. a fact that hardly supports the diary fiction, Hazard
Adams sees no reason to question its verisimilitude:

> In order to express this tension between past and present in
> Wilcher's mind, Cary chose the device of the journal because
> in it we can see Wilcher's finished, most complete attempt to
> meet his problem rationally while at the same time overpowering
> emotional complications shine through the effort.[13]

As the narrator's "journal" cannot, in reason, include the whole narration, Adams should rather have described the book as a continuous record
of daily events where, in the course of writing, memories of the past
surface to be interfoliated in monologue form. Still this is not strictly
true because, as we shall see, the narration often enough evidences no
clear line of demarcation between the present and the past.[14] If we are
to find the key to the form of this novel, we must look beyond the fiction
proper. This is what can be inferred from the view that Fred Stockholder
takes of the speaker's journal-writing. By pointing to how man's "choices"
remain constant irrespective of time, he actually explains what makes
the narrator suddenly turn his attention from past to present and conversely:

> . . . Wilcher's narrative, is more complicated. His story has
> two levels: the first is an account of his life at Tolbrook
> as he writes his journal, and the second a kind of remembrance-
> of-things-past. The life Wilcher observes as he writes the
> journal shows how the choices offered the characters in the
> older story remain constant despite historical changes.[15]

The fact that so many critics fail to sense the speaker's implied address
to a listening addressee apparently explains why so little has been
written on the identity of the voice who is in virtual charge of the
narration. As I hope to show,[16] the author frequently adopts a point of
view that, in reason, does not agree with the fallibility of the objectified narrator-protagonist. Cary once described narration in the first
person as "exceedingly limited in scope and content":[17]

> The first person has great narrative force, but is exceedingly
> limited in scope and content. The third, in its classic form,
> is immensely flexible and revealing, but by the very fact that
> it allows a writer to be everywhere, to see everything, it
> loses conviction and force.[18]

It should be observed that the author comments on the third-person
narration only in "its classic form" and by pointing this out he apparently wants to make it understood that his discussion does not include
Henry James who considered narrating in the first person "a form fore-
doomed to looseness" and, thus, attacked a narrative method on the very
same grounds as, obliquely, Cary defended it.[19] The important thing,
however, is that in To be a Pilgrim Cary proves that the limitations of
first-person narration need not imply a reduction of the author's
autonomy.[20] It appears that, whoever the virtual narrator may be, he
enjoys a perspective that is not only wider than the dramatized speaker'
but actually seems to agree with the author's. For all his objectified
fallability, he on these occasions turns out to be, in Wayne C. Booth's
use of the word, r e l i a b l e , i.e. "he speaks for or acts in
accordance with the norms of the work (which is to say, the implied
author's norms)".[21] This means, in fact, that we listen to two voices
one of which is less reliable whereas the other resounds with authorial
authority.

Cary draws not only an explicit portrait of his hero but, implicitly, he
also gives an inversion of the picture. As a consequence the narrator
proves not only a man of reason and orthodox faith but also an imaginati
"artist" and, in the literal sense of the word, a non-conformist. Throug
Cary's ironic undercutting of his speaker's consciously recorded reality
the reader is given an experience of "real" truth whose complexity the
fiction cannot allow of.

Whether in this way the author succeeds in conveying to his reader an
experience of his symbolist truth is, however, most uncertain. The fact
that, to all appearances, a large portion of his pattern-making has
escaped so many critics' notice does not support such a conclusion.
Indeed there is reason to believe the contrary, in particular as the
irony that has been pointed to has as a rule been taken to be a reflecto
on the objectified speaker's reliability. In this respect Hazard Adams's
view seems most representative although, unlike most of his fellow-
critics, he has understood that Cary's main interest lies in "the minds

(how his characters imaginatively construct their worlds) rather than
the actions of his characters".[22] Adams has realized that Wilcher's
life is a contradiction and that his world mirrors his mind. Still he
fails to do justice to the complexity of the conception that Cary's
novel substantiates:

> So if at first Cary here appears to be concerned with that
> part of the mind that moves above the surface, it becomes
> clear as we proceed that in Wilcher's pathetic and moving
> attempts to deal with his problem by writing it out we
> discover much more about Wilcher than even he is aware of.
> He confesses to more than he realizes; in attempting to
> bring his actions under some rational explanation, he dis-
> closes a gap between action and analysis. Wilcher does not
> really lie to us. Except for the sin of omission he is as
> candid as his emotions will allow but his life itself is
> a contradiction. As his journal proceeds, we realize that
> his eccentric brother and sister, Edward and Lucy, are
> really parts of himself suppressed in odd, unexpected
> ways.[23]

Hazard Adams does not question the speaker's identity. This is certainly
due to the first-person narrative mode where, of course, one of the
chief attractions lies in the narrator's unawareness of his own fallibility and consequent unveiling of character. In this respect To be a
Pilgrim makes no exception to the rule. But the fact that a great deal
of the author's irony is too subtle to alert the attention of several
critics   supports my view that Cary is not only concerned with his
speaker's mind but also with his reader's. Thus the very consistency
of Cary's comic irony testifies to his adherance to Blake's rule that
"that which is not too explicit is fittest for instruction".

In a short essay on Cary's use of form Barbara Hardy offers an analysis
in the light of which she tries to assess his achievement. She praises
the "order" that in, for instance, To be a Pilgrim he has restored to
the popular genre of the family chronicle by his use of the flash-back.
This technique makes it possible for him to show "the flow of generations"
not "consecutively" but "contemporaneously". Being like most critics
primarily concerned with the fiction she never questions the speaker's
identity:

> Cary, like Galsworthy, sets out to show the flow of a family's
> life, but he has the initial advantage of a more assertive theme.
> In his most successful novels he has his eye not on the family
> but on the age. The conflicts, losses and gains of social change

are criticized as they are chronicled, and the criticism is
made directly through character and obliquely through form.[24]

Granted that To be a Pilgrim should be considered a family chronicle,
Barbara Hardy's description is satisfying enough. In that case we can
easily subscribe to her definition of the pattern of the novel as "the
intersection and interruption of past and present" and her view of its
theme as "a fight between past and present".[25] She also gives Cary much
credit for his indisputable sensibility of vision which, according to
her, amounts to an organizing principle:

> It is the dominant sensibility which gives order and simplicity
> to the novel, though in Aissa Saved and The African Witch it is
> not enough to triumph over a crowded and episodic form. But at
> his best - in To be a Pilgrim, The Horse's Mouth, and The
> Moonlight there is not merely a painter's vision but the power
> of organizing the shifting life of pictures and conversations
> into a formal order which is both aesthetically pleasing and
> morally significant.
> . . .
> He is an excellent example of a writer as interested in form
> as a painter or a musician, and it may very well be the in-
> fluence of his painting which makes this conspicuous pattern-
> making. He seems to look on single characters and events with
> that double vision with which Jimson (in The Horse's Mouth)
> looks at his Adam and Eve. They are expressions of humanity:
> Eve leans away from Adam to fend off his first pass. They are
> also units in a pattern: Eve leans back because the composition
> demands it.[26]

Professor Hardy's description of Cary's visual sensibility in terms of
form is indisputably correct but she does not seem fully aware of how
thoroughly this organizing principle manifests itself in his view of
life as well as his art. The more aware we become of this, the more
obvious it will be that the speaker's situation is not only between past
and present but in the focus of various polarities such as individuality
and social allegiance, imagination and reason, dissent and orthodoxy.
Barbara Hardy describes the theme of To be a Pilgrim as "a fight between
past and present" and although this description gives only one aspect of
Cary's total conception, it serves as a sound basis for her analysis and
the credit she gives him for his use of form. The view she takes of his
form-making also helps her to the correct conclusion that his contrapunta
presentation of his hero's two stories implies "ironical portraiture"
as well as criticism of the present by the past:

> Personality is seen as growth and as constancy. The doddering
> old man who misbehaves in parks was once an uncertain child,
> once an excited innocent wondering how one set about getting

> a mistress. And the reader sees them all at the same time.
> . . . Age is only youth in a different body.[27]

Barbara Hardy praises Cary for "the rare enough esthetic pleasure of
assertive form" that some of his best novels give the reader. At the
same time she blames him for what she considers his inability to leave
oblique criticism without annotation. Comparing To be a Pilgrim with
George Eliot's Middlemarch "where contrasts and parallels between persons
and actions do much of the work of definition, and, more important, of
judgment", she makes the following observation:

> Cary is not a George Eliot and he sometimes makes judgment
> too explicit. Past and present show up each other's light
> and shade in a moving dance, but since the past is presented
> as memory it is hard for Cary to avoid explicit comparison.
> The pattern could say it all but since the past is contributed
> by Wilcher's memory, and since Wilcher, unlike Sara, is given
> the intelligence and the experience which can carry the weight
> of historical consciousness, his direct criticism is constantly
> supplementing the oblique comments of the juxtaposed actions.[28]

In Professor Hardy's perspective the speaker's comments on the implied
comparisons may sometimes seem as redundant as they are explicit.[29] Whether
they are "too" explicit or not depends on the reader's ability to adjust
his vision to the author's. They certainly sound too explicit to anyone
who is insusceptible to the division of the "I"-narrator's character
and the uncertainty of his identity. Still the inability of Cary's
critics to do justice to the complexity of his novel does not reflect
so much on their perspicacity as it draws our attention to his literary
theory and its application in practice.

Hardy's concern with the fiction proper and her consequent insusceptibility to the author's use of point of view should, however, in justice be
seen against the fact that her essay was published in 1954, four years
before the appearance of Art and Reality. In a work of more recent date,
Margie Averitt has based a study of the first trilogy on Cary's art
theory.[30] There she thoroughly examines his use of point of view and his
conception of symbolic form. She ascribes "the shift in tone" between
Herself Surprised and To be a Pilgrim to a basic difference in the two
speakers' attitude to life. In her view the former novel is a comedy
whereas the latter is a tragedy. Together they evidence "the unity of
complementary art forms" and she concludes:

> This effect is decidedly like the Blakean mythic interpretation
> of reality.[31]

Referring to a study by Albert Cook,[32] Averitt convincingly clarifies
her point. Cook discusses what he describes as "the great generic dualit
in art[33] by distinguishing between two basic types of human experience,
"the probable" and "the wonderful".[34] Under these headings Cook lists a
number of antipodal attitudes prevalent in either comedy or tragedy. As
the author points out, "each member" of these dualities "depends on and
implies the other, as day does night; man, woman; spring, fall".[35] There
fore Cook's distinction also helps Averitt to an explanation of Wilcher
spiritual conflict. Here follows an abridged and somewhat retouched version of Cook's table of "antipodal qualities":[36]

Probable	Wonderful
Society	Individual
Society	Artist
Rationalism	Idealism
Reason	Imagination
Manners	Ethics
Mean (Aristotle)	Extreme (Christianity)
Predictability	Nonpredictability
Concept	Symbol

Cook's dualities give a worthwhile approach to Cary's conception of
symbolic form even though it should be observed that, as the former make
explicitly clear, his base of discussion, unlike Cary's in Art and Reali
is not "the epistemological problem (reason-imagination)" but "the objec
as-perceived (probable-wonderful)".[37]

According to Cook, "the probable" is "in the realm of p u r e a c -
t i o n ".[38] It is a matter of predictable behaviour due to allegiance
to social norms.[39] In comic plots society adjusts the non-probable to
the probable, "and laughs in the process, because success is achieved".[4]
Tragedy, on the other hand, belongs to the realm of symbolic action. It
is, in other words, a matter of both action and thought, of individual
behaviour that is unpredictable because it disagrees with social norms:[4]

> The plot of tragedy is probable, and the protagonist a normal
> and successful aristocrat.[42] Gradually the individuality of
> his soul unfolds, the predictable becomes unpredictable, the
> wonderful is revealed beneath the superficial pattern of the
> probable, and the audience weeps in recognition of the mystery
> and tragedy of life. In comedy, almost never does a character
> represent the norm, which laughs at him and expels him as he
> implies it by his abnormality.[43]

What, thus, makes Averitt consider the narration of To be a Pilgrim an

"art form" complementary to the "comedy" of <u>Herself Surprised</u> is the
fact that

> . . . what the narration dramatizes is the attempt of the
> "artist" to answer his <u>wonderful</u> problems in <u>probable</u> terms.
> By living in the past Wilcher finally discovers, too late,
> that it is futile to try to expand the old concepts. They
> cannot be revitalized. The only hope for the imagination (and,
> hence, for civilization) is to relinquish them cheerfully.
> All his life Wilcher has felt the tension between these levels
> of reality expressed by Albert Cook in terms of individual
> and social attitudes.[44]

It is true that, as far as the surface narration goes, Wilcher's story
is a tragedy, but like so many other critics Averitt is not sufficiently
clear about the speaker's ambiguous identity and the range of Cary's use
of irony. She seems to be under the impression that it is the narrator-
protagonist's tension between duty to society and duty to himself that
makes the novel carry its point. This is, in my view, not quite true.
We must remember that the fiction proper is only part of Cary's conception and that it is the conflict between the conscious, unfree narrator-
actor and his unconscious, self-willed demon that ultimately gives the
narration its symbolic force. This means that the Blakean "unity of
complementary art forms" that in Averitt's view ties up the entire trilogy,
is also in evidence in <u>To be a Pilgrim</u> and, besides, in each of the
flanking novels as well. In the conscious narrator-actor Cary has in
other words explicitly dramatized an attitude towards life that in Cook's
distinction is "probable" whereas implicitly he objectifies in Wilcher
an antagonist who, giving rein to his "wonderful" demon, dissociates
himself from the golden mean of society.

Apparently Cary experienced a similar division in himself. Enid Starkie
who knew him well[45] found some resemblance between Wilcher and his author:

> The view generally held of Joyce Cary by his critics is that
> he was a rumbustuous man, with an immense love of life and a
> zest for living. I, however, saw him very differently. For me
> this gusto for life was, as it were, a kind of whistling in
> the dark . . . I felt, on the contrary, that he had a sad view
> of life . . . I always felt this pervading sadness beneath the
> gay and gallant manner. Wilcher in To be a Pilgrim seems to me
> to reflect him more fully . . . especially his attitude toward
> life . . . than Gulley Jimson in The Horse's Mouth.[46]

As I hope to show in my analysis of the character drawing, this division
is in evidence not only in the narrator-actor's experience of his own

dilemma and the author-narrator's strictly ambiguous vision of him. As
in A House of Children, a novel about Cary's childhood, it may, to some
extent, also account for the fact that an elder and more experienced
brother now and then relieves the nominal speaker of his function as
authorial mouthpiece. This does not, however, mean that we should disregard the possibility that this distribution of labour was made to
serve an indisputably practical purpose.[47]

Also the narrator's circle of relatives and acquaintances testify to a
similar division. As far as I can see no critic has realized that in
principle it is possible to refer the characters of Wilcher's world to
either of two contrasting somatypes, each tied up with a particular
attitude towards life. Thus ugliness is typical of those who behave in
accordance with Cook's "wonderful" norms whereas those whose actions are
"probable" are beautiful.[48]

An equally striking fact that in the criticism of the first trilogy has
not been commented on, is the apparent ambiguity of some signal words,
such as "faith", "madness", "religion", "responsibility", "grace", which
are too inconsistently used not to tell of the presence of two independent interlocutors in Cary's narrator. Nor has, apparently, any critic
been struck by the change of note in the speaker's voice that follows
every time this implicit dialogue demands a change of perspective. Thus
the voice in whose use "faith" equals dissent evidences a remarkable
self-assurance as contrasted with the anguish and diffidence of the
opposite party.

It is the dialogue that makes the speaker turn his attention from present
to past and conversely, and that, furthermore, makes the narration imply
far more than Wilcher is conscious of. By accounting for the author-
narrator's zigzag course between polar views, the dialogue gives both
shape and unity to the novel.

The more observant we become of the fact that the story dramatizes the
speaker's spiritual conflict, the more liable we may be to look upon the
narrative as allegory. As I hope my analysis will show,[49] all the characters of the novel have allegorical functions[50] which, besides, some
of the names seem to suggest. From this does not, however, follow that
they lack verisimilitude. Golden Larsen comments on this crucial point:

> However, an interpretation of the novel based solely on the
> actions of Edward, Bill, and Lucy [Wilcher's brothers and
> sister] is merely a cartoon of a more subtly realized and
> complex world of the narrator, Tom Wilcher. They can indeed
> be thought of as projections of Tom's own character even though
> such an allegorical approach would most certainly have been
> objected to by Cary. This is not only because he considered
> allegory fatal to art, but also because such an interpretation
> ignores the vitality those characters enjoy in their own right.[51]

In Averitt's view, too, Wilcher is an allegorist "creating the past in
the shape of his own soul".[52] As has already been pointed out, however,
she does not distinguish between the narrator-actor and the author-
narrator but identifies the former with the virtual speaker. Therefore,
in her eye, Wilcher himself cuts no allegorical figure. In my opinion
this is not quite true.[53]

Averitt describes Wilcher as a born but concept-ridden visionary who, in
the course of composing an "apology for his own life", becomes increasingly aware of the fact that "visionary art must reject the convention of
using mental forms already extant in concepts".[54] It is this Blakean view
of art that, according to Averitt, Cary tries to dramatize in To be a
Pilgrim.[55] Quoting a passage of Blake's description of his symbolic
painting "A Vision of the Last Judgment" Averitt offers a welcome epitome
of Cary's lengthy discussion of allegory. She clearly illustrates how the
former "owns the allegory in the middle book of Cary's trilogy":[56]

> The Last Judgment is not Fable or Allegory, but Vision. Fable
> and Allegory are totally distinct and inferior kinds of Poetry.
> Vision and Imagination is a representation of what Eternally
> Exists, Really and Unchangeably. Fable or Allegory is Form'd
> by the daughters of memory. Imagination is surrounded by the
> daughters of inspiration, who in the aggregate are called
> Jerusalem. Fable is allegory, but what Critics call The Fable
> is Vision itself. The Hebrew Bible and the Gospel of Jesus
> are not Allegory, but Eternal Vision or Imagination of All
> that Exists. Note here that Fable or Allegory is seldom without
> some vision. Pilgrim's Progress is full of it, the Greek poets
> the same; but Allegory & Vision ought to be known as Two
> Distinct Things, and so called for the Sake of Eternal Life.[57]

It is Wilcher's experience of what Blake calls "The Fable", i.e. mythic
truth, in his own story that makes him end his life in jubilant joy.
Averitt ascribes this transformation to "the mystery of vision present
in allegory", but for the sake of clarity she coins the term "creative
allegory" which undoubtedly suggests a view to which Blake might have
subscribed.

In my opinion, Blake's classification of allegory, fable, and vision
would have made an excellent preface to To be a Pilgrim because it would
have helped the reader to divine the "wonderful" nature of the insight
Wilcher finally arrives at. In his Fearful Symmetry Northrop Frye gives
an account of what Blake's "vision" amounts to and shows how easily it
lends itself to explaining what suddenly made Cary's hero, a staunch
champion of the Church, give up his orthodox belief:

> Now when something is revealed to us we see it, and the response
> to this revelation is not faith in the unseen or hope in divine
> promises but vision seeing face to face after we have been
> seeing through a glass darkly. Vision is the end of religion,
> and the destruction of the physical universe is the clearing
> of our own eye-sight.[58]

To be a Pilgrim makes a statement of Cary's belief in the Blakean doctrine
that the power of revealing truth solely belongs to the imagination.[59]
It is true that, unlike Blake, Cary was content to draw from phenomenal
life but being a symbolist he remains at the same time a celebrant of
the transparency that, below, the great poet-artist and mystic pays
homage to:

> I assert for My Self that I do not behold the outward Creation
> and that to me it is a hindrance and not Action; it is the
> dirt upon my feet, No part of Me. 'What', it will be Questioned,
> 'When the Sun rises, do you not see a round disk of fire some-
> what like a Guinea?' Oh no, no, I see an Innumerable company
> of the Heavenly Host, crying 'Holy, Holy, Holy is the Lord
> God Almighty'. I question not my Corporeal or Vegetative Eye
> any more than I would Question a Window concerning a Sight.
> I look thro' it and not with it.[60]

When, on the eve of his death, Wilcher has his Blakean Vision, it actually
has the form of a sunrise. It is, in Cook's use of the word, a truly
"wonderful" experience because, as in all tragedy, death cannot but
heighten its significance. Wilcher's revelation comes to him through the
eyes of a painter but unlike Blake he does not try to materialize the
"reality" of the spiritual forms he envisages:

> . . . to me death is a wonder. When I look now at the last
> horizon, I see him rise into the sky, more illuminating than
> the brightest sun, colder than the arctic moon; and all the
> landscape is suddenly altered. The solid hills melt into a
> cloud; and clouds affirm a reality. (p.339)

The insight that at last dawns upon the speaker is in fact what, in him,
the artist all along has tried to convey to his reason, i.e. the Blakean
view that "Mental Things are alone Real". It is in other words a symbol

fusion of fact and feeling, concept and experience, into the "dream"
that, in Art and Reality, Cary rates "truer than life" because it affirms
a reality that no concept can confine. Thus when in the passage below
death, like a rising sun, makes the shadows of the world shorten into
nothing and material things dwindle into "copies" of the immaterial
"real", Wilcher is well on his way into the realm of Unity where time,
space, and other dividers of life are suspended and where the Blakean
"One-ness of the Human and the Divine" is a fact.

> I admired Bill for taking death with such excellent manners.
> But now I see that he was doing something quite natural and
> inevitable. When death rises high above the horizon, the
> landscape draws in its shadows. It becomes flat and ordinary.
> Its details are even insignificant. But there is room for
> more of them and like small copies of the real, like miniatures,
> they become more dear. (p.340-41)

It is true that this statement of wonder may be too explicit to make the
reader share its impact of symbolic ambivalence on the speaker but undoubtedly it implies a homage to the man to whom the author owed his
idea of symbolism.

Thus, as will be shown in detail, To be a Pilgrim is a complex structure
of paradoxes and ironies that calls for an equally complex response in
the reader. It demands that we be susceptible to the novelist's unifying
sensibility or we are liable, like Bloom, to lose our bearings in a
pandemonium of ambiguities. In the latter's view, Wilcher is "an endlessly
divided figure":[61]

> Wilcher falls between two worlds and is in the strange position
> of advocating a life and faith to his niece Ann that he has
> himself never been capable of living.[62]

It should, however, be observed that, for all his inability to accept
the speaker's changing vision, Bloom does not experience a corresponding
cleavage of character in Wilcher:

> The triumph of To be a Pilgrim is that it holds its polarities
> together in the imposing tormented figure of its narrator. It
> is Cary's most sustained exploration of his divided and now
> barely distinguishable worlds.[63]

It consequently appears that, in feeling, Bloom is not unable to identify
himself with the speaker however foreign Wilcher's vision may be to his
mind. This gives us reason to believe that, at least as far as To be a
Pilgrim goes, Bloom is equal to the sympathetic response that according

to Cary the enjoyment of art demands from the reader:

> Without this power of sympathy there is no revelation. Sympathy
> is essential to the reader and writer. But by sympathy the
> reader can obtain from the created world of art a knowledge
> of truth, of the real world, with exactly the same sense of
> illumination as if he had discovered it by force of intuition.[64]

In his study of Cary's fiction, Kraus strongly supports the author's
claim on the reader's sympathy by considering it consequent on his firs
person narrative technique which he compares to Robert Browning's use o
the dramatic monologue, particularly in The Ring and the Book. There,
as in Cary's sequence novels, a group of speakers interpret the same
facts in accordance with their different interests and prejudices.[65]
Kraus bases his discussion on Robert Langbaum's The Poetry of Experienc
where the latter holds that the dramatic monologue cannot work, i.e.
show "facts from within" without the reader's sympathy and the conseque
suspension of his moral judgment.[66] This means, in other words, that th
reader will stand no chance to grasp the meaning of the poem unless he
adopts the speaker's perspective. Thus Langbaum writes:

> By seeing what the speaker sees we are able to identify our-
> selves with him, stand in his position and thus inside the
> poem where meaning resides. Since the projective leap is more
> apparent the more different from our own the view we take, the
> communication is likely to be more emphatic, the more partic-
> ular, the more extraordinary even, the perspective.

> Thus, the dramatic monologue specializes in the reprehensible
> speaker because his moral perspective is extraordinary; and it
> specializes for the same reason in the extraordinary visual
> perspective as the objective counterpart of the extraordinary
> moral perspective.[67]

However "reprehensible" Browning's speakers may be, they strictly obser
their individual viewpoints. "The consistency of the distortion," Langb
writes, "gives unity to the poem by establishing the singleness of the
point of view."[68] The significance of the dramatic monologue consequent
lies in the reader's understanding of the speaker or what, more exactly
Langbaum describes as "the effect created by the tension between sympat
and moral judgment."[69] It is true that, in contrast to Browning's monologues, Cary's trilogy narration allows of dialogue scenes and even
conversation where the primary speaker has no part, but in both, nevertheless, the dramatic element is what Langbaum calls "truth as perspective".[70] Like Browning's monologists, Cary's speakers are "reprehensibl
and, in both, the fact that each maintains his individual perspective

so consistently makes the reader's "condemnation" his "least interesting response".[71]

In Langbaum's view, Browning's use of dramatic monologues in The Ring and the Book is "the first sign of the poem's relativism":

> Such a method can be justified only on the relativist assumption that truth cannot be apprehended in itself but must be "induced" from particular points of view to make each repetition interesting and important as a psychological fact.[72]

This statement equally well applies to Cary's trilogies and reminds us of the fact that, in him, form and meaning amount to the same thing. In both Browning and Cary, the parallel monologues make a joint expression of an epistemology that disbelieves in social and moral absolutes but celebrates the revealing power of art.[73]

Kraus holds that "within the covers of the trilogy there is no Cary" because "he has abdicated the third-person writer's opportunity to make authorial comment".[74] As we have seen, however, this is not true. Thus, in To be a Pilgrim, Cary lets his speaker and the latter's brilliant brother deliver by turns authorial commentary with the same impunity as, in The Ring and the Book, Browning allows himself and, above all, his Pope to shape the reader's experience of the relativist truth the poem dramatizes.[75]

Kraus's analysis of Cary's trilogy technique is interesting because it agrees very well with the author's art theory and therefore throws light on how it works in practice. Unfortunately his concern with the entire trilogies does not make him give sufficient attention to the separate novels. Thus he fails to see the full complexity of To be a Pilgrim. Like so many other critics, Kraus does not question Wilcher's identity and realize in full the speaker's division of vision as well as the protagonist's division of character. Kraus is, in other words, not fully observant of the fact that the portrait of Wilcher, the conformist, suggests the view of a dissenting contrary who is equally "reprehensible". This ambiguity of identity serves, in my view, the important function of making the reader shrink from passing any unequivocal judgment. It makes him feel that, in the speaker's divided world, the pursuit of justice and truth in conceptual terms is bound to lock up judgment in a vicious circle from which there is no escape unless reason is tempered with

sympathy. Therefore the whole novel acts as an object lesson in the
toleration that makes the basis of Cary's ideal of freedom.

In To be a Pilgrim, Tolbrook, the Wilcher family estate, has a history
of constant change that makes it act as a true symbol of England, Cary's
"Protestant" world. Even the name of Tolbrook has the ambivalent make-
up of his symbolism because to tolerate or not to tolerate - or brook -
meant to Cary a conflict.

PART TWO

A STRUCTURAL ANALYSIS OF TO BE A PILGRIM

CHAPTER 1 INTRODUCTION

To be a Pilgrim, the second piece of the trilogy, differs remarkably
from the preceding novel though they share some basic characteristics
and though, ultimately, they reflect a similar view of life.

The Wilcher of Herself Surprised whom Sara Monday, the narrating heroine
served and robbed is the speaker-protagonist of the present novel. Like
Sara, he relates his past and does so in a situation of restraint. However, whereas the hale and hearty Mrs. Monday's lack of freedom is only
physical and temporary, Wilcher's imprisonment extends to the core of
his soul. Thus both narrators live under circumstances that make them
turn in on themselves. They are, however, people of imaginative power,
but whereas Sara plunges with zest into the lush affairs of her past,
Wilcher is on the serious errand of getting in touch with an invigorating
sense of life that never has been his but that, even as a child, he could
experience and admire in others. Sara had this quality, too, and it was
for this reason that he wanted and still wants to start a new life with
her. While, consequently, the buxom cook narrates her story with a show
of morality, Wilcher's narration is a serious pilgrimage undertaken in
order to achieve the freedom of his soul, and the latter's anguished
intellectualism is a far cry from the former's unquestioning exuberance.

In his prefaces Cary describes the trilogy as a set of character novels,
and as regards Herself Surprised he admits that he even went so far as
to cut out his heroine's "notions of history and art" so as not to have
"the essential Sara" "diluted". Whether or not a picaresque story makes
it possible for an author to maintain the rule of "character first" is
not to be discussed here, but the ambiguous portrait she draws of herself leaves it open to doubt if her book can be described as "soaked in
character". In the present novel the reader is faced with the same
question for, in principle, the same reason. Although the narrator is a
man of true intellect and equal to judicious self-criticism, his character is by no means unequivocal. As far as the first novel goes, the
ambiguity of the narrator's self-portrait can be passed off as a true
reflection of the baffling character of the human mind or, possibly, the
eternally feminine; but in To be a Pilgrim it becomes more and more obvic

that an explanation on similar lines does not hold the whole truth as
Cary uses this per se plausible duality to expound, in pros and cons,
his private view of what makes the essence of life. This means that
Wilcher's function is to act out, in his own "life", the author's vision
of values, and that the drawing of his hero's character must be sub-
servient to what the exposition of this view demands.

CHAPTER 2 THE EPIC SITUATION

THE EPIC ILLUSION

In To be a Pilgrim the narrator dramatizes himself in a role that hardly
allows of any sustained writing. Wilcher never evidences any explicit
awareness of the fact that he is relaying his experience to an implicit
à-vis, let alone claiming the authorship of the book, but nevertheless
Cary tries to make up for the absence of a convincing epic frame by
supplying some circumstantial evidence in support of his narrator's
authority. Sometimes we learn that Wilcher is actually holding a pen:

> I did not know that a woman was capable of this careful approach
> to an historical problem. I had almost written too careful, too
> balanced. (p.236)

> And our discussion of the subject gave me the happiest evenings
> of my life. I write advisedly. (p.262)

> . . . he [Edward] had already fitted up his study behind the
> stairs, where I now write. (p.266)

What form Wilcher's writing takes on these occasions remains an open
question, but as there is no other alternative, the reader is apt to
believe that the narrator is committing his thoughts to a diary, i.e. his
"note-books", which he sometimes refers to. Apparently he cannot do without
these as we are made to infer from a description of his hurried prepara-
tions for his visit to London:

> I went upstairs, dressed in my town clothes and packed a bag
> with my notebooks and a clean shirt. (p.300)

The reader is also invited to imagine a very good reason for Wilcher to
keep a diary:

> "You don't really think I am trying to poison you, uncle?"
>
> In my astonishment I jumped to an unlucky conclusion. I said
> that she had no business to read my note-books.
>
> "I don't read them," she answered. "Have you written me down
> as a poisoner?"
>
> "Certainly not. I wouldn't dream of such a thing."
>
> "Do, if you like. You ought to write everything down. It's
> good for you. I kept diary myself once, and it was so awful
> I had to burn it. But it did me lots of good." (pp.89-90)

On none of the above occasions does Wilcher's writing indisputably refer
to the composition of the present novel. Therefore this epic uncertainty
is liable to make the reader welcome any odd bit of information that may

clarify its origin and verify its authenticity.

We are, for example, tempted to believe in an epic illusion which ultimately depends on ourselves as readers. This does not necessarily mean
that Cary tries to seduce the reader into believing in Wilcher's authorship but rather to suspend his judgment by means of some ambiguity. After
quoting a letter to Sara, Wilcher comments:

> Or did I write this? It is always difficult for me to remember
> whether I have actually written to Sara; or only composed a
> letter in my head. (p.37)

These words certainly hold an authorial warning to the reader not to ask
for a verification of authenticity. Anyhow, Wilcher's writing by no means
affects the structure of the novel and at the very end it
becomes perfectly clear that the factual narration is not to be found
within the covers of a note-book:

> Ann came in to put me to bed for the night. She found my note-
> book on the bed and silently removed it. She did not reprove
> me for breaking her order to lie flat and do nothing, and in
> her silence it was understood between us that whether I die
> to-day or to-morrow, does not matter to anybody. But for her
> that is a defeat; for me it is a triumph. (p.342)

This farewell scene proves that the narration is not in the protagonist's
hands. If any reader should believe in Wilcher's diary-keeping as a
plausible form of composition, the removal of his note-book will come
as unexpectedly as the exposure of a counterfeit pianist performing on
a mechanical instrument which refuses to stop playing. In all likelihood,
however, few readers will be surprised at this manifestation of the
virtual speaker's factual autonomy. Throughout he evidences a remarkable
detachment from his experience as if he were a producing dramatist watch-
ing himself acting from the obscurity of the wings. On the other hand we
cannot, of course, expect even a glimpse of this virtual narrator within
the material world of the fiction as he simply does not belong there.
When for once we think we can, behind the words, make out the picture of
a man writing at his desk, we bump unawares into a soliloquizer wandering
about the old house:

> Lucy was strange to both of us. And yet, as I say, every word
> she said, however unexpected, found in me a response; some
> secret nerve within me was excited. To what? I was going to
> write, to the love of God, of religion, to some grandeur of
> thought. But now, as I pace restlessly through the lower rooms,
> I feel it as something deeper, more passionate. The life of the
> spirit. (p.89)

It is true that Wilcher's memoirs lie, so to speak, embedded between the leaves of his note-books, but the basic story by no means fills the sole function of sketching an epic background. At the same time it is integral to the narrative mainstream where past and present contribute, as it were contrapuntally to the illustration of a central theme.

THE INDETERMINATE EPIC "NOW"

It is true that in space no epic situation can be defined, but the fact remains that in time the narrator often seems indisputably removed from what he relates. As far as the memoir narration goes, this is, of course quite natural, but to some extent it also applies to the frame-story. On both narrative levels, however, Cary now and then tries to give the reader the illusion that he is reporting from an epic "now" or, rather, from each of a whole series of similar moments that closely follow the progress of his vision. To give an impression of epic simultaneity this "now" has, of course, to be rendered in the present tense:

> Now that I begin to get used to this girl, I see that she is like Edward in many ways, even in looks. (p.13)

> I thought this couplet in Edward's first book of epigrams, a typical piece of his cynicism; but now I see it's truth. The secret of happiness, of life, is to forget the past, to look forward, to move on. The sooner I can leave Tolbrook, the better, even for an asylum. (pp.34-35)

> And the next day when I had to pass her in the corridor, she pressed herself against the wall and looked at the floor. We were alone, and there was no reason why she should have behaved so respectfully, except her own idea of what was right and proper. I felt then for her an impulse of gratitude and affection, so strong that I feel it now. (pp.77-78)

> This morning, now that Ann has pulled my curtain, I see a sky as pale as Bill's eyes . . . (p.108)

> But even then she did not cry. As the train moved, I saw the narrow, pale oval face, as white as paper, behind the window glass, and the peculiar intensity of her look at Edward. She was frowning as if to concentrate on something that she could not grasp. She was not sure, even then, that she had enough of him to remember. I suppose for all her love of Edward, she had never come very near to comprehending him. And now I see that concentrated frown again when the woman stands before some new task, some new problem. Yesterday it was . . . (p.273)

As contrasted with the present, the use of the past tense tends to remove the observer from his vision, but still the illusion of a diarist's short

narrative distance can be maintained. For this end Cary sometimes inserts
statements of time that, beyond dispute, indicate that the epic situation
is not far behind the action relayed:

> This week, next year, when Sara comes out of goal, shall see
> my salvation. As I wrote to her last night, "With you I can
> make a new life . . ." (p.36)

> When I awoke last night, at half past four, and found myself
> alone at Tolbrook, I felt that I should have to get up and
> knock my head against the wall. (p.38)

> To-day, at luncheon, she said to me abruptly, "Molly's going
> to have a baby." (p.274)

> . . . she is still, three days later, pondering day and night.
> You can see the questions passing round and round her brain,
> like coloured chemicals in an apparatus. "How did Robert do
> such a thing . . ." (p.274)

> To-day, after fiddling about for ten minutes with my pulse,
> temperature, pillows, etc., she plumped out, "I suppose Mr.
> Jaffery wanted to see you about your will." (p.335)

As, however, the novel has no explicit chronology along which the
position of similar statements can be determined, they do not contribute
to the reader's knowledge of the epic situation. Still they heighten our
sense of its existence. After all it takes no exact information of time
and space to give us such an experience. When, for example, the speaker
uses phrases such as "I remember", "I can see", "I admit", "The truth
is", etc., we are reminded of being in the presence of a controlling
narrator.

IMPLICIT SUPPORT OF THE DRAMATIZED NARRATOR'S EPIC AUTHORITY

It has not been possible for the author to devolve, in unequivocal
terms, the formal responsibility for the narration on his chief character.[1] On the other hand Cary gives his dramatized narrator's epic identity
a great deal of indirect verification by now and then making his speech
testify to a restricted perspective that agrees with his role within the
fiction. It is true that, in the two following passages, it is hardly
possible to determine the time that separates the speaker from the
facts he relates, but in either case the narration implies a compara-
tively short narrative distance, and by reflecting his mood at the
moment of telling it makes the reader experience an epic atmosphere

where the speaker addresses him as if he were familiar with his present
circumstances:

> I believe I have been more agitated during this last week in
> Tolbrook than any time since before the last war. For one
> thing, there is a new war fever about; and this time a true
> fever; a disease, a distemper of the blood. I can't bear to
> read all this stuff about Hitler and the Nazis, as if that
> set of cunning rascals were likely to contrive their own ruin
> by provoking war. Thus I cannot look at the morning papers.
> And, for a second thing, it seems that Robert has actually
> gone off with Molly Panton, a thing I could not believe. (p.223)

> Ann has written two letters. It appears that this girl is one
> of those who do not know how to show affection, save with a
> pen. But this very kindness convinces me that she will not
> come back. My happiness with her was illusion. (p.298)

Often enough the narrative distance is so short that it is virtually
negligible. Then epic and drama seem so perfectly wedded that the speaker
who now both relates and acts at, apparently, the same time is hardly to
be distinguished from the objectified actor who, by his very appearance,
verifies the narration. This does not, however, mean that the relation
has lost its original epic character and unequivocally turned into drama.
This is, in fact, scarcely possible as long as, by offering a sequence
of well-organized information, the speaker seems not completely unaware
of the reader's existence which consequently makes the narration still
bear an implicitly epic stamp:

> I stand in my mother's room now. It is a small room opening
> out of the big state bedroom on the second floor. It is the
> only room in the house which remains as it was. I stipulated
> that it should be left untouched.

> I believe my tenants showed it off as a Victorian relic. But
> to me it is a holy place. In this cold morning light, I look
> at its faded hangings, its worn carpet . . . (p.32)

> It is not yet eight o'clock and still gloomy; a cold winter
> morning, but I cannot stay in bed. I get up and go along the
> corridor to the linen room. The baskets ranged beneath the
> shelves, and the linen lying in the close warmth of pipes,
> have the air of all things seen at night, of having been
> interrupted in their private thoughts and memories. (p.76)

> But I can't go to sleep. I cover my head with the bedclothes,
> but still my ears strain, my heart beats; I catch myself
> holding my breath. (pp.23-24)

This reduction of the narrative distance to virtually nil seems to make
the narrator less extrovert or, rather, suspend his awareness of the
reader as if he were an actor appearing before an audience. Again, this

actor is also a dramatist. In the still vital core of his aging brain
the narrator appears to be a man of not only intellectual but also imaginative power who, before "his mind's eye", can conceive what his failing
eyes deny him. At the very end of the novel he draws a remarkable picture
of his imagining self placed in the hub of his own subjective vision:

> As I lie with nothing to do but feel the world agitating round
> my bed, not only the fields about this house are present to my
> mind's eye but the moor, the Longwater, Queensport, and beyond
> them, all the villages and towns of my country, with their
> spires and towers and chimneys standing under this broad day-
> time of eternity, their streams reflecting its face, in the
> innocence of creatures dependent on the whims of the spirit. (p.341)

This scene visualizes the narrator's relation to the wide-scale vision
of British life that he unfolds, but it by no means answers any questions
about the epic origin of the narration.

CHANGING DISTANCE, TIME, AND THE EPIC CHARACTER OF THE NARRATION

In To be a Pilgrim the narrative distance is subject to considerable
change on the level of the memoir as well as in the "diary". The narration
often changes from the present tense into the past or conversely. This
means that in order to sustain the reader's interest the narrator or,
rather, the author avoids sticking to a single mode of narration. If we
compare passages where similar scenes have been reported in different
tenses, the contrast is obvious. Still we can hardly say that the present
testifies to an unequivocal reduction of the speaker's epic concern. On
the other hand the past may heighten the reader's awareness of the virtual
existence of an epic situation:

> In the morning, I lie half asleep . . . (p.46)

> I found myself lying on my bed . . . (p.119)

> But I can't go to sleep. I cover my head . . . (p.23)

> I was far from sleep. I got up and went downstairs . . . (p.161)

So far we have only considered the basic story as, contrary to the memoirs,
it has some epic bearing on the narration. Also when Wilcher deals with
his past, however, he makes frequent use of the scenic present. This
applies above all to the early episodes of his life:

> Nurse's voice says outside, "All right, Miss Lucy - I hear you
> - your papa shall know about this."

> I know that I shall not be whipped while I am ill, so I do
> not care. I am still grinning, full of delight, of the myste-
> rious senseless glory which issues in my laughter and violence.
> I take a firmer hold, and Lucy beside herself, beats at my
> face, with the book. Suddenly the flannel gives way and leaves
> a huge rag in my hand. (p.47)

> We enter a gallery, where, under shaded lights there is an
> exhibition of French prints and pictures. Edward presents me
> to small ugly woman with a snub nose and brown eyes. I notice
> her bad skin, pale and covered with small pits; her prominent
> chin and her darting glance. "Mrs. Tirrit - my brother Tom."
> She raises my hand in the air with a quick pressure, and then
> looking sharply at me says, "Not the soldier." (pp.72-73)

It is true that here the factual narrative distance is indisputably
longer than in the "diary", but whether the narrator's identification is
as a consequence, less intense will possibly remain an open question. In
the main, anyhow, there seems to be little difference as, in the crucibl
of the experiencing narrator's creative mind, past and present run into
a confluence of unique vision. The variation of distance gives variety
to the narration, but even if we allow for the fact that the choice of
tenses seems independent of any dramatized changes of the speaker's
situation, Cary lets him change from present into past or conversely
with such apparent ease that in the course of the narration it tends to
suspend the distinction:

> Amy was a devoted mother; but again, in her own way. An early
> question of hers to my mother was, "How young do you smack
> them?" I remember her as she sat nursing her baby, and looking
> down upon it with an expression I haven't seen for many years;
> a smile of detached calm amusement, as if the baby were a joke,
> of good quality, but too familiar for laughter. And even as I
> look, her hair becomes white, her broad cheeks darken; she is
> an old woman, looking, with exactly the same smile, at another
> baby, whom I do not recognize, a small sickly creature with
> bluish skin and eyes so pale that one cannot call them grey
> or blue. This baby gazes upwards with a fixed look of grave
> curiosity.

> Who is it? It could not be Amy's youngest, who died at three
> of Malta fever.

> I went to look at the old screen, close stuck with family
> photographs, which once stood in the nursery, and now in the
> attic. It was not there . . . (pp.112-13)

> Lucy smiled at me and took my arm. I had forgotten that. But
> now suddenly her arm glides into mine and I perceive how I
> loved Lucy then; . . . (p.21)

> I began to squeeze Lucy and punch my head into her chest, and
> all the time I am laughing. (p.47)

In one and the same context Wilcher sometimes uses the present tense to describe both his actual situation and a distant experience. This does not unequivocally mean that his sense of time has been suspended. In the following passages his use of the scenic present rather helps to dramatize both the ease with which he passes the gulf between past and present and the intensity of his retrospection:

> She [Lucy] darts round the corner, a rosy child in a white fur tippet and a blue coat. She seizes my hand, jerks it violently, and yells, "No, he isn't ready - and his face is s t i l l dirty. Oh, you are a nuisance."
>
> The jerk still jerks me now. (p.25)
>
> In the morning, I lie half asleep, and the pillow frill tickles my neck. Lucy returns to me, no longer a savage with gap teeth, wriggling with mocking laughter or shrieking in rage; she is a warm presence. We are lying in the dark, in this old iron bed where I lie now . . . (p.46)
>
> . . . having tapped the coal on all sides, he [Edward] gives it such an expert stroke that it flies into thin pieces. I see him still, in the glow of the blaze, smiling at his own feat, with the air of one who laughs at his own childishness. (p.76)

If we are to determine whether on the memoir level Wilcher assimilates himself to his vision with less reserve than in the basic narration, we must consider the duality of Cary's speaker who, throughout the whole novel, has not only the ultimate control of the relation but also has to submit to his story by acting it out. In principle, therefore, Wilcher's use of the present tense is both "factual" and "historic" or "dramatic" at one and the same time. The more aware we become of the narrator's self-dramatizing response to his own more or less distant experience, the more apparent becomes the ultimately epic character of the narration.

In principle this answer also applies to the basic narration, but here the epic effect tends to be blurred by the, at least seemingly, factual proximity of the narrator's vision.

CHAPTER 3 THE CENTRAL THEME AND THE VARIABLE OF VISION

About Tolbrook Manor we learn:

> Although it stands high, it has no view. (p.11)

Significantly enough the narrator is at a similar disadvantage. He describes himself as "short-sighted" (pp.80,142) whereas his sister finds him "blind" (pp.21,22,290). It is true that Wilcher has weak eyes, but his deficiency of vision is primarily a manifestation of his frame of mind which, tying him to the past, has made him blind to life and left in a twilight world of anxiety and bondage. The neglected Tolbrook is the navel of his life and a symbol of his world. There he was born and there he is to end his days. It is true that the Manor is so submerged in the gloom of ancient trees that "it has no view", but to the old man it makes an entrance to the past. As the purblind Wilcher's journey through life is slowing down towards its final station, he enters a world of memories that quickens his spirit and lengthens his sight, and finally when past runs into present, life appears to him in a new light that, on the verge of death, makes him experience a new birth. Under the spell of history the narrator changes from a bewildered outsider in the present into an initiated describer of the past. The cheerful vitality he evidences on his first morning at Tolbrook is as astounding as it is significant:

> I slept deeply, my first good sleep for months, and when I
> waked, early as usual, a short enquiry revealed that I was
> still in good health and excellent spirits. Neither Tolbrook
> nor Ann had upset me. On the contrary, I was excited by the
> thought of exploring the old house, after so many years. I
> opened all doors to these memories, from which, in my late
> mental anxiety, I had fled, and at once my whole body like
> Tolbrook itself was full of strange quick sensations. My
> veins seemed to rustle with mice, and my brain, like Tolbrook's
> roof, let in daylight at a thousand crevices. (p.14)

In his narrator-protagonist Cary has, indeed, provided himself with a narrating medium of great versatility. Not only does his narrating "I" keep the close perspective of the dramatized alien at Tolbrook, but at the same time he offers the sovereign views of an enlightened commentator. Outside the realm of fiction this dichotomy may hardly seem valid, but as it is it makes the essence of Wilcher's character and the character of his life. He is a man of true intellect and free views but also of strong sentiments which far too easily invert his bold outlooks into anxious myopia or as Cary's preface has it:

> . . . he has grown up, like many Englishmen, Liberal by con-
> viction but Conservative in heart. In him, that is, the at-
> tachments of sentiment, which are the perpetual root of Con-
> servative feeling, are stronger than the drive to adventure. (p.7)

In fact, Wilcher has been granted to voice this prefatorial insight himself, and his despair at the fickleness of his vision certainly helps to
reconcile the warring elements of his character:

> Why do I ever forget that the glory of my land is also the
> secret of youth, to see at every sunrise, a new horizon. Why
> do I forget that every day is a new landfall in a foreign
> land, among strangers. (p.109)

This constant battle between spirit and sentiment, detachment and attachment, is reflected in Wilcher's contradictory use of the word "faith".
Sometimes his allegiance to the past prevails on him to use the word in
a narrow, i.e. dogmatic, sense:

> . . . I remembered that only that morning I had been speaking
> to her [Ann], perhaps too insistently, about the necessity of
> religion. "The world is senseless without faith," . . . (p.174)

Often enough Wilcher's sentimental "myopia" makes him unable to distinguish
between the doctrine and the spirit:

> "You shouldn't talk about faith arising from chairs as if you
> were a savage. Faith is an act of the intelligence, as you
> ought to know," etc.
>
> For I value very much the girl's intelligent and honest mind
> . . . (p.238)
>
> . . . on one of our afternoon walks, I took occasion to remark
> on the importance of religious education for young children.
> "They cannot, of course," I said, "understand the a r g u -
> m e n t s for the existence of God, simple and irrefragable
> as they are. They can be taught only to recognize the e x -
> p e r i e n c e of God, of goodness in their own hearts, and
> in other people's acts, so that when they grow older, they are
> ready for those proofs upon which faith must stand, unbreakable
> and triumphant. (pp.79-80)

On other occasions, however, the narrator evidences a detachment of
vision that makes "faith" equal the unquestioning trust in life from
which free and enterprising characters, such as Lucy and Sara, have drawn
their power and bliss. Though Wilcher thinks he lacks this spirit himself,
he can recognize and admire it in others. Defending Sara against Ann's
charges of hypocrisy he takes a view of religion that altogether disagrees
with the norms of his conservative self:

> "Sara seems to have got a hold on you, uncle."
>
> "She is a remarkable person."
>
> "She rather affected the religious, didn't she?"
>
> "No, you are quite wrong. She never affected anything, but she
> is deeply religious. She is one of those people to whom faith
> is so natural that they don't know how they have it. She has
> a living faith." (p.11)

In fact, Sara is an incarnation of "living faith". She is an itinerant
servant without a permanent abode. Unlike her master she is a free soul
and in her humble labour for her daily bread he finds a manifestation o
life in "faith":

> . . . I saw, as by revelation, that deep sense from which Sara
> had drawn her strength and her happiness, the faith of the
> common people. That faith which is expressed in so many proverbs,
> "A great inheritance; two of each and one gullet." "Give me
> hands, give me lands." And I entered into the minds of those
> who for generations have known life as an enterprise for their
> bread. Who do not think in terms of inheritance or profession,
> but of a temporary shelter and a month's wages. (p.130)

As a matter of fact all the characters of the novel contribute to this
exposition of "living faith" either by their abundance of this quality
or by their manifest lack of it. It is true that, time and again, the
narrator claims to be inbued with this spirit, but at the same time his
i n c o n s c i e n c e makes it clear to the reader that the view he
takes of "faith" makes him blind to his dramatized self. In short,
Wilcher's portrait of his past ego is still as valid as ever:

> The truth is, that when Sara came to me, I was a lost soul. I
> had become so overborne by petty worries, small anxieties,
> that I was like a man lost in a cave of bats. I wandered in
> despair among senseless noises and foulness, not knowing where
> I was or how I had got there. I loathed myself and all my
> actions; life itself. My faith was as dead as my heart; what
> is faith but the belief that in life there is something worth
> doing, and the feeling of it. (p.35)

Although the narrator is not unaware of the impermanency of his vision,
he does little to reconcile the opposite views he maintains. The dualit
of his vision does not, however, only lie in the ambivalence of his
character but also in the fact that his travelling both past and presen
splits his identity and helps to make the discrepancy between his senti
mental myopia and his intellectual hyperopia the more apparent. Actuall
these two conflicting manifestations of the narrating "I" usually evide
little awareness of one another. From the very outset it has been grant
to the narrator's intellectual self to aquaint the reader with a view

that his sentimental ego does not attain until his passage through the
past has brought him back into the present. Only when Wilcher comes to
relate a beloved nephew's remarkable failure in life, does his myopic
vision extend to admit a deeper perspective:

> How does faith fail? Why does its sap cease to run? Not by age
> or disease. John was young and strong. When I said prayers
> this morning, I said to myself "I must love these words, I
> must rejoice in truth." But in that act, I felt my spirit
> withdraw from them like leaves touched by frost, some devil's
> breath from the perverseness of my will. (p.288)

When, eventually, "living faith" fills his soul, Wilcher's emotional
self exults as if he had never been aware of this view before. Still it
amounts to what his intellectual "I" has been expounding from the very
beginning:

> "What does that matter whether you're a Christian or not?" I
> said. And I was so much surprised by my own words that I
> suddenly began to smile, like someone who has made an epigram
> by accident. (p.340)

Thus Cary's exposition of "faith" follows the course of a variable
evidencing both positive and negative aspects, and as a consequence of
the narrator's fickle vision the reader will hardly be apt to share
Wilcher's surprise at the sudden release of his spirit. At the beginning
of the novel we are, in fact, given to understand what his return to
Tolbrook is going to mean:

> An old house like this is charged with history, which reveals
> to man his own soul. (p.26)

This remarkable versatility of vision makes the narrator harbour both
dramatized "inconscience" and authorial insight. This means that although
the author has objectified himself in the role of a fictive narrator and,
consequently, withdrawn his real self into off-stage anonymity, his voice
can still be heard commenting on the significance of his hero's situation.
Before Wilcher starts narrating the story of his life, the reader is
granted an argument that gives the key to his character and maps the
course of his life:

> And is not that the clue to my own failure in life. Possessions
> have been my curse. I ought to have been a wanderer, too, a
> free soul. Yes, I was quite right to break off from this place.
> Although I have loved it, I can never have peace till I leave
> it. (p.16)

In practice, Wilcher gives himself up to the preservation of his property,

notably the old house and its shading trees, but nevertheless he now and
then brings up the authorial view of love as a burden to the mind:

> I told Ann Tolbrook would kill me, and I was right. I have
> never had peace or comfort in this house. I have been too fond
> of it. To love anything or anybody is dangerous; but especially
> to love things. (p.34)

> But I thought, "It is my own fault. Haven't I known all my
> life that it was folly to give my affections to sticks and
> stones and all that helpless hopeless tribe," etc., etc. (p.119)

Though the privileged narrator is well aware of the fact that his own
life-long attachment to the past is antagonistic to "living faith", this
insight cannot transform his sentimental self until, towards the end of
his re-experience of life, it matures into a truly spiritual experience:

> For the truth is, I have always been a lover rather than a
> doer; I have lived in dreams rather than acts; and like all
> lovers, I have lived in terror of change to what I love. (p.333)

CHAPTER 4 NARRATIVE MODES AND THE VARIABLE OF CONSCIOUSNESS

In the preceding chapter we saw how the author expresses his theme by shifts of point of view. These shifts also evidence a division of character in the speaker. This cleavage may raise doubts about his identity when his vision seems more privileged than the fiction can reasonably allow of. The narrator's character is, however, an aspect that should be kept apart from the character of the narration although there is an obvious connection. Therefore the best approach to Cary's use of his "I"-narrator is an examination, not of the shifting vision but of the speaker's varying consciousness of his narrating role. This variability should be represented as a gamut ranging from complete unconsciousness of any reader's attention to passages of an indisputably epic character. Yet the intermediate stages between these extremes are often difficult to define, and so I prefer, for the sake of clarity, to split up the following survey of Cary's use of various narrative modes into four main parts: formal soliloquy, self-objectification, controlled scenic exposition, and epic narration. Under these headings we have to consider various mixed forms. Last but not least we must bear in mind that the study of epic awareness always implies some discussion of vision.

FORMAL SOLILOQUY: THE OMNISCIENT AUTHOR TURNS HIS SPEAKER'S SELF-ABSORPTION TO ADVANTAGE

It is true that at Tolbrook the narrator's days are spent in isolation and idleness, but none the less the relation holds an implicit epic address that runs counter to the view of the circumstances that he conveys to the reader. Only occasionally and in passing does the narration evidence an introversion that completely agrees with his explicit self-description. The following passage reflects a gradual toning down of the speaker's epic awareness until we are faced with a rather self-absorbed actor.

> So, too, when I came home and related the story to Edward, I made it out a victory for myself, as a reasonable, a civilized person; a lover of justice and decency. But, in fact, I had not dared to wait another moment in case I, too, like the Jones', had fallen on my knees and confessed myself a miserable sinner. The dark wave was rising over me, and I had longed to drown in it; to get rid of self; to find what? A cause. Excitement. The experience of suffering, of humiliation, so attractive to my sense. Above all, an answer to everything. (p.69)

This dramatic effect is achieved by a change of style. What makes the
speaker seem to be absorbed by his own thoughts, lies in the abridged
utterances and his manifest predilection for rhetorical questions. On
the other hand, these moments of slackening consciousness are too brief
and few to affect the general character of the narration. Their chief
function is to give objectifying reminders of the speaker's fictive
identity, and soon enough the reader is usually back in the narrator's
conscious care. In the passage below we can follow how Wilcher's conscious
ness runs low indeed until, all of a sudden, it resumes its original
tension:

> And my reward for years of heavy soul-destroying worries is to
> be thought and called a usurer.
>
> The love of possessions. It is spoken for a reproach, and I feel
> it like shame. But what are these possessions which have so
> burdened my soul. Creatures that I have loved. The most help-
> less of dependants. For their very soul, their meaning, is in
> my care.
>
> A woman loves her baby in its weakness and dependence, but
> what is more dependent than a house, a chair, those old books,
> a tree.
>
> In these savage family quarrels of 1913, I would clap on my hat
> and go out to walk under the trees. (pp.219-20)

The introversion that the narrator thus evidences varies considerably,
but, on the whole, it is not far below the level of conscious narration.
Wilcher is liable to soliloquy, but his isolation makes it fair to assume
that sometimes it is not failing self-control but an urgent need to argue
himself out of his affliction that, for want of another listener, makes
him talk to himself:

> I am an old man, and I have not much longer at Tolbrook. This
> is April, and before next April I shall have left for ever. I
> want to use every moment of these last months at home with
> those I love, with Lucy and Amy, Bill and Edward. (p.114)
>
> And as for a plough or so, temporarily deposited in my house,
> why should I quarrel with them. Taken in the proper spirit,
> they can be an inspiration. I must not forget my first visit
> to Sara . . . (p.129)

Only on very few occasions does the narrator seem completely oblivious
of his epic role and then his eyesight becomes a visionary's. In the
following monologue the narrator's awareness of his epic function has
subsided to a low-water mark but at the same time the soaring elocution
resounds with the voice of his spiritual father:

The monk, in his sleepy routine, who seduced my weakness just
now, where is he? A new vigorous generation snatched his peace
away; the generation of my ancestors, who made a farmshed of
his chapel and bore their half-pagan children in his holy cell.
Who once more pulled up England's anchor and set her afloat on
the unmapped oceans of the West. Why do I ever forget that the
glory of my land is also the secret of youth, to see at every
sunrise, a new horizon. Why do I forget that every day is a
new landfall in a foreign land, among strangers. For even
this Ann, this Robert, are so changed in a single night, that
I must learn them again in the morning. And England wakes
every day to forty million strangers, to thousands of millions
who beat past her, as deaf and blind as the waves. She is the
true flying Dutchman. (p.109)

SELF-OBJECTIFICATION

The "I" who commands the author's vision can be justly described as the
v i r t u a l speaker even when at times he reduces his perspective
and thus leaves for the stage of action. The more aware we become of
the fallible actor's "myopia", the more easily we retain the author's
vision, however true it may be that it is now no longer stated explicitly
but is only implied. As, even in his absence, the privileged speaker's
existence remains so obvious, I often find the proper term "implied author"[1]
somewhat inadequate. Therefore I frequently, though not consistently,
call him "the virtual speaker". The latter's relation to his acting
self is subject to considerable variation. However, Cary objectifies his
hero in two principal ways. Either he blunts his consciousness of his
own acting self or he makes him unconscious of the ambiguity of his own
speech, not to mention his inconsistent use of some ambiguous words. In
the chapter on "the vision variable" I discussed the dual meaning of
"faith" and in the last two chapters I will present numerous other
instances of verbal irony. Therefore I will here be mainly concerned
with cases of self-objectification for which, primarily, the actor and
not the speaker s e e m s responsible.

1) The virtual speaker removes himself from his self-objectification

While Wilcher is pursuing his pilgrimage for his lost soul in the autonomous realm of his mind, he usually evidences little concern with his
present life unless it is integral to what appears to be the author's
ultimate vision of "faith". We learn very little about the narrator's

"stage-costume" apart from a few occasional glimpses that give a somewhat bizarre sketch which, like a caricature, settles his appearance in
the eyes of the other characters at the same time as it removes his
recording presence.

Throughout his life Wilcher has stuck to the fashion of his day. In the
main he seems aware of the fact that time has marooned him in a foreign
generation and that the values of the young are beyond him. On the other
hand he cannot sufficiently dissociate his observing self from his acting
ego and watch the aging man of superannuated fashion through the detached
eyes of the silent author. Thus, although Wilcher fully realizes the
gulf of time that alienates him from the young, notably Gladys, John's
wife, and Ann, he cannot explicitly share their feelings before this
Victorian version of Brummel released from a panopticon:

> Then suddenly she [Gladys] became animated, jerked her shoulders
> one way, her behind the other, laughed in my face and said,
> "That's all right Uncle Lucifer. You needn't be afraid for
> your precious infant - it's not John would be ruined if we
> clicked," and she told me she wouldn't dream of marrying a
> man who couldn't afford even to keep a car.
>
> The strange appellation, Lucifer, startled me as much that I
> did not know how to answer. It was only afterwards, from Julie,
> that I discovered it to be a reference to my legs, or rather
> trousers. My good city tailor quite agreed with my dislike of
> seeing men drape their legs in two skirts, and my trousers
> were cut on the old manly basis, to show the limb. The infantile
> mind of Gladys had found this reasonable fashion, or rather,
> principle, amusing; and she was accustomed to refer to me as
> Lucifer legs, or more formally, as Uncle Lucifer. (pp.272-73)[2]
>
> If I ordered to-morrow a young man's suit, with enormous
> trousers and a tight waist, and put on my head a little Amer-
> ican hat like a soup plate, or one of those obscene objects
> called a Tyrolese hat, I should look and feel so disgusting
> to myself that life would not be worth living. Yet when I
> examine myself, as now, in a long glass, with Ann's eyes, I
> see that I must be a queer object to a stranger, and a young
> stranger. (p.10)

In the focus of his own conscious observation Wilcher objectifies himself
on the line suggested by his dress. This means in other words that here
actor and narrator seem so perfectly agreed that the latter fails to see
what in the author's eye ultimately justifies the appellation "Lucifer".
His conceited contempt of the present hardly makes him a prepossessing
figure. Still the lonely man's blind attachment to bygone values endears
him to the reader. Indeed his failing control of the narration too clearl

points to authorial dispensation to reflect on the speaker's character. Often Cary reminds us of his hero's norms by not making him live up to them. Here, for example, the staunch Liberal unconsciously manifests a nettled sense of class that hardly agrees with the ideals of his conscious self:

> . . . in my rage and alarm, I put on my hat and took a taxi to John's place of business. It was one of the smaller shops, of highest distinction. Its showroom was furnished luxuriously with fine rugs, cut chandeliers, palms, and so forth. John was engaged with a client, a woman. But his fellow salesman knew me and did not trouble me. I pretended to examine the cars. John affected to enjoy his work, but it always made me uneasy to see him humouring his clients, whether they were of his own class, who were excessively polite and smiling, as with their servants, or some rich woman, of a lower class, insolent and mannerless. At the moment, he was dealing with two such women; mother and daughter; a fat beast with the bulging jowls of a French pug, and a skin like a leper, whose expression, as she looked round, was so ridiculous in its arrogance, that one would have laughed at her, if it had not been for the cruelty of her stare, her crooked mouth; the young girl had the smooth mask of profound stupidity, ignorance and conceit, painted to give the idea of luxurious perversity. But it was marked already with the peevish ill-temper which goes with small minds and petty selfishness. Both women wore furs and jewels of great value. (p.285)

In this way the narrator unconsciously draws a self-portrait whose scenic objectivity cannot be disputed. Below we recognize the Wilcher of Herself Surprised who there solicited his Sara with Jamesian circumspection with a view to putting an end to the lumbago that in cold weather followed on his visits to his mistress:[3]

> We were sailing in his cranky little boat, a pursuit which caused me acute misery. For wet, especially in the seat, always gave me rheumatism; the motion of a boat, even on a calm day, made me ill; the necessity of continually getting up and moving across to the other side of the boat, and ducking my head under the boom, at the risk of my hat, broke up every conversation and exasperated me extremely; and, finally, I could conceive nothing more stupid than to proceed by zigzags, from nowhere to nowhere, for the sake of wasting a fine afternoon. Neither, if I might mention such a point, though it is probably unimportant, have I ever been able to understand why there was no accommodation provided on small yachts, for things like sticks and umbrellas; whereas land conveyances, such as gigs and even governess carts, always have a basket designed for their proper storage and protection. (p.246)

The umbrella seems to make him a true companion through life. With snobbish conceit he handles this baton of distinction:

> John and I protested with force. I at once measured the floor
> with my umbrella, which was exactly one yard in length, with
> inches nicked on the handle. I have all my umbrellas made to
> this pattern, which has shown its worth in many a family
> discussion. (p.281)

Even at more critical moments his umbrella comes in useful. Here
he flaunts his skill at using it as a pointed weapon while fighting a
dubious cause with the determination of an erring Quixote:

> I had my narrow escapes. I was assaulted and threatened. A
> young man who intervened on one occasion when a young woman
> showed offence, attacked me with a stick; but I nearly ran
> him through with my steel umbrella. I remembered Edward's old
> advice, founded on the history, that, with the white arm, the
> thrust has always defeated the cut. So in this little battle,
> the force of evil, better instructed, utterly defeated that
> of virtue, which was left breathless on the ground. (p.308)

This interlude of somewhat conceited triumph is set in a context of
contrition from which it diverges jarringly enough. To all appearances
Cary has given in to the temptation of making more fun of his hero than
his character allows of. In the following passage the author
even goes so far as to shed his humour not only on Wilcher's queer appa-
rition but on his whole existence of dissolving values:

> The thunder did not break. Instead, the drops increased in
> number and suddenly became a flood. The trees, the hedges and
> the fields, the sky itself and all its gesticulating silent
> mobs wavered like reflections in a stream, suddenly touched
> by a breeze, and then dissolved into an air which was largely
> water. I found myself alone among warm cataracts, with no
> distinction of material for the senses, except the variety of
> noise; the dashing of leaves, the roar of boughs, the hissing
> of a copse, the rustle of hedges, the tinkle of drains. Which
> proved so delusive that in the thickened twilight I lost my
> way and found myself walking in the stubble, mixed with new
> clover, of a field already cut; an accident not surprising on
> such an evening. But now of such bewildering effect that, as
> I stood, with every clover leaf pouring its waterfall into my
> boots, I felt as if the very earth were liquifying under my
> feet, as if the familiar trees, fields and sky had actually
> melted into some primitive elementary form, and that the world
> of German philosophy, in which everything can be anything else,
> as the philosopher pleases, had actually realized itself in
> a universal nothingness, whose very colour was uncertain. And
> I, the very last individual being of the old creation, though
> still solid in appearance, and capable of supporting a hat;
> as I ascertained by touch; trousers, umbrella, etc., as I
> perceived by sight, was yet already wavering in essence, be-
> ginning to lose the shape of my ideas, memory, etc., prepar-
> atory to the final and rapid solution of my whole identity.
> (p.277-78)

For all Wilcher's seriousness before life he occasionally evinces a
sense of humour to justify this deluge of levity. Here, however, the
virtual speaker very clearly dissociates himself from the actor by making
fun of the symbolism that his novel so seriously celebrates.

2) The action affects the narrator's control

So far we have examined cases of self-objectification where the virtual
speaker seems to have removed himself from the actor and by letting the
reader share his privileged perspective invites us to laugh at his hero's
lack of self-criticism. To some extent, however, this dramatization of
pedantry, conceit, etc. can also be seen as the result of the actor's
influence on the narrator. This is what we are given to imagine when the
recording of an exasperating incident makes him re-experience the incident
so vividly that he flies into another uncontrollable fit of passion. Then
the narrator is so vehemently carried away by his own feelings that his
lack of control seems to objectify the action. Thus his version of an
upsetting visit that Jaffery, the Tolbrook estate manager, paid him on
the day of the actual narration, is still resounding with the indignation
he experienced on the occasion:

> And when I began to shout that I knew all about his plots with
> Robert and Ann, to put me out of the way and get hold of my
> property, he was fairly beaten. He jumped up. Ann came quickly
> in with a look which meant, "There; he is insane after all,
> what a bore." And Jaffery retreated at full speed. But I could
> tell by the way that he moved his turkey's neck that he was
> frightened. Which gave me some satisfaction. And might give
> me some more, if they lock me up. Who can tell? (p.34)

In the above scene the narrative distance is very short but time seems
immaterial since a far more distant, though partly similar, scene exerts
an equal influence on him. Thus a heated dispute with a clergyman of a
less orthodox turn touched off such a violent temper that its reverber-
ations are still ringing in his version of the affair:

> I . . . approached the fellow, a lanky tallow face from Cam-
> bridge, asked him to tea, and brought up the subject of evil.
> I suggested that the modern church did not lay enough emphasis
> on the positive nature of evil, etc. He answered that in his
> view the Church ought to go in for socialism.
>
> I saw, of course, that he was trying to evade my point, and
> I put it to him plainly, "Do you believe in the devil or don't
> you?"
>
> To which, twisting up his mouth into a conceited knot, he

> answered that, even in the Fathers, the reality of the devil
> was not so strongly developed as laymen supposed. He was
> regarded rather as a negation of God, or a general name for
> the characteristics of man's fallen nature, and so on, a heap
> of heresies.
>
> . . .
>
> "The devil," he answered in his abominable accent, "is said to
> be a gentleman, and therefore probably supports the government,
> so that I certainly disapprove of him."
>
> This horrible levity upset my temper, and I said that the
> matter was scarcely one for raillery, and that if he were not
> my guest, and entitled to special consideration, I should be
> obliged to tell him what I thought of his hypocrisy, manners,
> appearance, etc.
>
> He withdrew then at speed. For I admit that I had now lost my
> temper and uttered some abuse of which I was afterwards ashamed.
> But it was untrue, as reported in the village, probably by the
> wretched creature himself, that I had threatened to mutilate
> him. Though it has occurred to me since, that emasculation would
> have been the appropriate fate for one who had performed a
> similar operation on the doctrines of the Church.
>
> I had silenced the Judas, but he was not to be defeated for,
> as I might have reflected if I had not been led away by the
> dispute, he was already sold to the devil's service, who had
> armoured him already with the inpenetrable brass of intellectual
> conceit. He actually preached against me. I could no longer
> read the lessons in church, and finally was obliged to cease
> from attendance. For I could not take communion from the hand
> of a blackguard who had betrayed the creeds, and denied the
> devil, at such a time of crisis. (pp.247-48)

Although, on the one hand, the narrator is judicious enough to regret hi

behaviour and realize that behind his aggression was fear, his emotional

self, on the other hand, remains blind enough to indulge in the passion

of the moment and, before he leaves the episode, to serve his off-stage

adversary a final kick:

> This separation from my beloved church was a great grief to
> me and I blamed myself for my impatience with a wretched
> nincompoop who was perhaps, from education, incapable of that
> moral courage necessary to acknowledge the evil nature of man;
> as well as the good.
>
> My excuse is that my friends were being killed and, above all,
> I felt that secret fear which is a much more powerful motive
> than the strongest principles. (pp.248-49)

If the above scene should not convince the reader of the devil's existenc

it certainly proves the presence of the author who, with a fiendish smil

makes his poor Oxonian give away his blinding conceit at the same time

as he prompts the benighted man's Cantabrigian opponent. And who knows?

Perhaps, after all, Wilcher did threaten to emasculate him.

3) The insufficiency of the narrator's local awareness

Wilcher's chief characteristic is his instability. As we have seen, it
affects both his vision and his consciousness and in his latter days of
developing asthenia and decrepitude it has become even more pronounced.
His occasional losses of self-command are typical manifestations of his
unsettled mind and may explain his inability to verify the threats that
he was said to have uttered against the clergyman, and it seems to give
the key to his surprise at his dawning awareness of finding himself in
a place where his steps have taken him:

> And I distinctly heard Ann's voice say something about the
> time. "Perhaps," I thought, "she is talking to herself; and
> in any case, I'm not going to expose myself to ridicule by
> any further interference with these children. They have their
> own ideas about things."

> But a moment later, to my own surprise, I found myself in the
> passage, at the door of the nurse's room. (p.38)

> And early in the morning, I found myself in Robert's little
> orchard, on the site of the old shrubbery. The cold spring
> wind blowing round my legs and up my dressing-gown awoke me.
> (p.210)

A similar insufficiency of consciousness is also reflected in the narrator's somewhat mechanical way of relaying to the reader an, apparently,
passively experienced vision of his physical presence outside the privacy
of his introvert world. Wilcher can be so lost in his thoughts that we
know nothing of his epic whereabouts until some voice calls him back to
reality. He certainly makes no secret of the fact that at night he is
sometimes so restless that Ann has to lock him up to make him stay in
bed as otherwise he is liable to stray away, and that on other occasions
he is in a state of what he well describes as "tranquil weakness" (p.119)
that rules out any precaution. When, however, voices from outside break
in upon his introversion and alert his awareness enough to make him join
the outside world, the scene that presents itself to the reader seems
not perfectly within his own epic control:

> Ann left this morning, in snow, a quick heavy fall which has
> given us a blue sky. All the rooms in the house are filled
> with its reflection.
> . . .
> Only the plaster work remains from the magnificence of the
> past; some absurd cherubic angels blowing trumpets and playing
> dulcimers and zithers on the ceiling. Who, in this borrowed
> light of the sky seem to give out from their bulging cheeks
> and dinner plate halos, a faint radiance of pale blue light,

> as if some angelic essence, transmitted from above, made
> them recall their birth, in an age of romantic faith.
>
> "Excuse me, sir," Mrs Ramm is peeping round the door.
>
> "Yes, yes, yes." I jump off the bed. (p.292)
>
> No one appreciated comfort and luxury like Lucy. But she left
> them in a moment. Why? Not for love; not for charity: Not
> because her conscience troubled her. Not for the sacrifice.
> But for the adventure. Lucy was one of those whose faith is
> like a sword in their hands, to cut out their own destinies.
> That faith has come to me now. At least, I hope so.
>
> "Who are you talking to, uncle?" I am sitting in Lucy's arm-
> chair looking at Ann in a blue dressing-gown. (p.55)

In the last passage, for example, the narration suggests no complete
self-absorption until the unexpected discharge of Ann's question sudden
lights the reader's insight. It consequently rests with the imaginative
reader to develop the significance of the scenic vision the author is
holding out to him. Even if, as in the two following cases, the use of
the past tense gives the narration some stamp of epic control, the ultimate effect of the narrator's words is implied in what seems to be an
involuntary materialization of his epic circumstances. Whether, therefor
the reader shares the dramatist-author's conception of a scene, as in
the above present-tense cases, from the negligible distance of the or-
chestra stalls or, as below, he has been removed to the upper circle, is
immaterial to his realization of the effect the author aims at:

> Passionate Lucy threw herself upon the dark wave of fate, of
> God's mysterious will; and in the presence of the little maid,
> part of me cried, "Foolish and wicked boy, you are destroying
> the peace of your home and your heart." And another part, "Be
> reckless, have faith - take no thought for the morrow - cast
> your bread upon the waters."
>
> "Hullo, uncle, I was wondering where you'd got to." Robert
> stood before me, but his eyes did not look at me. He did not
> wish to show any surprise at my position, with outstretched
> arms against the wall. (p.78)
>
> This was no romantic freak. To Amy and Bill, I am sure, it
> was the common thing. To simple-minded persons, miracles appear
> like nature. In the same way, they expected to be happy, to
> love one another, etc., and therefore they did so.
>
> "A kind of faith cure," Ann said to me, and I thought I must
> have been speaking aloud. (p.104)

It must, however, be pointed out that the narrator also evidences the
same passive or matter-of-fact attitude to his experience of the past
when, on some occasions, unreported speech pops out of nowhere and,

consequently, helps to dramatize the confluence of past and present that seems to raise his experience of faith above the vicissitudes of time:

> As I stand here at the door of the nursery staircase, collecting my strength for the climb, I hear Lucy's voice screaming to me furiously, "Tom-my, Tom-my. Aren't you ready?" (p.25)

> My battles with Lucy were a family joke, and even I could not understand why I fought her; why once, at six years old, I tried to kill her. Indeed, I often tried to kill her. But the reason was, that she made me murderous with her devil.

> "What an extraordinary boy you are, Tommy." Her voice flies at me out of the dark like a snake out of ambush. (p.27)

4) The habitual meddler's blunted sense of self-criticism

It is true that the insufficiency of Wilcher's consciousness is due to failing health and power, but then we must consider that his life has rutted into habits so deep that they have blunted his ability to judge, on some points, his own doings. Wilcher has always been an inveterate meddler and still he cannot help interfering, at least not in Ann's and Robert's family affairs. On Ann his influence turns out to be considerable. By and by he signally wins her over to the values that make the basis of his life. She starts redecorating the old house to what it was a generation before and she even has a hand in restoring Tolbrook to the Christian regimen of Wilcher's childhood. As a consequence there is a widening gulf of alienation between Ann and her husband. The choice of names for the christening of their child and his education become points where the old man enforces his will without realizing to what length he is going against Robert's:

> Robert came to me this evening when I was sorting some of Edward's papers, and said to me, "I don't want to be a nuisance, uncle, or ask too many questions, but I've been wondering just what your idea is in getting at Ann."

> "What do you mean, Robert?"

> "Well, I mean just the whole thing, uncle. First, it was the nursery chairs and the nursery wallpaper, and then it was the names, and now it's the kind of way she should bring up the boy. You've got her kind of switched back." (p.173)

How far Robert's complaints are justified may, however, be somewhat uncertain as to some extent Cary wants the change in Ann to illustrate his narrator's dictum that

> "Marriage, to a woman, is a conservative education." (p.174)

Nevertheless Wilcher's responsibility for Ann's switch-back should not
be underrated even if his predominant concern with less temporal matter
tends to blind him, as well as the reader, to the fact that he very well
knows how to have his way. Thus Ann's view of him makes him surprised:

> "You think we're all mad. You think me mad."
>
> "Never, uncle. you are much too clever at getting your own
> way."
>
> I was astonished. "So you think me cunning. Lunatics are famous
> for their cunning."
>
> "Well, look. Robert meant to go back to Brazil, but here he is
> tied to Tolbrook. And I meant to be a distinguished pathologist,
> and here I am, a silly little wife with a big tummy, also tied
> to Tolbrook."
>
> "And I did all this - why, it's perfectly ridiculous."
>
> "Perhaps you didn't know you were doing it. You only suggested
> that I should see Robert again if we came to Tolbrook. And you
> knew I had fallen for his nice eyes. And then you happened to
> catch us together. And then you gave Robert all these new toys
> to play with - a little at a time. Like giving cut wool to a
> kitten till it's quite tied up. And now you have got the baby
> you wanted and you have decided that it's going to be an Edward
> or a Lucy."
>
> "What nonsense, what nonsense. Though these are good English
> names. And I suppose, if you have a son, he will be in the
> eldest line, and they are all Edwards."
>
> For it was true that I had sometimes hoped for another Lucy
> or Edward. And I had perhaps shown my preference to Ann. (pp.104-0

As the author signals to the reader by inserting a significant "perhaps"
the old meddler is still at work. Perhaps, after all, Lucy did her broth
some justice by calling him a "pettifogger" (p.161). However that may
be, to gain his end Wilcher does not even stop short of playing on his
heirs' anxiety about his will:

> "This poor child," I thought, "is lost already - she is blinded
> by prejudice and ignorance. And if I speak to her of God, she
> probably imagines an old man in a grey beard and a very bad
> temper. It is useless to appeal to her on religious grounds.
> But there are others." And drawing up my chair, I said, "My
> dear, I understand your difficulty about religious instruction.
> But let us make a bargain. If you will allow this child to be
> brought up in a reasonable Christian faith, I shall settle two
> hundred a year on him, in your trust. Yes, and you know," I
> said, "he would have a very good claim to Tolbrook. I might
> even undertake to leave the place to him. I should be glad to
> find in Edward's and Lucy's grandchild a successor," etc.
>
> "But I'm not sure if I want him to be a Christian," Ann said.
>
> "Wait a minute," I said, perhaps too hastily. "Of course, you

won't be forgotten. Not at all. I have already made some pro-
vision . . ." (p.83)

By the same means Wilcher tries to save the young couple's marriage from
impending divorce:

"I see you think I am a kind of moral idiot," I said to the
children, to all our surprise. For all at once I had lost my
temper. "An old miser who can only think and talk about money
and shake his will every time that he's crossed. But it's you
who are the idiots, yes, perfect idiots - not to know that money
is important - extremely important. I've had to do with money
all my life, and I tell you that it's not only the root of
evil, but the root of good, too," etc., and so on.
. . .
" . . . the truth is that I ought to leave the place to Blanche.
She may be a prig, but she's a Christian at least, and knows
how to value the things of the spirit, and a family property,
which is one of them." (pp.181-82)

Wilcher's attempt to bribe Ann and Robert reflects an uncompromising
resolution that makes him blind to the changing standard of his morals
On some occasions, however, this determination is conveyed with such
conscientious calculation and skill that we have reason to ask whether
the speaker is deceiving himself or the reader. The following prayer-
scene is, anyhow, a superb piece of ambiguous narration:

The room was very warm and smelt of the baby, which was lying
in a peculiar cot, made of canvas, next Ann's bed; a little
thin creature with black hair and a sharp nose. He was sucking
his fist and uttering now and then an impatient cry. The morning sun threw the shadows of the square window panes upon the
floor, and the bath and a towel-horse opened before the fire-
place. The nurse, in her blue print, knelt at a chair and thrust
herself out behind in a fervent manner. Ann, wearing a lace cap
which I had never seen before, and which made her resemble the
portrait of my great-grandmother, propped herself on one elbow
and kept putting out her hand to disentangle the child's
fingers from the hem of his sheet.

From outside we could hear the hens clucking, and one of the
men stumped across the yard in his long boots. A horse standing,
perhaps by the gate, now and then threw his head and made a
sudden loud rattle of trace chains. Now it happened that the
day was that of St. James, and the collect that which describes
how the saint left all to follow Jesus; but as I turned to it,
I came in the page before on the gospel for St. John Baptist's
day, and since it seemed to me appropriate to the scene, I
read it. "Elizabeth's full time came that she should be
delivered and she brought forth a son. And her neighbours and
her cousins heard that the Lord had showed great mercy upon
her; and they rejoiced with her. And it came to pass that on
the eighth day they came to circumcise the child; and they
called him Zacharias, after the name of the father. And his
mother answered and said, Not so, but he shall be called John.
. . ."

> . . .
> So strongly was I made aware of God's presence and visible
> deed in the quietness of the room, broken only by the clucking
> of hens outside, the snuffling of the baby, the sudden clank
> of the horse's chains, that tears were forced to my eyes, my
> voice wavered, and I was obliged to break off from my reading.
> (pp.126-27)

Of course, it seems by no means unnatural that, as he is turning the
leaves of his prayer book, his eye should fall on a page before the
collect of the day. Furthermore, the presence of Ann and her new-born
makes his temptation to break the order of Common Prayer plausible enough
Less plausible is, after all, the fact that the conscientious man of
regular habits does give in to his temptation and on the spur of the
moment at that. It seems, therefore, reasonable to believe we should not
be blind to the fact that behind his choice of gospel text there may also
lie some of his aversion to the evangelist Brown, his brother-in-law,
and the name of Matthias as Robert wants his boy to be christened after
his father.[4] What, to this effect, stirs the reader's suspicion is,
moreover, his predominant concern with the staging of the scene which
makes him indulge in a peripheral setting of rustic sounds as if, by
imbuing it with the sanctity of stable-yard nativity he unconsciously
tries to seduce his experience of the moment into the final significance
of divine inspiration. This means, to put it bluntly, that each time the
horse clanks his chain, the implied author winks at his reader.

By undercutting the surface narration Cary inverts his speaker's character. Within the fiction there is certainly room for Wilcher's scheming
and hypocrisy but as his double-dealing affects his function as both
actor and narrator we have reason to wonder which of the two is the
greater rogue. In chapter 6 the division of Wilcher's character will be
dealt with in further detail.

5) Development and change in the narrator

When after his calamitous visit to Sara, Wilcher returns to Tolbrook, he
is in the same plight that took him there at the beginning of his story.
Now that his journey through the past gently launches him into the prese
and his strength is ebbing out, he is surprised to find himself released
from his hampering allegiance, and as he reclines in himself, a mighty
swell of confidence carries him away into the unquestioning independence

of those to whose lives his own has made a tragic foil. Still the reader
will scarcely share the narrator's surprise at his jubilant finale though
it is by no means the outcome of a continuous process that can be followed
through the narration. As may be inferred from our discussion of "the
vision variable"[5] the author's variations on the paradoxical "faith"
theme hardly make it possible for him to let Wilcher's attitude to life
be subject to any consistent change. Furthermore we must consider that
it is the past, rather than the present, that makes his principal concern.
In fact, it occupies two thirds of the narration. In the former half of
the novel where past and present frequently intersect, Wilcher's disposition to scenic identification is apparent enough, but it markedly
abates in the latter part where, for extensive spans of retrospection,
the past tense largely holds the field and, as a consequence, settles the
epic character of the narration in so far as it helps to remove the vision
of the dramatized narrator into the outskirts of the reader's awareness.
Thus the sliding identity of the narrating "I" hardly paves the way for
any progressive character-drawing.

In the course of the narration Wilcher does not explicitly evidence any
awareness of a gradual change in his present circumstances at Tolbrook
although there seems to be some development. From the fact that he is
apparently becoming less and less tied to his bed and also increasingly
forgetful of his decision to join Sara after her release from prison, we
can infer that he is slowly recovering from his exhaustion. Anyhow he
has indisputably regained some vitality when, by leaving Tolbrook, Ann
gives him up to himself. The narrator does not seem completely unconscious
of this development, but as a rule his short perspective of himself tends
to blind him to the fact that by accumulating a rising fund of information
his narration may continuously imply some development. This applies in
particular to his attitude towards Ann whose presence he at first looks
upon with unqualified distrust:

> I do not like this girl. I prefer my other niece and several
> of my honorary nieces. (p.9)

Before long, however, Wilcher seems to have become conscious of his prejudice:

> There is I know some anxiety about the future of the property.
> I have two nephews and a niece, all with equal claims. Perhaps
> Ann, having been almost unknown to me, now wishes to make up
> for lost time. I do not blame her. She has every right to her
> share of the booty. (p.12)

Although Wilcher has now placed his heirs on a par, this turn of the
tide has hardly affected his basic distrust. Anyhow he is deeply suspi
cious of the girl and determined to brace himself against her affectio
as we can infer from his irritation and disdain:

> Now that I cannot bear the sight of Ann, she is beginning to
> run after me. She kisses me good morning and shakes up my
> pillows. She takes me for walks and tries to amuse what she
> thinks are my prejudices. She has brought up the old nursery
> chair from the back passage to the day nursery, and cleared
> out the beds, saying, "We'll make it as it used to be, and
> have it for our own sitting-room." But all this affection
> does not deceive me. (p.39)

Nor does Wilcher's cross-grained vexation deceive the reader. Between
and Ann mutual understanding and sympathy are arising. Her attachment
appears to be genuine enough and testifies to an increasing identifica
tion with Wilcher's own values of life. This development is brought in
sharp relief during her pregnancy and alienation from her husband:

> And Ann, with her unexpected power of knowing my feelings, if
> not my thoughts, said to me one evening, "I wonder will this
> baby be sitting here in another fifty years or seventy-one
> years."
>
> I was surprised by such an idea in Ann's head. But it gave me
> a keen pleasure. (p.82)

Soon after, Wilcher's reserve admits a first note of positive recogniti

> I believe Ann to be, at bottom, a good creature, . . . (p.92)

It takes, however, the birth of a son to bridge the full span of the o
man's distrust and make him express his unqualified affection:

> She was rougher, ruder to me, and yet she seemed more affec-
> tionate, more like a daughter. (p.131)

Of course, it is the use of the present tense that largely supports the
illusion of a short narrative distance whereas the past makes it subjec
to some modification. Nevertheless it remains short enough to make the
narrator seem so involved in the present that he fails to share the
reader's experience of some gradual change.

CONTROLLED SCENIC EXPOSITION

Although the speaker's unconscious self-objectification is what primari
justifies a novelist's use of the first-person narrative mode, it does
not, of course, rule out scenic exposition that is under the "I"-narrat

conscious control and whose reliability need not always be questioned. Throughout To be a Pilgrim there is a fluctuation between summary (or commentary) and scene. At intervals the epic pace seems crisp enough but then, like the stream of a widening river, it occasionally slows down to make the narration enlarge upon scenic detail. In fact, the novel holds an abundance of consciously narrated scenes of various kinds. Some of them can be considered complete units in so far as they contain not only elaborate dialogue but also a detailed setting and well-directed action. Wilcher can go to great lengths to evoke atmosphere and set the reader right about his sentiments. The following passage makes the beginning of a scene where he turns up to tell the improvident Edward his mind. Waiting for him the narrator has ample time for close observation:

> I found his big room, on the seventh floor, with an excellent view of St. James's Park, crowded, as usual at his parties, with very incongruous guests. Some, to judge by their uneasy and pompous solitude, were from the constituency; some, by their tweeds and ties and hair, from Chelsea; and some, as obviously, were ladies of the highest fashion, moving quickly here and there and darting quick glances of recognition at nobody, to hide the fact that for the moment they knew only nobody. Two young officers chatted together like polite conspirators; a famous millionaire looked at the pictures with the face of one who asks, "Ought I to invest in these absurd things?" and two political groups, all of men, talked vigorously among themselves. All these latter, young and old, had the same kind of assured manner, which was quite different from the unassuming social confidence of the guardsman or the arrogance of the rich merchant. One could tell at once that they were all used to playing the statesman, in some circle, large or small, and to public speaking. They threw into their voices notes of geniality, indignation and importance.
>
> Edward's secretary, a very fair young man, with the manners of a bishop, came up to me and asked me if I knew where he was.
>
> "No, isn't he here?"
>
> "He isn't at Mrs. Eeles?"
>
> "No, I saw her just now."
>
> There was a slight pause, as if we might come to some understanding about Julie.
> . . .
> "Exciting times," I say, to relieve our mutual embarassment.
>
> "Oh, yes, this Williamson letter."
>
> "I meant, about the peace," and as one of the political group turns to include the secretary, I say, "What terms are we going to give them?"
>
> "Terms? No terms at all."

Another exclaims warmly, "I'm not going to deal with people
who shoot our men under a white flag."

"Is it quite certain that the letter was meant to be private?"

The discussion breaks out again with still more energy, and
gradually I perceive that it is all about a bye-election, . . .
. . .
The door opens and Edward comes in with Bill. Edward is always
late for his parties. He seems as usual, both busy and unruffled.
He carries a portfolio under his arm; but he is dressed as for
Ascot, in a pale grey frock-coat, with an orchid in his button-
hole.

I push up to him and he greets me with an affectionate smile.
"How nice to see you, Tom. You're staying?"

But I'm not to be cajoled any longer. I answer angrily, "Did
you get my letter about the agency?"

"Just a moment." He turns aside and at once he is surrounded
by the fashionable ladies, the young politicians. (pp.166-68)

The genre of the fictitious memoir, in principle, rests on the reader's
unquestioning acceptance of the infallibility of the narrator's memory
even if, as in the present novel, the author does not provide it with
memoranda, letters, pictures, and other forms of substantial support.
It is true that the scenes which Wilcher consciously builds up are
presented with an unswerving precision of detail that, after all, might
have sapped the reader's credulity but for the immunity from disbelief
that the narrator's scenic participation, at the same time, confers on
him. We must consider that what the dramatizing narrator offers his
reader is not simply a chain of unambiguous reconstructions viewed from
a certain distance, but often enough it rather seems to mirror an actual
experience staged, above time and space, in a mind of ultimately irre-
pressible creativeness. Wilcher fills the dual function of observing
narrator of the past and autonomous dramatist-actor in the present, and
often these cooperate in next-to inseparable conjunction. This means that
when Wilcher relates an experience of the past, his disposition to imaginative identification tends to suspend the narrative distance and,
consequently, turn a memory into a present experience:

It was true that I was in pyjamas, but I had not meant to go
out of my room. I said that I had thought to hear voices in
the nursery.

"Voices," she said, and blushed. She always colours when she
thinks me strange or mad.
. . .
"It was my own voice," I said, "as a child, and your father
Edward's and my brother Bill's and my sister Lucy's."

"You are dreaming, uncle."

"No, they were here - this was our nursery, you know." (p.15)

Within the autonomous enclave of Wilcher's creative mind reality is, consequently, not always to be distinguished from imagination. As we have already seen,[6] he seems not quite unaware of this fact when on one occasion he suddenly begins to question the existence of a letter he is quoting. Besides we are reminded of the ambiguous nature of his experience whenever he surprises the reader by representing his epic self as a soliloquizer or whenever there is an apparent confusion of distance.[7] It seems, in fact, that Wilcher's communion with the past is not always accidental but is a contact that can be sustained by force of will and may, if lost, be sought and gained:

> I murmured my apologies, for I did not want to lose my discovery.
> A real discovery is not a thought; it is an experience, which
> is easily interrupted and lost. (p.16)[8]

> In spite of all my precautions, when at last I was left alone
> in the dark, I had lost touch with Amy. I couldn't even recall
> the shape of her face, or the dressing of her white hair. Yet
> her presence was close, and all night, while I dozed or waked,
> I felt as if she were in the house, upon one of her long visits.

> "My dear," I thought, "if you were here and I could see you,
> I should ask you to forgive me - or perhaps you would not
> understand such a request. It might frighten you after all
> these years when our relations had been established in a form.
> You knew me even longer than you knew Bill. Yes, long before."
> Then to my surprise I thought I saw Amy standing before me,
> not as an old white-haired woman, but as the young rosy, too
> rosy and too plump young girl, who had once romped with me at
> Christmas parties, until her nose and her forehead shone like
> apples. She was laughing at me . . . (p.114)

Most of the scenes draw their vitality from the dialogue which they usually contain. As we have already seen, the abundance of quoted speech hardly alerts the reader's disbelief in so far as it tends to tighten his awareness of being in the presence of a dramatizing speaker who, irrespective of the factual narrative distance, enjoys a dramatist's licence to produce as much dialogue as he needs. Indeed, this privilege makes him even go so far as to quote words that were never voiced in reality. Thus he puts other people's thoughts into articulate speech:

> But now, when I remember my father's eyes, as he watched the
> syringe brought towards his helpless body, I feel such a pang
> of grief that my own heart knows the pain of death. For I
> know what he was saying to himself, "Now they are putting me
> to sleep, because I want to tell them this thing, which only
> I can tell. Only a dying man, upon his death bed, can know it.

And because they do not know it, they don't know its importance,
they don't want to hear it. And they will keep me asleep till
I die." (p.158)

We spoke trivialities, about Edward's triumphs and an Ibsen
revival in which Julie had been asked to take a part. "But I
could not act Hedda Gabler - I should feel ridiculous waving
a pistol now." Her eyes meanwhile asked me, "Why have you
come?" She said, "I like your morning visits," meaning, "you
have come for some special purpose." (p.190)

This does not, of course, necessarily mean that the narrator presumes to
know what is beyond his range but rather that he translates his own
articulate impressions or reactions into speech. On a few occasions he
therefore makes even lifeless objects speak:

. . . I lay in perpetual winter, frozen still, without hope of
spring. I breathed in the air of infinite resignation, sad
and clear, through which all objects appeared in their own
colours; neither gilded by the sun, nor glorified by autumn
mist. All appeared small, distinct, separate; and charged with
several mortality. "We die," they said to me, "we die alone
and all our hopes die with us. Anger is foolish, struggle is
useless, and self-pity is self-torture, for there is no help
from anywhere." (p.119)

I see the chairs, tables, pictures; and even my London office,
with its worn carpet and ink-stained waste-paper basket,
standing in dumb patience, as if waiting upon my decision.
They have already that dejected look of things at a sale,
where everything seems to say, "We are betrayed - there is
no faith or trust in the world." (p.176)

This dramatizing disposition, above all, manifests itself in Wilcher's
presentation of his own thoughts as if the workings of his mind equalled
a kind of soliloquy. Then "think" and "say to oneself" seem largely
synonymous:

She [Ann] was perfectly grave, but I could see that she was
laughing at me, and this made my head swim. But I said to myself, "Serve you right, you old fool, if you drop down dead.
Don't you know how to mind your business yet. And what if
Robert does go to her room. Does that prove that he goes to
bed with her. What do you know about this new world of morals,
or immorals, which has floated out of the German boxes, like
the ghost dancers of the high moor, who, they say, come smoking
out of the earth on mid-winter night, to prance and jibber
round the standing stones of phallic cults older than the
human brain." (p.26)

And I thought, "In fact, I have been ungrateful to these young
people, especially to Robert. For he has at least set me free.
I need worry no more about those old tottering relics in the

fields. Let him respect only the house, for his own son's sake, and I shall be a fortunate man." (p.136)

And then at once I thought, "Suppose next time we passed, I said something to her - some little compliment, or perhaps something more particular, even a little startling."

"Pooh," I said to myself, "you old fool - she would just think you a nasty old man or she would call for a policeman. And, besides," I said to myself, "I shan't see her again. That's four times. Even a goose like that can't walk up the path for a fifth time, with a face like an unaddressed envelope. No, no," I said to myself, "You won't see her again." (p.305)

Whether Wilcher takes part in a conversation or soliloquizes, his ulti-mately epic control of the scene remains unchanged. Therefore the quoted thoughts that the narrator often interpolates rather integrate into the dialogue than break it up:

Edward jumped up and said, "Have my chair, Julie - aren't you cold there?"

"No, thank you - it's too hot." And she said in the same voice, "After all, we are evil ourselves - we have plenty of bad thoughts."

"Not you, Julie. You are the best friend anyone could hope for."

"No, no," in a voice so passionate that both of us were si-lenced.

I thought, "She wants Edward, and she is angry that she can't have him - she has always been in love with Edward," and I became still more impatient with these triflers. I said, "All this seems to me pretty wild stuff. . . ." (pp.226-27)

She [Ann] did not answer me, and I thought, "There now, we're quarrelling, And it's your fault, you old fool. You ought to be more careful. But what is one to do? Why must these children always talk rubbish? Why must they make everything more con-fused and more perplexing?"

But Ann, after knitting half a round, answered only, "And, of course, there's the Maginot Line."

"I agree with you, my dear. . . ." (p.239)

I saw that the boy [Robert] had tricked me. But I said to myself, "There's nothing to be done. Nothing is to be gained by anger. On the other hand, I can still save something by diplomacy, by tact." So I said, "It's a wonderful change - you have certainly done great things here." (p.118)

The narrator effaces his controlling self by staging his commentary in the protagonist's private asides. By reproducing his own thoughts Wilcher also acquaints the reader with notions that he might as well have pro-nounced in his own epic person as they make part of the author's ultimate

view of life and, consequently, retain their validity throughout the
narration. In the following cases this course of communication seems the
more circuitous as the passage of time that parts the primary speaker
from his "thinking" secondary self is inconsiderable:

> "Yes," I thought, "that was the clue to Lucy, to my father,
> to Sara Jimson, it is the clue to all that English genius
> which bore them and cherished them, clever and simple. Did
> not my father say of Tolbrook which he loved so much, 'Not a
> bad billet,' or 'not a bad camp'; and Sara? Was not her view
> of life as 'places' as 'situations' the very thought of the
> wanderer and the very strength of her soul. She put down no
> roots into the ground; she belonged with the spirit; her
> goods and possessions were all in her own heart and mind,
> her skill and courage." (p.16)

> But I thought, "It is my own fault. Haven't I known all my
> life that it was folly to give my affections to sticks and
> stones and all that helpless hopeless tribe," etc., etc. (p.119)

> This was no romantic freak. To Amy and Bill, I am sure, it
> was the common thing. To simple-minded persons, miracles
> appear like nature. In the same way, they expected to be happy,
> to love one another, etc., and therefore they did so.

> "A kind of faith cure," Ann said to me, and I thought I must
> have been speaking aloud.

> "I don't know what you would call it." But I thought "Not a
> cure for anything. It was the whole idea of an age, and how
> could I convey that, or its strength. For only the idea can
> fight against the cruelty of fate. It is in some strong well-
> founded idea that men and women, and whole nations, float as
> in a ship over the utmost violence of chance and time." (p.104)

In the following cases the two voices are so confusingly alike that, as
may be inferred from the capricious use of quotation marks, the author
does not take particular care to keep them apart:

> And now I think, "How did Lucy know at twenty-one, even in
> her whims, what I don't know till now from all my books, that
> the way to a satisfying life, a good life, is through an act
> of faith and courage.

> But then, where was my faith? I was a child . . . (p.55)[9]

> When, on these mornings, the window arches of the old cell
> frame a cold spring sky and the first buds on the great lime,
> I think, "The mediaeval monks who looked out of these windows
> at sky and buds did not see them with clearer eyes than Bill's."
> Both looked out from a security and faith as strong as a child's
> surrounded by the unseen care of its mother. (p.108)[10]

By letting Wilcher project himself into a secondary ego the anonymous
author makes the virtual speaker help himself to some of that substan-

tial identity he may need to support his own authority.

Throughout, the narrator evidences a marked predilection for unreported speech, and only occasionally does he mix it up with the oblique mode. This does not, however, mean that within the dialogue he tries to efface all traces of his epic control, for instance speaker-indicating clauses and other interpolations made for the reader's benefit. Now and then the narrator even supersedes the dramatist before their acting self has finished his speech. Thus Wilcher's utterances are often dissolved in a careless "etc.", "and so on", "etc., etc.", "etc. and so on":

> "You have been very smart, Jaffery," I said, "but I'm not dead yet, and Robert need not think so," etc., etc. "Perhaps after all, I shall decide to get rid of the place. It's always been a curse to me." (p.33)

> "But don't you think it will be better when marriage is arranged more on stock-breeding lines," and so on. All very reasonable and scientific. And so, as Ann, I suspect, well knows, the more upsetting to me. (p.101)

> "If God is immanent in the world, then He is not only in experience, but in reason," I say, "for if we find Him in experience as love and altruism, it is only by reason that we distinguish this love, this goodness, and resolve that it is good, not only in itself, but for the world," etc., and so forth.
> "What do you mean by immanent," . . . (p.139)

Only occasionally, however, is the narrator's reporting self in predominant charge of a scene where, consequently, the direct speech is rare and reduced to a subsidiary function. In fact, the only exceptions occur where little, if any, interchange of words is possible or where for once in a while Wilcher happens not to be one of the (usually) two participants of a dialogue. Notable scenes of this kind are Lucy's attempt at suicide and Bill's proposal.[11]

EPIC NARRATION

When an author hides behind a dramatized narrator, he gives his composition an epic basis of formal objectivity which, however, hardly affects the narration. What has happened is, in fact, only that he has substituted the subjectivity of his fictive ego for that of his real self.[12] In the present novel, the narrator spends his days in a state of idleness and introversion that allows of no conscious communion with a prospective

vis-à-vis outside the fiction, but throughout the narration there runs
an epic undertow which proves that whoever the virtual speaker may be,
he is certainly not unaware of the reader's presence but anxious to act
as his friend and guide. This obliging attitude is in evidence from the
very beginning where Wilcher initiates the reader into his own world by
linking it up with Sara Monday's:

> Last month I suffered a great misfortune in the loss of my
> housekeeper, Mrs. Jimson. She was sent to prison for pawning
> some old trinkets which I had long forgotten. My relatives
> discovered the fact and called in the police before I could
> intervene. They knew that I fully intended, as I still intend,
> to marry Sara Jimson. (p.9)

Indeed, the more the narrative pace quickens for crisp epitomes, the more
aware we become of being in the narrator's conscious care. When, for
example, Wilcher sums up a year's war service in a few lines, he seems
to have slipped out of his dramatized self as completely as an actor who
appears before the curtain after the show:

> I was sent to France in 1916 as a stretcher bearer. I was too
> old for the infantry, and I refused a commission.[13] But the
> last weeks of that bitter winter in the Somme trenches gave
> me pneumonia and left me with a damaged heart. I was invalided
> out of the army in September, 1917, and came home to Tolbrook
> after more than a year's absence. (p.241)

In principle, the narrator's control of his narration is apt to abate,
the more he falls in with the protagonist's role, but as far as the
scenic dialogue goes, the reader is seldom left alone for more than brief
moments. Whenever necessary, the speaking actor proves ready to jump into
the role of a helpful commentator inserting an informative aside:

> "Is old Jaffery still running the place?" he asked.
>
> Jaffery is the estate agent in Queensport, and my local manager.
>
> "Yes, yes, more or less," I said. "Did you know Ann was here?"
> (p.18)

> "But Lucy, for God's sake, be serious. This is some of your
> nonsense."
>
> "Yes, it's some of my nonsense."
>
> For of course I was quite right. Even Lucy knew it was some
> of her nonsense. To amuse herself or to shock us, or both at
> once.
>
> "Then tell me the joke. I'll not say a word."
>
> "I told you the joke, Tommy. Puggy Brown has called me, and
> I'm going to him." (p.54)

"What nonsense, what nonsense. Though these are good English
names. And I suppose, if you have a son, he will be in the
eldest line, and they are all Edwards."

For it was true that I had sometimes hoped for another Lucy
or Edward. And I had perhaps shown my preference to Ann.

"But I'm not blaming you, uncle, for wanting the family to go
on. The family is like you, isn't it, and of course you want
to go on." (p.105)

Of course, a narrator only has to change his mode of narration to tell
the reader of his presence. This becomes apparent enough when, for
instance, as in the following account of an individual episode, the
narration quickly passes from scene via summary into comment and then
the same way back into scene:

I was too busy. So I opened no more of their letters.

"I must have forgotten them," I said.

"But, uncle, you really can't ignore people like that. Here
is Cousin Blanche's writing. Yes, she has written to you almost
every week - there must be twenty from her alone."

"You read them for me."

"I couldn't do that. Cousin Blanche wouldn't like me to. She
hates me, and I can't say I like her."

To keep the child quiet I promised to read the letters, but
I did not do so. I put them into a broken ventilator and by
God's mercy I forgot all about them again.

An old man is obliged to be a coward, not for his essential
self, his mind and will, but for his body which may betray
that will. He is like a general compelled to fight his last
campaign, with weak worn out troops, badly equipped and liable
to run away at the least reverse. He must use all his self-
control, his ingenuity.

I had executed a skilful retreat. But I had not allowed for
Ann's new coarseness of mind. Two days later she told me
that Blanche was coming to see me. "I telephoned to her and
said that it wasn't my fault if you refused to have anything
to do with her."

"I do not refuse," I said, "a soldier does not refuse to be
shot. But he doesn't desire it. No, I can't see her. It is
impossible for her to understand me or for me to argue with
her. She is as stupid as a horse."

"But, uncle, it's not fair to let her think that I keep her
away."

"No, no, certainly not. But I can't see her - I have to see
Mr. Jaffery first."

"I don't mind in the least what you do about your will, but
you mustn't get excited. Having babies is too much for you
altogether."

> "I'm not excited. But I won't see Blanche."
>
> "Well, I've asked her to tea with us to-day." (pp.131-32)

What considerably adds to the epic quality of the narration, is the
wealth of incidental information that seems to be there only for the
reader's benefit as it hardly agrees with the "note-book" fiction:

> Tolbrook Manor house has no beauties except two good rooms
> by the Adams brothers. Although it stands high, it has no
> view. It is an irregular house; a three-storey block with
> one long east wing and on the west an absurd protrusion, one
> storey high, ending in a delapidated greenhouse. (p.11)[14]

> I found myself in the dining-room, which still has its old
> chairs, too big and clumsy a set for a modern house, and I
> began to hunt for those two, at which Lucy and I, side by
> side, always prayed. (p.89)

> Julie suddenly returned to England, in the middle of Edward's
> most ferocious election. This was in 1900, during the Boer
> War, at Ragworth, near Liverpool. (p.153)

> William, now acting Major, with an D.S.O. and M.C., was killed
> a few hours after the armistice in one of the last actions of
> the war. (p.257)

It is true that the fiction cannot admit an explicit recognition of the
reader's presence, but occasionally the narrator seems so steeped in his
concern about his vis-à-vis that an unconsidered "you" slips his lips
telling of a virtual epic situation beyond the fiction:

> Ten years ago I would have told you that my childhood was
> peaceful and happy. At that time, a very unhappy time in my
> life, I often took refuge in the idea of my happy childhood.
> (p.34)

> Sometimes Julie did not speak to me for weeks; yet every
> Friday or Saturday, I would stay the night with her. Why did
> I perform an act become so hateful to me. You say it was
> habit. But habit is not whim. (p.304)

What, however, makes the narrator give away his epic concern the more
positively, is his frequent use of "I remember", "The truth is" and
similar governing clauses which hold an indirect but evident address to
an off-stage vis-à-vis:[15]

> When you are old, they throw "conservative" at you as a
> reproach. But I can remember very well when Robert himself,
> as a small child, in this very house, would not go to bed
> without a certain lump of wood, the remains of a toy horse,
> in his arms. He loved his horse, and to protect that horse
> he would fight with his own mother, whom he also loved.
>
> I remember . . . (p.24)

Throughout Wilcher's narration manifests a modest restraint that adds to
the impression that it may have not been only for his own edification
that he wrote his "journal". Thus he comments on his indecent behavior:

> I was not only astonished at my conduct with the young girl
> in the park; I was horrified at myself. For I had used some
> phrases to her which were calculated to shock her modesty,
> and which, it seemed to me, I had chosen for the purpose. To
> wake her up. To excite her. To make something happen, for
> myself as well as for her. I could not believe how such words
> had passed my lips. (pp.306-07)

In Wilcher not only the epic narrator but also the dramatist shrinks
from the risk of causing offence. Here he tells Ann his mind:

> ". . . Our childhood was good for us, whatever it would have
> been for you ninnies in your fog of flummery, it was perfect
> for us - I could not wish anything better for any child. We
> knew where we were and what we had to do, and what was right
> and wrong - all the things you silly geese have muddled up
> till you don't know your etc. from an etc." A very coarse
> comparison, such as never before, except when I was in the
> army, had I used to a woman, much less a niece, however
> disreputable. (p.40)

Indeed the narrator's observance of propriety sometimes makes him seem
not quite unfamiliar with the idea of publication. In some cases this
may explain his tendency to leave out names:

> At this time the governess was a certain Miss C., a fair,
> pretty mild creature, who was some distant relation of my
> mother's family. (p.42)

> "But Gladys is not that sort, uncle - her people think no end
> of themselves, I can tell you, and she went to school at ——"
> - a famous school of which I cancel the name, in justice. (p.264)

The narrator's discreet unveiling of his own indiscretion brings out the
full paradox of his situation or, rather, the indisputable existence of
a virtual epic situation beyond the limelights of the fiction. In addition to the dramatized introversion of his soliloquizing self, the
speaker is consciously acquainting the reader with the changing vision
the progress of which equals the old man's belated pilgrimage.

CHAPTER 5   THE CHARACTERS OF THE MEMOIRS AND THEIR FUNCTIONS

The different people who fill the narrator's memories fall into two
principal groups. Some of them enjoy a sense of spiritual freedom whic
is the hall-mark of "faith" whereas others prove remarkably deficient
this respect. All the characters serve symbolic ends and therefore ma
of them are rather types, if not cardboard figures, than truly life-l
individuals. They have been moulded on a simple typology that helps th
reader to a great deal of information about their spiritual status an
helps him to realize how each character has a perfect contrary in the
opposite camp. These opposites form polarity groups which give dual
aspects of concepts, such as "freedom" and "dissolution".

THE "FAITHFUL" AND "FREE"

1) Physical characteristics

Cary's "faithful" characters bear a strong resemblance to the physica
type that Kretschmer describes as "pycnics". They have a broad trunk.
Bill is described as "broad" and "tall"[1] and Brown is "short and squat
Like Kretschmer, Cary ascribes particular importance to the shape of
the nose. Sara's nose which, before Jimson's deformation of it, in
Herself Surprised, was "broad and snub"[3] is, now, simply "broad".[4] Bro
has been blessed with a "pug nose" or a "short pugnacious nose",[5] and
Amy's nose, too, has apparently the same pycnic lack of prominence as
it makes her look like "a sucking pig".[6]

The characters of "faith" are not beautiful people, but their bodies
have a powerful build which seems to raise them above the common run o
men. Thus Amy manifests a motherly mightiness that at once damps the
coxcombical heat of the political drawing-room scene where an aggressi
pacifist has cornered her good-natured military man:

> Suddenly Amy appears beside him, carrying her baby in her arms.
> The politicians gaze at her in astonishment. She is dressed in
> electric blue, which gives to her high complexion the brilliance
> of a ribstone pippin. She is almost cubical in shape, as always
> when she is nursing; and her hat, of the largest size, is perched
> upon the top of a roll of hair, so high, that it is nearly as
> long as her whole face. (p.170)

In fact, the very ugliness of these characters makes them radiate powe

Brown, the Lord's champion, looks frightening enough. He has

> . . . the shoulders of a giant, or a dwarf; and the face of
> a prize fighter, pug nose, jutting brows, thick swollen lips,
> roaring over all the noise of bullocks and sheep. (p.20)

2) Personality characteristics

All the characters who, according to the narrator, have a living "faith"
are also "pilgrims" in so far as they have no permanent abode in this
world but are always ready to move on. Contrary to Wilcher, who desperately clings to the old family estate which he wants to preserve by all
means, his father takes quite a different view:

> "Not a bad billet, but I've been here too long." (p.150)

Throughout the novel Cary gives varied expressions to his view of life
in "faith" as a pilgrimage:

> But now I saw that to the wanderer all his world is home. He
> is the least homeless of men because he possesses all, the
> earth and the sky, the houses and the trees, with the eyes
> of a homekeeper, and all men and women are his familiars. (p.301)

This itinerancy is reflected in the lives of all those who abound in
spirit. Lucy and Brown are travelling evangelists. Service takes Bill,
the army officer, and his wife to India. Farming makes Robert leave
Tolbrook for Canada. As a consequence, Cary is anxious to make it clear
that the word "pilgrim" is to be taken in the widest possible, i.e. in
a non-religious, sense:

> ". . . and Sara? Was not her view of life as 'places' as
> 'situations' the very thought of the wanderer and the very
> strength of her soul. . . ." (p.16)

What applies to Sara, also applies to Amy whose "pilgrimage" seems to
have started early enough:

> Amy, without mother or any relation in England save the old
> vicar and two maiden aunts in Yorkshire, was ignorant even
> for a girl of those days. But her ignorance did not oppress
> her. She advanced through life like an explorer through un-
> known country, ready for anything; not in conceit of herself,
> but in the belief which says, "It's all happened before, so
> it can't be so terrible." (p.112)

A "pilgrim" equals a "gypsy" as Cary makes it clearly understood in his
description of Lucy:

> I had not set eyes on Lucy for nearly four years. And when,
> in the dim-lit hall, I saw near the door a poorly dressed
> woman standing in silence, I took her for some beggar or gypsy,
> come to ask a favour. She had the look of gypsy women as soon
> as they cease to be girls; thin and nervous. No one can tell
> what age they are. At twenty they have the thin dry wrinkles
> which will only be deeper when they are eighty, and show
> already bitter experience and strong will. (p.84)

> She looked up at me and I saw again the gypsy face, calmly
> impatient of the protected, the comfortable, the self-deceivers.
> (p.96)

On its way through history, Tolbrook, like England itself, is referred
to this category of "gypsies", "adventurers", "travellers in the world",
"men upon a journey", "private soldiers", "flying Dutchmen", and "wander
ing Jews", which also includes "Mother Carey's chickens" (!):

> "It is as if Tolbrook itself were on a pilgrimage," I said.
> "It is like a gypsy van, carrying its people with it." (p.136)

A missionary is a "pilgrim", too, though in Wilcher the calling was not
strong enough to make him stake his life on adventure, i.e. follow the
catch phrase that even as a child tied him to Lucy in secret communion:
"To be a pilgrim!" (p.16). Thus on his deathbed, Wilcher sums up his
life:

> The truth must be confessed, that I am an old fossil, and
> that I have deceived myself about my abilities. I thought I
> could be an adventurer like Lucy and Edward; a missionary. I
> shouted the pilgrim's cry, democracy, liberty, and so forth,
> but I was a pilgrim only by race. England took me with her on
> a few stages of her journey. Because she could not help it.
> She, poor thing, was born upon the road, and lives in such a
> dust of travel that she never knows where she is.
>
>> "Where away England, steersman answer me?
>> We cannot tell. For we are all at sea."
>
> She is the wandering Dutchman, . . . (pp.341-42)

To the "faithless" Wilcher's mind these followers of their own spirit
often evidence a lack of judgment that makes him describe them as "mad"
and their actions as "nonsense". By and by, however, it becomes clear
that the narrator is made to use these words in a sense that is not
unequivocally negative and narrow but that, ultimately, amounts to carefree confidence or unhampered vitality which gives the "faithful" courag
to "break the pattern" (p.310) of ordinariness. The implied dramatist-
author makes this point clear indeed in the conversation between Wilcher
and Ann quoted on p.68 above.[7]

Time and again the narrator returns to the "nonsense" of the "faithful" whose judgment does not "spring from logic but from sense, the feeling of the world" (p.320). To the young Wilcher, at least, Lucy's runaway match is "nonsense" though later on the privileged narrator looks back upon her resolution in a different perspective:

> I had not appreciated her; and I did not understand her non-
> sense. For Lucy's nonsense was her own nonsense, and therefore
> it had courage and faith. (p.55)

A similar act of truly instinctive "nonsense" is Robert's running away with Molly to start a new life as a farm labourer:

> And when I express my wonder that Robert should leave Tolbrook
> for such a position, Ann says only, "It's just like him."
>
> "What is like him? - he is a skilled farmer, and a very ambi-
> tious one."
>
> "It's this Adam and Eve idea," Ann says, "which is going
> about. When Adam delved and Eve span. Men must work, if pos-
> sible, in a muck heap, and women must weep, if possible, into
> a new baby."
>
> "What fearful rubbish - what is all this. Do you mean Robert
> models his life on Genesis?"
>
> "No, but Genesis came out of the ideas of people like Robert."
>
> "My dear Ann, you are a great donkey - to talk such stuff.
> It's the kind of stuff which poisons everything with its stuff.
> Because it sounds like sense." I was angry with the girl. And
> she answered me:
>
> "Yes, perhaps it is nonsense. . . ." (pp.223-24)

During his spells of privileged insight the narrator does not only do justice to the characters of spirit for all their maddening "nonsense" but he also praises them as people of "principle":

> Four years ago I was shocked to find that some of my trifles
> had passed into Sara's keeping. But now I was not only amused;
> I felt a secret exultation in Sara's impudence, and more than
> impudence. Something far deeper. Something that had come to
> me also from Lucy. A freedom. An enterprise. And looking round,
> I saw a dozen more objects from forgotten corners of Tolbrook
> and Craven Gardens; an engraving of Wellington at Waterloo;
> a glass picture, cracked in four places, of Cherry Ripe; a
> little tripod table with one foot broken short. Apparently
> Sara had permitted herself to take nothing that was in use,
> or in good order. Everything was cracked or chipped. A woman
> of principle. (p.316)
>
> But Lucy, the rebel, began in revolution against the new. She
> did not think that all change was progress. She discriminated,
> even at six. She knew the value of order, of a routine, even

in our rebellious nursery. I daresay Nature had taught her
that it is precisely the stormiest spirit, which needs, upon
its rough journey, some rule of the sea and road. "The love
of routine," a scientific friend said to me once, "is nothing
to be ashamed of. It is only the love of knowing how to do
things which Nature plants in every child, kitten and puppy."
(pp.24-25)

We laughed at them [Bill and Amy] both, but now, remembering
Amy's untroubled expression before Bill's anger and terrible
suggestions, I ask, "How was it that Amy always knew what
she ought to do, and did it, and so calmly accepted the con-
sequences?"

I thought her simple. No one is simple. But I can see now that
Amy, in the very conflicts of her duty, as wife and mother,
had strict though complex principles. Sometimes Bill came
first, sometimes a child. But Amy was a woman of principle,
and what strength that gives to the humblest soul, what wisdom
to the most modest intelligence. (p.165)

Cary makes it perfectly clear that by "principle" he understands a rule
of conduct that does not come from reason but from instinct and, therefore, makes no restriction of man's individual freedom. By Sara's con-
fining her stealing to "cracked and chipped" things and by Lucy's
"routine" the author, of course, understands a simple principle in the
accepted sense of the word. When it comes to Amy's "strict though comple
principles", he makes it perfectly clear that they have a pliability tha
simple logic cannot allow for. Therefore he does not take the trouble to
help John explain why, for all his wife's unfaithfulness, he finds her
"rather strict, in her own way":

. . . when Gladys or even John spoke to me in those years, I
was not sure that I understood. I was not deaf, but I felt
the uneasiness of the deaf, who strain to comprehend something
which eludes them.

One day, John, in a moment of confidence, said to me, "Of
course, Gladys has her own morals - she is almost systematic."

The word systematic seemed to offer me a chance I sought, to
tell him that Gladys was consistently unfaithful. But John's
next words, in a dreamy voice, were "Yes, she's rather strict,
in her own way." (p.284)

It seems indeed that Cary wants John's words to sound like mere nonsense
to make it the more apparent that they can only be understood in a wider
perspective over and above the premises of the fiction. What makes Wilch
describe Amy and Gladys as women of "principle" is the consistency or,
rather, persistency with which their uncompromising spirit manifests
itself and, as in Herself Surprised, Cary lets "obstinate" appear often
enough to stress its own status as a highly significant key-word:

But Amy would not accept the money, even on the most business-like terms. She said in effect: "If I borrowed all this money from you I'd never know how I was going to pay it back."

I accused her of being too particular, and we had a little argument. For Amy was an obstinate woman. (p.261)

And yet Sara had her faults. She had her obstinacy, . . . (p.320)

. . . she [Ann] did not seem to hear me. She is as obstinate as a mule, as Lucy, as Sara, as Amy; . . . (p.332)

"When are you going to make up your mind about Molly, Robert?"

"I made it up a long time ago. I like Moll. May be a bit obstinate, but a good girl." (p.192)

Robert was an energetic child, obstinate but always good tempered, and with all a small boy's power of amusing himself. (p.217)

For all their obstinacy these people are, as a rule, in excellent spirits. Either they "smile" or "laugh" and in the latter case they often do so with a vengeance like the Sara of Herself Surprised:

"He's on the railway," she [Sara] explained to me, . . . and she laughed, while she dusted down a chair for me with her apron. When she laughed, she shook all over. (p.314)

Amy, whose laugh was a private convulsion, as if a silent earthquake was heaving at the rocky bondage of her stays, would make her chair creak so loudly that Bill would cry, "Easy, old girl - take the sofa if you want to laugh. It's stronger." (p.251)

Lucy fixed her eyes on me and smiled as she sang. And in her smile I saw the mischievous girl who had so often, in so many ingenious ways, used me and made a fool of me. It was that smile which saved me, or damned me, I cannot tell which. (p.68)

I was shocked when I first saw Robert, on his return. At twenty-eight, he looks like forty. His face is like a peasant's, thin and hard, coloured like the inside of an old rein; and seamed as if by cuts.

But even when he does not smile, he has always a smiling air. He has the habitual expression that I saw once on the face of a successful young pugilist, . . .

Robert has the little smile of that scarred young boxer; at once melancholy and knowing; as if he said "All the same, I do the fighting." (p.17)

A strange young woman in nurse's uniform came into the room, smiling. Even her walk was like laughter. (p.125)

Gladys, who seldom laughed, but often smiled, with much good humour, now smiled upon us all as if to say, "We're all friends here, aren't we?" (p.272)

3) The female incarnations of "faith"

Within the fiction Sara Monday plays a remarkably modest role. Thus
Wilcher's memoirs offer only brief glimpses from the many years when she
was his servant and mistress, and on the diary level she does not appear
until the old man's journey through the past is to launch him into the
present for good. However, his spiritual release would hardly have been
possible but for his confrontation with her because not until then does
he learn to distinguish between Sara, the individual, and the spirit and
"faith" she embodies. Her restricted appearance in the story proper
makes the narrator the more free to provide her, explicitly, with all
the essential qualities that make up the perfect "pilgrim". Unhampered
by fictive realities he thus sums up her character:

> ". . . and Sara? Was not her view of life as 'places' as
> 'situations' the very thought of the wanderer and the very
> strength of her soul. She put down no roots into the ground;
> she belonged with the spirit; her goods and possessions were
> all in her own heart and mind, her skill and courage." (p.16)

> She had her own mind. She kept her own consel. She was devoted
> but she was never servile. And I rejoiced in her quality which
> belonged to my own people, whose nature was rather affection
> than passion, whose gaiety was rather humour than wit; whose
> judgment did not spring from logic but from sense, the feeling
> of the world. Only to hear Sara's step in the passage was a
> reminder of the truth, which was the tap-root of her own faith,
> that we were travellers in the world, . . . (p.320)

By and by, similar summary views accumulate into a growing body of commentary in which all the characters can be seen and judged. Thus Sara
has a rhetorical function that gives her a predominant role in the
narration that is out of proportion to her limited part in the fiction
proper. There, however, her material self re-appears in a number of
women who bear a striking resemblance to her. Amy is one of these and,
as far as Wilcher's story goes, she is the chief exponent of "faith".

Amy evidently was Wilcher's first and diffident passion and when, finally
he is ready to start his own "pilgrimage", it is she, and not Sara, who
engages his thoughts:

> And now lying here, I miss Amy more than all those whom I
> have known. I know why Amy sent away that curate and why she
> would not let me talk to her about the consolations of relig-
> ion. She did not want them; perhaps she did not altogether
> like them. Perhaps in her shrewd mind, as simple and strong
> as Sara's, she was sceptical of Heaven. (p.339)

Wilcher's portrait of the young Amy is quite like that of Sara, the "village girl" of <u>Herself Surprised</u>. She is "rosy, too rosy and too plump" and though Wilcher once entertained the idea of marrying her, he dismissed it on second thoughts as he found that he "might as well marry any plump milkmaid" (p.115).[8] Like Sara, this sovereign mother is a true servant and even in her old age she goes on waiting on others:

> She did not seem to stoop, but she had a rounded back, broad and soft, and she complained of breathlessness. Her hair was the silver white of an old woman; and she had an old woman's deliberate cautious movements, exasperating to the older Lucy. But she would never sit down if there was anyone to be waited on. At Tolbrook she was once more the servant. (p.293)

Amy's life, like Sara's, is a journey. As a soldier's wife she has become used to having no permanent abode and, as a consequence, she is always prepared to move on. After her husband's death she refuses to listen to Wilcher's reason but sells her house. Significantly enough this true pilgrim ends her days in a boarding-house. Like Rozzie in <u>Herself Surprised</u>, Amy declines, on her deathbed, the consolations of the Church but evidences great concern about her "stays".[9] Only now, i.e. at the very end of the novel, does the narrator seem to become conscious of her close resemblance to Sara and the more anxious to point out that, as an exponent of "faith", she is the latter's equal:

> "Yes, what does that matter - faith is nothing to do with Christianity. Look at Sara and look at your Aunt Amy. Yes, look at Amy. . . ." (p.340)

> Amy and Sara, coutrywomen both. They didn't submit themselves to any belief. They used it. They made it. They had the courage of the simple, which is not to be surprised. (p.339)

Thus the implied author passes the reader the key to the ambiguous title of Sara's book of whose existence the narrator seems completely ignorant.

By creating Amy, Cary has made it possible for the essential Sara to act a principal part on the social level of the Wilchers. The more apparent their close resemblance becomes to the reader, however, the less do they stand out as particular individuals in their own right. Throughout, in fact, the author does not let individuality blur the general significance of his characters. To this end Cary has filled his narrator's world with a number of sketches of women who all bear a striking likeness to Sara and Amy.

At Tolbrook a certain Agnes Ramm has taken over Sara's duties as house-
keeper and cook. She is now exactly the age at which the latter entered
Wilcher's service. To all appearances she is identical with the Aggie
of Herself Surprised, who disclosed to the young Sara her master's
"philanderings" with great gusto:[10]

> Agnes Ramm had been at Tolbrook twenty years, and I remember
> her when she first came, as kitchenmaid, a round, blooming
> young girl. Agnes had turned out a good maid, but not of the
> best character. She had had two illegitimate children before
> she was twenty, and once at least she had attempted some
> approach to myself. A hussy. But now at forty-six, after
> severe illness, a sad woman with strong religious feeling. (p.79)

Molly, the farm pupil with whom Robert has an affair, comes, like Sara
and Gladys from a somewhat better family than might have been expected.[11]
Like the young Sara, she is "shy" and "sly". She shares her healthy
looks and powerful build, and, of course, she has her "snub" nose.[12]

When on one occasion Wilcher's mother fails to put an end to a nursery
row, a "Sara" enters the stage making a parallel to Amy's intimidating
appearance in the midst of the political drawing-room dispute:[13]

> Nurse appears, a countrywoman, low built and broad. She tears
> us apart with her powerful arms and says, "That's enough -
> I've had enough, thank you. . . ." (p.28)

The little "between-maid" who helps the narrator to his first sexual
experience is also "shy" and "shrewd".[14] Like the other females of
"faith" she is rather possessed with health than with beauty. Despite
her dubious character she is, like Sara, an incarnation of domestic
virtue:

> I tremble again before that little maid whose very name has
> gone from me. She was a little fat creature with a face like
> moulded soap; and the nature of a bird in a cage, chirping
> with all domestic music. You heard her voice everywhere but
> always with some other voice, or the sound of a kettle singing,
> a grate being scoured. (p.76)

Nor does Ann's new nurse win Wilcher's fancy by her looks alone, but her
abounding vitality makes her attractive enough and reminds the reader
of Sara and her biblical namesake who laughed before the Lord.[15] In fact
the bouncing girl seems to make an incarnation of laughter:

> "A charming child," I thought, "her face too square, her cheeks
> too plump and rosy; but what a wife for some lucky man; what a
> companion and a mother. It is a pleasure to have her in the
> house." (pp.125-26)

4) The rankers

Amy has a dual role in so far as she has not only to live up to Sara's
sovereign power but also has to match her husband, the army officer who,
in Cary's world of paradoxes, is the archetype of "the private soldier"
who like Wilcher has been given a humble role in life but who, unlike
him, accepts it as a matter of course:

> Forty years ago, when I complained to Edward of my lost career,
> he smiled and said, "You've got what you wanted. You always
> meant to live at home. It's a shame the place wasn't left to
> you."
>
> I raged against him. To a man like Edward, I was one of those
> poor creatures, lawyers, bankers, the little clerks, who
> haven't the spunk to take a risk. And what is the truth? That
> all these quiet little men are the victims of ideals, of pas-
> sions. They are the lovers, the pilgrims of the world, who
> carry their burdens from one disappointment to another, and
> know it is useless even to complain. For their own comrades
> will despise them.
>
> They are the private soldiers who do the hard fighting, while
> the generals take the glory.
>
> Bill used that very image to me on the evening of Edward's
> party. "You and I are rankers to Edward." (pp.175-76)

Bill and Amy evidence the very antithesis of the meticulous old lawyer's
laming anxiety and, as a consequence, they lead a life whose virtues
Wilcher can experience in fancy though never accept in reality. They
marry, beget, spend their money, and die with an unquestioning confidence that is truly naive or as the narrator has to admit in spite of
all the worry they have given his "faithless" mind:

> Bill and Amy had the unbreakable faith of children who come
> home every day to a new world; and from that faith, they looked
> out, as monks once looked from this room, at the world as a
> spectacle. They did not need to think of themselves, for they
> knew exactly their purpose and their due. (p.106)

To these unassuming people life makes an open book holding all the answers
they need. This means that, to Wilcher's mind, they simplify matters
beyond the logic of his bearings. Thus, while he tries to start a discussion on the relation of philosophy to religion, a favourite topic of
his, Bill's speech certainly makes more sense to the reader than it does
to the narrator:

> Amy would read: "Here are two contemptible fellows, a philo-
> sopher without courage and a Christian without faith." And

Bill would take his pipe out of his mouth and say, "It's stopped."

"What's stopped?"

"The rain - no, it hasn't," and then, "Johnny might have said that - it's true, too."

"Do you think so?" I would ask. "Is John a convinced supporter of the Church?"

"But he's very philosophic - takes the rough with the smooth. Poor chap, he's had to."

"Good heavens, Bill, but that's not what the book means. It means that a philosopher must be honest even if his conclusions expose him to ridicule or lead him into pessimism."

"Yes, the rough with the smooth. What a gust. Thank God the leaves aren't out." (pp.251-52)

When, to please her brother-in-law, Amy tries to differ with her husband she proves beyond doubt how well matched they are:

"I think Tom's right. John was not really so philosophic. Too particular about his food. . . . (p.252)

Bill has eyes "like a retriever" and on one occasion Amy is happy to be delivered by a veterinary.[16] These references to the world of zoology are certainly not accidental as they both evidence an animal innocence which opens a well of comedy that the author is not always able to dam:

They were not a sentimental couple. Lucy used to say that when Bill left Amy for the first time, her last words, called after the railway carriage, through her tears, were, "Where did you leave my bicycle pump." And that Bill answered at the top of his voice, "Don't forget you're punctured behind." (p.107)

However foolish Amy and Bill may seem in the limited perspective of the fiction proper, their stupendous simplicity tends to raise them above the common run of mortals. After all, they are symbols and, often enough, Cary seems anxious to temper the reader's smile with the insight of their ultimate significance. They are "private" but, as in the case of "nonsense", their specific quality must be seen in the original sense of the word to be properly understood:[17]

Edward used to say that Bill and Amy's conversation on any subject, but especially a political subject, explained to him the history of the Greek word "idiot." "They are the most private citizens I ever met, even in a village pub." (p.165)

5) The militant leaders

Though Brown and Lucy share Amy and Bill's "privateness", they incarnate
rather spirit than "faith". They show the militant mettle that is signally missing in the, at heart, pacifist major and his wife. There is
surely an authorial pointer in the fact that, during Lucy's illness,
Amy acts as her nurse[18] and when for a brief encounter the professional
soldier and the champion of God appear in one and the same scene, it is
made perfectly clear which of the two incarnates the true servant:

> Brown was seen at the turn of the stairs, carrying a large
> trunk upon his back, like a professional porter. Lucy called
> out to him sharply, "Careful - don't break the balusters." She
> spoke as to a slave. But Bill, exclaiming, ran to take one
> handle of the trunk, and said, "You mustn't do that, sir. Let
> me help you." He was full of compliments and apologies, and
> when they had brought the trunk to the hall, he reproached
> the visitor. "Shouldn't have done that, Mr. Brown - a great
> effort - but you might have strained yourself."
>
> He laughed and straddled his legs like one talking, not per-
> haps to a bishop, but a dean; a reverend person who required
> special treatment, special protection, but not the highest
> kind of respect. (p.98)

It is also significant that, in Wilcher's earliest vision of the power-
ful evangelist, he should appear before the sign of the "Wilcher Arms".[19]
As we have already seen,[20] his looks are hardly human, but undoubtedly
Cary wanted him to incarnate Bunyan's invincible pilgrim:

> No foes shall stay his might,
> Though he with giants fight;
> He will make good his right
> To be a pilgrim. (p.20)[21]

In a later description the face of the roaring beast is largely retouched
possibly to admit some resemblance with Bunyan himself.[22] Thus the originally "thick swollen lips" have tightened into a "huge thin mouth". To
make up for this occasional concession to normality, however, Cary rounds
the description off by re-stating his monstrosity:

> Brown, as I say, was an ugly man, all body and no legs; not
> very short, but shaped like a dwarf. His head was extremely
> big, and he had the face of so many great orators and preach-
> ers, advocates and demagogues, a political face; short pug-
> nacious nose, long upper lip, huge thin mouth, heavy but
> shallow chin, deeply cleft; hollow deep-set eyes. He was as
> formidable as a gorilla, and seeing his threatening movement
> towards my father, . . . (p.95)

Brown is the leader of a dwindling little sect of undaunted souls, and
at the same time that Wilcher voices his disdain for his teachings, he
feels, at heart, his powerful attraction:

> Why was I afraid of Brown. I was a clever young man who was
> reading Kant. Brown had no arguments that did not fill me
> with contempt. But when he sang these verses from Bunyan,
> his favourite hymn and the battle cry of his ridiculous little
> sect, then something swelled in my heart as if it would choke
> me, unless I, too, opened my own mouth and sang. I might have
> been a bell tuned to that note, and perhaps I was. (pp.20-21)

Unlike Bill and Amy, the reckless evangelist and his equally strong-
willed wife make no well-tuned couple. The opposite sex has to Brown an
attraction that lays him open to Lucy's revenge and with fiendish delight
she saps his belief in himself and his Lord. For all the strain of their
"partnership" they stick together, however, because it makes a mutual
challenge, and, consequently, an inspiration and a wellspring of strength

> "I'm glad you're not going back," my mother would say, "I
> don't think Mr. Brown's religion makes anyone much better or
> more charitable."
>
> "Good Lord, no," Lucy would answer. "Puggy doesn't bother much
> about tea-table virtue."
>
> Lucy was strange to both of us. And yet, as I say, every word
> she said, however unexpected, found in me a response; some
> secret nerve within me was excited. To what? I was going to
> write, to the love of God, of religion, to some grandeur of
> thought. But now, as I pace restlessly through the lower rooms,
> I feel it as something deeper, more passionate. The life of
> the spirit. (p.89)

6) The rebel of principled freedom

Lucy has "faith"[23] but her excess of spirit makes her radically different from the characters previously discussed as can be inferred from
the fact that in her earlier days, at least, she was considered a "belle".
Her temperament is, however, not equally prepossessing even if Wilcher's
admiration for his sister makes him apt to parry the fact:

> When Ann came to put me to bed, take my pulse, mix me a
> draught, and so on, she began to ask me about Robert and his
> side of the family. "I was always told that Aunt Lucy was
> rather fierce."
>
> "Fierce. At your age - no, six years younger - Lucy was one
> of the belles of the season - a charming girl. But she had a
> strong will. . . . ." (p.19)

Wilcher loves his sister in particular as her presence releases the
self-confidence without which no "pilgrimage" is possible and the lack
of which brings her husband back to her in spite of all that she makes
him suffer:

> My attachment to Lucy was a country legend. I see myself
> joined to her as if by a string; . . . I am always running
> at her heels, clasping at her hand; or anxiously hunting for
> her, with the anguish and despair of a lost dog. I cannot be
> happy without her. (p.25)

> But suddenly my love seemed to expand and burst into a fit of
> laughter. I began to squeeze Lucy and punch my head into her
> chest, and all the time I am laughing. The shy serious little
> boy, making his anxious and careful way through a world full
> of older brothers and sisters all capable at any moment of
> the most unpredictable fits of violence or mockery, gives
> place, like a magic-lantern slide, to a stranger. I see the
> serious face split by an enormous demoniac grin; the tufted
> hair speaks no longer of disability and ugliness, but of an
> unruly coarseness. I am full of violence and rebellion. (p.47)

> And Lucy, when she gave me power, gave me anger. (p.297)

> And through Lucy's eyes, I saw again the richness which had
> been given to us; the fortune of those who have had a lively
> childhood and who have never lost their homes.

> Lucy made it for me by the power of her spirit, which created
> again that beauty. For I did not see then that beauty must be
> made again and that when love dies, the form that expressed
> it is also dead. (p.291)

Lucy incarnates rebellion. Early enough she shows her mettle by opposing
her father as well as the Lord:

> Lucy returned a message that she wasn't coming to prayers;
> she would never again attend prayers or go to church. Miss C.
> went up to reason with her, and Lucy gave her reason, that
> she hated God, who was nothing but an old Jew.

> My father then sent an ultimatum to which Lucy answered that
> she hoped she would go to hell. The devil was a devil, but at
> least he was better than God. And she did not care for any-
> body or for anything they said to her.

> This of course, was a direct challenge to my father and all of
> us understood very well that he would not care to beat her
> twice in the same day. That such a beating might have serious
> consequences for Lucy and therefore for him and for all of us.
> And that Lucy was counting precisely on that point to defeat
> him. (p.43)

As, by the way, her name suggests, Lucy is possessed with a devil, i.e.
in the "diabolos" sense of the word. She is an "accuser" or "slanderer"
and her function is, in other words, to remind people of the fact that

there are two sides to a matter and to rouse them out of the stagnancy
of appeasing beliefs:

> When I intervened on Amy's behalf to point out how important
> it was for John to get a scholarship, Lucy answered me, "Why
> shouldn't you pay with all the money you've made out of
> Edward?"
>
> I knew that this was a deliberate provocation. Yet I always
> lost my temper. I would cry, "That's an abominable slander,"
> etc., and I should have liked to kill Lucy. Her poisonous
> tongue made wounds that nothing could heal. No one was more
> quick and clever in twisting malice and truth, falsehood and
> injustice, into one burning dart and feathering it with a
> plume drawn from the victim's own breast. She had a devil's
> genius in striking at the very roots of the soul, and para-
> lysing its nerve.
>
> It would flash upon me, "It's true. . . ." (p.219)

Wilcher loves his sister because of her "faith" but being susceptible
to her "devil" he is also equal to hatred because, at bottom, he also
feels the fear that made Brown "howl" to his Lord to be saved from "hel
or "her":[24]

> "What an extraordinary boy you are, Tommy." Her voice flies
> at me out of the dark like a snake out of ambush. Devil's
> words. For Lucy did not believe them; she meant them to stab
> me, to destroy my faith in myself, and to increase her own
> importance. (p.27)

As in the case of Lucy's namesake, her power manifests itself as pride.
By "fighting pride with pride" (p.161) she serves the Lord "out of
devilry" (p.48). However well the narrator knows to describe her "faith"
as well as her "demon", the author's dual view of her nature remains
beyond him even when Edward displays his superior judgment on this poin

> ". . . And look at Lucy, she doesn't believe in anything."
>
> "She's given up everything for God,"
>
> "Do you think so? My impression is that Lucy hasn't any relig-
> ion at all. But she has a great sense of class. She has turned
> herself into a char because she feels that her own class is
> finished. She doesn't feel grand enough as a mere lady. She
> has flown to the arms of Puggy to give herself the sense of
> nobility."
>
> "I think that's nonsense."
>
> "Yes, quite probably - like most other things." (pp.75-76)

When Cary introduces a new character, he is, as a rule, eager to descril
his physical mould. In this respect Lucy makes a notable exception. In
fact, Cary lets his initial statement concerning her beauty remain

unattested by close description until her days are virtually out. Probably he found it difficult to conceive a portrait matching her fierce spirit. Possibly he also wanted to keep the reader in suspense to heighten the effect when, at last, her visible self comes out in Cary's merciless limelight. It should, however, be observed that the author does not let his speaker's silence pass without annotation. On one occasion he actually makes him admit his inability to convey her looks:

> I let Ann have my own photograph of Lucy, from my mantelpiece. It is better than the one downstairs. And I don't like photographs. They are dangerous. They serve only to hide the real people from me. When I look at Lucy's picture, faded and pale, she disappears behind it. (p.52)

When owing to her husband's unfaithfulness Lucy returns to Tolbrook, she is no longer the sparkling beauty who had run away to marry Brown four years earlier. Evasively Cary stages her reappearance in a "dim-lit hall" where the bad lighting gives the narrator an excuse to withhold from the reader her real looks. What he describes is a "pilgrim":

> This woman under the hall lamp which made deep hollows in her cheeks, looked at me, in my dinner jacket and white shirt, as gypsy women look when they beg from the gentlemen on Epsom Downs. Their hard filmy gaze puts gentlemen into a glass cage like wax figures in a museum. (p.84)

Only when Lucy returns to die harrassed by privation, toil, and illness, does the narrator find her physical destruction advanced enough to make a proper incarnation of her destructive spirit:

> She was white-haired, shrunken, with cheeks so thin that one saw through them the shape of her gums, and the dry corded muscles of her jaw. Her nose was like a finch's beak, hooked, yellow and shining. The blackened skin round her eyes gave them the piercing brightness of lights behind a dingy curtain. (p.289)

Above all her bird-like nose warns the reader of her particular position among the characters of "faith". When, soon after, the narrator sketches her again, the "dingy curtain" of physical decay has definitely given way to the demonic lucidity of her essential self:

> . . . I got up and went to her room. But before I had opened the door it sprang open before me and Lucy stood there laughing and holding up her arms. It was strange to see in the little old woman, dried as a mummy, with her witch's nose and chin, her fierce eyes, the gestures of the beautiful young girl, frank and coquettish. "I heard you coming, Tommy. I knew you would have to come . . ." (p.297)

It should be pointed out that Lucy's destructiveness makes her keep a
perspective that is as close as the "myopic" Wilcher's. As her role can
hardly maintain its significance outside the light of "faith", the
narrator is as apt to see in her a "hypocrite" as, in her eyes, he himself is liable to make a "pettifogger":

> Lucy could always enrage me by calling me a pettifogger. As
> I could anger her by calling her a hypocrite. For both words
> came so close to the truth of our natures that they took its
> light and cast a shadow on our souls. (p.161)

To Wilcher the nature of evil makes a problem in which he has taken a
life-long interest. He has even written a book on the subject. Unfortunately the duality of the concept remains beyond him as the facetious
Cary makes it implicitly clear by his narrator's infelicitous use of the
ambiguous "positive" in what seems to be the very title of the work:

> . . . it was John who urged me to publish my book on the need
> for a new statement of the Christian belief, with special
> regard to the positive power of evil; and the real existence
> of the devil. (p.262)

What in the author's eye gives Lucy's life validity enough to save it
from any final charge of hypocrisy, is her "principle", i.e. her proud
"come wind, come weather" course through life. It is true that this
course testifies to little sense in so far as her stubborn refusal of
medical treatment brings about her own destruction. At the same time,
however, her very stubbornness is a triumphant manifestation of the
"pilgrim's" powerful unconcern and bliss. While, before his death, the
"faithless" Edward is seen sitting fast asleep in the family trap while
the horse is listlessly taking him along the roads,[25] Lucy enters the
same apocalyptic vehicle in quite a different spirit:

> "Why does a religion die, Lucy? It's very strange when you
> think of it. Why do people cease to take any interest in God.
> Even the simple people who know nothing about theological
> quarrels."
>
> "The people only want something for nothing," Lucy said. "We
> are well rid of them, as I tell the master."
>
> "Then your sect will die."
>
> "I believe. And the master, bless the lamb."
>
> "You aren't a religion."
>
> "Drive, Tommy, drive. Get her head up - make her go." (p.290)

7) Dissolution as a releaser of life in the post-war generation

Gladys, John's wife, is a true member of the young generation which has a need to manifest its independence vis-à-vis a society that has let them in for so much suffering and loss. Wilcher is not only scandalized by these young people's contempt of established norms but, at heart, also frightened because he fears it will bring about the dissolution of the basic values which he has given all his life to defend. Consequently he is at first not very happy about John's associating with a girl whose very appearance gives offence to propriety. From the beginning, however, Cary makes it implicitly clear that this piece of buoyant vulgarity has not lost her faith in life as, besides, her name gives us reason to believe:

> Her figure was slim and flat; her face disproportionately large and round. In repose, with its small features, large blue eyes and brassy hair, it reminded one of those dummies put in hairdresser's windows. But it was seldom in repose. Gladys was always jerking her head, twitching her little mouth, rolling her eyes and humping her shoulders. In conversation she would wriggle her behind as if it itched; and frequently she plunged her hand into her breast or down her back in order to scratch herself. Her voice was the chatter of a colobus monkey; her laugh the shriek of a cockatoo. She was daubed like one of Edward's pictures; and her nails were always dirty. (p.264)

Like Sara and Molly, Robert's snub-nosed mistress, this girl comes from a family of a higher social status than might have been expected.[26] Being an exponent of "faith" she has, of course, no need of "stays" as Cary lets her husband intimate to the reader in a typical display of ambiguities:

> ". . . She's really rather a good soul, and she has a lot of guts, too."
>
> "I see them only too plainly," I said. "But I suppose stays are out of date, like my prejudices."
>
> John smiled and answered that Gladys did not need stays; her figure was so good. (p.264)

Gladys is a post-war version of an urbanized Sara. She never gets "stuck" because she has the mettle of the little sparrow to whom life is tight enough never to make it forget the art of surviving.[27] Therefore the preservation of the past makes little sense to her, and therefore she laughs at Wilcher's dated fashions.[28] Consequently her husband's classical erudition means nothing but wind to her:

> He would lie across a sofa, unbuttoned, his long hair falling
> down his perspiring face, and throw out, with lazy grin, some
> classical allusion, which the others neither understood nor
> heard. Unless Gladys catching it up could turn the sound of
> it into an obscenity. (p.284)

Like Sara, Gladys deceives her "long-nosed" husband and separates him
from his mother, but at the same time she proves the only pillar of
their home and remains his servant till his death. Then, however, she
feels no scruple to join another man without delay. Wilcher never seems
fully aware of the parallel Gladys's character makes to Sara's but,
however that may be, he grows "almost fond" of the girl whom at first
he took for "a young prostitute from the cheaper streets" (p.264). As
after John's death there is nobody young enough to stand up in defence
of her ways, Cary makes her pass a final judgment on herself in words
that resound with authorial conviction:

> "You've got me wrong, Nunky - I'm not going to the devil. I've
> got a good grip on things. I'm not like that old soak, Julie
> - I'd be ashamed." (p.288)

8) The past generation and the law

Time and again the reader is given to understand that the Wilchers and
Tolbrook are as old as the English and their England. In fact, this
ancient West-Country family symbolizes the whole nation it makes part
of:

> For the Wilchers are as deep English as Bunyan himself. A
> Protestant people, with the revolution in their bones. (p.21)

In the novel Wilcher's father appears to the reader as a four-square
country squire whose "flat-topped hat" seems to crown his plausible
affinity with the accepted picture of John Bull:

> My father, in a flat-topped felt hat, and my mother in a
> tight-waisted sealskin and little round ermine hat, are al-
> ready fifty yards down the drive. My father holds himself
> very upright; but rolls a little on his short thick legs.
> He is still a soldier in his back, but his legs are growing
> farmerish. (p.25)

By having the narrator's father firmly rooted in his native soil the
author makes him appear a true representative and worthy head of the
Wilcher family, but for the very same reason he must also evidence the
makings of a "pilgrim", and by conceiving him as a Christian Liberal

and a retired soldier with a distinguished war record at that Cary has
made him, at least formally, qualified to symbolize the Nonconformist
spirit. As far as the action of the novel goes, however, Colonel Wilcher
does not primarily incarnate boundless "faith" as, in the narrator's
eye, he rather makes an administrator of religious observance and
discipline. Within the little community of the Tolbrook nursery he
maintains strict rules:

> Prayers were at a fixed hour. And it was a crime to be late.
> All quarrels to be made up, and all repentances spoken, before
> the last prayer, at the bedside; on penalty of drum-head court
> martial; that is, an immediate slap on the behind, so conven-
> iently reached at that hour. And three complaints from nurse
> in one week, meant a whipping. (pp.29-30)

It is true that Colonel Wilcher's "law" does not seem to violate young
Wilcher's sense of freedom, but it should be observed that it altogether
disagrees with the implied author's norms, e.g. his view of "principle"
as founded in individual responsibility and "faith".[29] Whether the
"principle" that the author lets the narrator's father embody, makes
him rank second to the other exponents of living "faith" remains an
open question. As far as the story proper goes, he represents a generation that, like the narrator's own, is getting out of touch with time.
For all the generosity of his Christian Liberalism, he fails to extend
his full sympathy to any other denominations than churches of established
standing,[30] and being a staunch supporter of Gladstone he is shocked at
the young Liberals' condescendent attitude to the "Grand Old Man" (p.124).

However, when it is time for the master of Tolbrook to take farewell of
the world, the author makes him an incarnation of unqualified "faith".
Lying, most significantly, on a "camp bed" in his "dressing-room" the
old "pilgrim"-soldier awaits the call for him to break the deadening
inactivity of his Tolbrook "billet". His last will turns out to be an
act of perfect intuition and "faith" as it devolves the burden of all
his real estate on the "faithless" Edward whom he despises and whose
spiritual destitution the legacy is meant to symbolize and seal whereas
the other children are set "free" by receiving a most modest sum each.[31]

THE "FAITHLESS" AND "UNFREE"

1) General observations

Although in principle the "faithful" and the "faithless" categories have
been conceived on an antagonistic basis and consequently correlate, the
characters of failing "faith" form an incomparably smaller group. It
comprises only two principal roles, Julie and Edward, and two subsidiary
ones, Wilcher's mother and his nephew John. Their contrasting relationship to the characters of "faith" is reflected in the fairly uniform
typology that can be derived from the narrator's description of their
characteristics and qualities. Certain physical and temperamental traits
make it fair to presume that Cary moulded them on Kretschmer's asthenic
type even if, like Lucy in the opposite camp, Edward breaks the pattern
owing to the exceptional position he holds.

Physically the "faithless" are very attractive[32] even if, as we shall
see, the narrator's judgment on this point seems subjective enough and
liable to change. They are all "slim" or "thin".[33] Furthermore, Julie
and John who, contrary to Mrs. Wilcher and Edward, suffer from next to
total exhaustion of spirit, have been provided with "too long" noses.[34]

These four characters are all highly gifted people and represent a level
of civilization that has risen too high to remain saturated with the
sources of life. Contrary to Cary's snub-nosed uglybodies they are unhappy, irresponsible, and weak because their lives have not been chan-
nelled into restraining principles and, consequently they have not become
primed with determination and meaning. They are, in other words, too
free to identify themselves with life and so get "stuck" in a self-centre
of isolation where they give themselves up to their own refined tastes.
Thus Edward's room mirrors his lack of originality and spirit:

> We are back in Edward's room among his beautiful books, his
> first editions, his ivories and china, his French impressionist
> pictures which seem even to his friends still an affectation. (p.74

Julie's room is a similar ivory tower:

> I jump up, trembling with excitement and audacity, to explore
> the room. It seems to me beautiful and strange. On the walls,
> covered with a plain brown paper, are Japanese prints in white
> frames, and a few drawings, signed by the artists. A Beardsley,

> a Beerbohm print, an impressionist sketch by Manet. . . .
> Along one whole wall, a low white bookcase is full of books
> in bright bindings. . . . And when I open them, I find many
> of them inscribed, "To dear Julie," "To dearest Hedda," "To
> my old friend, Julie," with the signatures of the authors
> and artists.
>
> I had never seen a room with plain walls, plain curtains, with
> no gilt frames or silver ornaments; with no decorations but
> the austere prints. For even Beardsley in his black and white
> was priest-like. I thought, "It is like a cell, of one whose
> faith is in beauty and love, but a noble beauty, a proud and
> reserved passion." (p.148)

Even Wilcher's mother who makes the least pronounced case of "faithlessness", lives in a sanctuary of refined beauty. Like John, all these
characters "stand aside"[35] and their alienation turns out to be so
unqualified that it tends to suspend the verisimilitude of their lives.
On the other hand, they seem human enough in comparison with their
"faithful" counterparts whose infallibility raises them above the common
run of men.

2) Two female exponents of failing "faith"

a) Wilcher's mother

The narrator concerns himself far less with his parents than with his
brothers and sisters. The portrait of his mother is vague indeed. Still
her spiritual status becomes evident enough in the parallels or contrasts
that other characters provide. She is her husband's perfect opposite,
and often their polarity is so apparent that it tends to make the reader
unduly aware of the implied author. In accordance with Cary's strict
observance of antitheses this wife of a West-Country soldier and farmer
has been made a descendant of East-Country Quakers and scholars. Her
maiden name is not the spirited "Wilcher" but "Bowyer" as the facetious
Cary has christened her apparently not very militant family.[36] Contrary
to her husband, she loves Edward.[37] Like the latter she is not only
physically attractive but also witty and flirtatious.[38] Like Julie, her
son's mistress, she is a lonely and unhappy fin-de-siècle woman whose
room makes a statement of her ethereal mind:

> I seemed in that room to be existing within my mother's being,
> an essential quality, indescribable to me then, and not easy
> to describe now; something that was more grace than happiness,

> more beauty than joy, more patience than rest, a dignity
> without pride, a peace both withdrawn and sensitive. (p.31)

She also resembles Julie in so far as she is too gentle a soul to stand
her own ground. When, as a little boy, Wilcher makes a mess of her room,
she fails to scold him.[39] Like Edward she is a parent whose love for
her child is not strong enough to break through a crust of formal duty.
When, for once, she lets her frightened little son sleep in her bed,
there is a lack of intimacy comparable to what many years afterwards
the narrator is to experience in the congenial privacy of his mistress's
boudoir:[40]

> I remember my fascinated delight in the glossy red satin lining
> of the curtains, and the tall mountains of pillows, like a tor
> under fresh snow, which stood over me when, having slipped to
> their foot, I waked in the morning. I was in paradise. And yet
> I knew, even then, that kind as she was, my mother suffered
> me with difficulty in her bed; and that she had never cared
> greatly for my plain face, my awkward ways, my spectacled
> eyes. I got on her nerves, as they say. (p.334)

Though Mrs. Wilcher makes a striking parallel to both Edward and Julie,
the fact remains that, being a married woman and a mother, she enjoys
the "stays" of limited or, rather, principled freedom and, consequently
she is saved from swerving into their "sloth and decadence". Like her
husband in the opposite camp, she does not make a fully convincing
exponent of the spiritual category she belongs to. This becomes clear
enough when, on a small but significant point, the author contrasts her
with Julie so signally that the reader can hardly refuse the implicit
comparison he has been invited to. Thus after describing his mother's
frequent charity visits to a slum area the narrator makes Julie declare
her inability to do similar work.[41] Furthermore, in contrast to the
"faithless" Edward, her favourite son, she remains herself to the very
end of her life:

> My mother never became an eccentric. If she could not sleep
> she lay patiently in her bed, or read a book. She was too
> considerate of others, too proud, to give way to singularity.
> But Edward, in his loneliness, soon fell into strange habits.
> He would spend half the night walking, or even driving, across
> the lanes and over the moor roads. (p.268)

b) Julie

In every respect Julie is an anti-Sara and together they thus represent
the full polarity of the concept "faith". Contrary to Sara, the servant
of life, Julie incarnates death, and to nurse a dream of love that never
came true she has withdrawn into a private world of her own where life
seems to have ceased to tick.[42]

Julie leads a life of form without substance and this explains why Cary
has made her a Catholic and an actress. She is completely "stuck" in
her adoration of Edward, her irresponsive god to whose whim she is any
moment ready to minister in a sanctuary of the fin-de-siècle letters
and art to which her lover has given his heart. In fact, with her
aestheticism and loneliness Julie evokes the "Yellow Book" circle of
writers and artists whose works adorn the walls of her shrine-like
dwelling:

> Julie was intelligent as well as beautiful, and her mind, at
> that time, had the same forms as her body; an austere grace,
> a balanced quickness. She had all the qualities of a great
> actress; above all, that seriousness before life which we saw
> again in Duse. She had all, except ambition. (pp.148-49)

As a matter of fact the thin Julie's dark and pale beauty seems easily
to lend itself to the ornate black-and-white style of Beardsley. Thus
the narrator describes his first view of her:

> Inside I found a thin pale girl, who jumped up and looked
> angrily at me. She seemed to me, as far as I could see in the
> dim light, very plain. Her pale hair was drawn smoothly back
> into a style quite new to me; her small round forehead pro-
> jected in two shiny bumps, her eyes, very large and black, . . .
> (p.144)

When, in his portrayal of Julie, the narrator compares her attitude
toward life to Eleonora Duse's, he makes a reference that is certainly
not accidental. Julie's story holds certain particulars that may have
been taken from Duse's biography. Like Cary's tragic actress she was
a most famous "Hedda Gabler". Furthermore she came to hinge her life
and career on a man, D'Annunzio, who like Edward, was not only a dare-
devil politician and a nationalist war-monger but also a ladies' man,
an aesthete and poet. Duse died during an American tour and Julie's
spiritual death takes place under similar circumstances.[43]

Julie remains irrevocably tied to the object of her devotion. She tries
to rid herself of him but has not "faith" enough to stand her own. At
the same time her physical mould is subject to continuous change. Returning from her American tour to see her lover she is no more a pale
ethereal "nun" but seems to be well on the way to equal Amy and Sara if
we disregard her beauty which, as we have seen, can hardly indicate
"faith":

> I had never seen Julie so beautiful or so magnificently dressed.
> She had had a great success in America. She had a new reputa-
> tion, new clothes, new jewels; even a new appearance. She was
> heavier, more imposing. (p.155)

Furthermore, vis-à-vis Julie, Wilcher seems to make as ill-matched a
partner as, in Herself Surprised, the colourless Matt (!) Monday to
Sara:

> Julie looks at me. I am sitting on the bed among the dresses
> which swell up on each side of me, and my feet, of course,
> do not reach the floor. Probably, in my frock coat and patent
> leather boots, my high collar and formal tie, I appear a little
> absurd in this situation. Julie suddenly begins to laugh. She
> stoops down, red with laughter, and I see her breasts, now
> plump and round, within her wide-topped stays. (p.178)

On the eve of her attempted suicide the original Beardsley girl has
developed into "some dark Creole beauty", and as we have every reason
to believe that her body still has a spiritual correlate, we are led
to presume that Julie's desperation now has given her a "gypsy's" spirit
strong enough to break her bondage. Anyhow, this is what can be inferred
from her cryptic use of "disloyal", "religious", and "stand aside":

> ". . . She hated me to say that I was going to be a nun."
>
> "Do you still wish it?"
>
> "No, I don't think so. I should have to forget so much that
> I don't want to forget. I should feel so disloyal."
> . . .
> And I said in a voice carefully respectful, "I'm glad you're
> not going to leave us, Julie. We need you."
>
> "Only the religious are happy in a world like this. But I
> haven't the right to stand aside." (p.191)

Julie fails to gas herself to death because, for all her new spirit, her
symbolic role makes her destined for failure, and by letting the scandal
of her attempted suicide hurry Edward into marrying another woman the
author ingeniously seals her fate in tragedy. Julie's degradation is,
however, a process that can be traced much further back. We must not

forget that Julie's physical change by no means detracts from her beauty
and consequently cannot signify an unambiguous development towards the
incarnation of "faith". Even if Wilcher's description of the successful
actress returning from America[44] gives a picture of health in blossom,
the adjacent comparison to a fruit liable to overripeness has, to my
mind, a slightly jarring note:

> And her face had that special look which belongs to much-
> flattered women like the radiance of peaches which have been
> warmed in sunshine. (p.155)

Soon enough it actually appears that Julie's plumpness has none of Sara's
muscular firmness but an increasing "softness" matching the dissolution
of her character:

> Julie comes in, dressed with a splendour suitable to her new
> stately beauty. And that growing softness of her figure seems
> to have invaded her glance, her expression. What had been
> passion and fire in the young girl was now more tender, more
> gentle and resigned. (p.179)

In fact, even the portrait of the "dark Creole beauty" bears marks of
the spiritual death whose consummation is to follow on the attempt at
suicide that she premeditates. Apparently she is already in the Valley
of the Shadow of Death:

> She seemed like some dark Creole beauty while she strolled
> under the arching palm leaves and pondered, with downcast
> eyes. Her long lashes threw a green shadow on her cheeks.
> Little beads of sweat stood on her round forehead. (p.191)

When after her "suicide" Wilcher succeeds his brother as Julie's lover,
her gentleness quickly develops into apathy numbing her whole life.
Sharing her bed the narrator might as well have made love to a dummy:

> . . . when, by her silence, however melancholy, she permitted
> me first to stay and then to enter her room, I affected to be
> carrying out the old routine. I allowed myself to believe,
> when I climbed at last into her bed and took hold of her and
> arranged her body to suit my purpose, that I was performing
> a trivial act which might, for a moment or two, take from our
> minds the weight of our anxieties. But the truth was, I was
> trying to fly out, by that door, from oppression and fear.
> And Julie's gentle acquiescence hid from me the violence of
> my deed. (p.229)

This listlessness seems to deprive her existence of its verisimilitude
and leave her in a haze of unreality. When the porter of her house is
caught in the act of stealing her silver, she refuses to have him pros-
ecuted (p.207). She takes to drinking but, eventually, no amount of drink

can make up for her total lack of spirit. Instead of enlivening her
body her intemperance quickens its dissolution:

> . . . Julie did not get drunk. She became only blowsy and
> red.
> . . .
> Julie, in the morning, when her head ached and her whole
> flabby body seemed to be dissolving in self pity, would say
> to me . . . (p.284)

At the same time as her physical condition mirrors her spiritual death,
her dwelling makes an emblem of hell as can be inferred from the interlocutors' disagreement about the temperature of the place:

> Edward and I, in the golden light of the fire, seemed to be
> in a different world, and I think we both felt it. Edward
> jumped up and said, "Have my chair, Julie - aren't you cold
> there?"
>
> "No, thank you - it's too hot." And she said in the same
> voice, "After all, we are evil ourselves . . ." (p.226)

In addition to this drastic pointer the author elaborates a view of hell
that amounts to a restatement of Milton's "darkness visible":

> The rest of the room was felt rather than seen; and Julie was
> only a shadow among the thick uncertain shadows of furniture
> in the background. But the sky through the dark frame of the
> window had become brilliant with the strange light of a London
> dusk, neither blue nor green, gloomy but limpid, like a clear
> sheet of glass, apparently transparent and profound, but
> showing no star. It was like some vast shallow jewel lit by a
> cunning arrangement of lights hidden behind it. Its beauty
> gave no sense of expansion to the spirit, but only oppression.
> (p.227)

This hell is, however, no place of eternal damnation but rather a pur-
gatory-like melting-pot where the unfree are dissolved and, consequently
freed. It equals a process of revolution in a "crucible" where people
as well as societies are transformed. When the narrator compares Julie
to a peach "warmed in sunshine" the author behind him apparently tries
to intimate to the reader that she has already experienced a blast from
the "furnace door" of her inevitable damnation, i.e. the "bar of heat"
which, according to Edward, heralds "revolution", i.e. in Julie's case,
"the wrath to come" (p.275). When eventually Julie evidences a "sullen
rage against the world", she is consequently well on the way out of her
private hell into "freedom". It is true that she apparently is to end
her days in the asylum where her "rage" finally takes her, but on the
symbolic level this makes a happy ending as the reader by now can hardly

be in doubt about what the author means by "madness".[45] Besides, for
all his fear of being "certified" himself, Wilcher, at a very early
stage, takes an equally ambiguous view of asylums:[46]

> The secret of happiness, of life, is to forget the past, to
> look forward, to move on. The sooner I can leave Tolbrook,
> the better, even for an asylum. (pp.34-35)

To what extent Wilcher is able to take a positive view of Julie's dissolution, i.e. consider it a "revolutionary" process is, of course, a
question to which we can find as many answers as there are different
"points of view" in the author's narrator. As, in principle, Cary's
symbolism is out of bounds to his narrating "I", the latter is never
given to realize in full his indisputable susceptibility to the varying
"faith" that the other characters have to incarnate. This, above all,
applies to Wilcher's attitude towards Julie. Thus he is by no means aware
of what ultimately makes him take such a sudden dislike to a liaison
that, before it became a fact, had tickled his fancy as the perfection
of bliss, however well he knows how to describe the lack of intimacy he
experienced even on their first night together. Therefore, for all the
plausible objectivity of his first picture of Julie after her "suicide",
it also manifests his own instinctive revulsion to the spiritual death
that her bloated body incarnates:

> She received me with a kind of calm, gentle surprise which
> gave her, I thought, a stupid look. Indeed, I thought, seeing
> her again, that she was growing plain. Her plumpness was
> unbecoming. Her pallor had an unhealthy look. Her eyes and
> forehead were full of fine wrinkles. And while we were waiting
> for tea I felt sorry for her. I thought, "She is finished -
> she has let her life ebb away," and I said with a roughness
> which surprised my own ear "You should take more exercise,
> Julie, you're getting too fat." (p.228)

However true it may be that Cary cannot let his narrator acquaint the
reader with any explicit knowledge of the symbolic significance that
Julie's life serves to express, he cannot, on the other hand, make her
tragic end leave a lasting burden on his sensitive mind. Most probably
Cary had some difficulty in tempering the narrator's limited understanding with his own authorial intelligence. This is what can be inferred
from the well-calculated dose of commentary that the author lets his
narrator administer to the reader on Julie's commitment to her mental
hospital.[47]

Wilcher's account of Julie's life is interspersed with literary references which, without exception, make convenient vehicles of authorial
commentary at the same time as they seem to mean nothing to the narrator himself. This communication is, of course, conditioned by the
observant reader's acquaintance with the works in question. Thus the
former "Hedda Gabler", the Ibsen exponent of "faith", has Ernest Dowson
"decadent" poems in her bookcase to define her own feelings of love,
longing, and loss and, furthermore, the equally congenial John Davidson
plays to stress her desire for spiritual freedom.[48] On another visit she
appears to be reading Dorothy Osborne's love-letters, and by making
Edward quote them Cary gives utterance to Julie's feelings. Significant
enough she cannot understand what made Miss Osborne stick to Sir William
Temple, "that stick". Nor is she aware of the wisdom of her own "state-
man's" answer which holds an implicit reflection on her inability to
make her own fortune. What Cary wants to say is simply that in the "ear"
times" of Lady Temple there was no fin-de-siècle "decadence":

> "Why is she so attractive?" Julie asks, "and how could she
> love that stick Sir William Temple?" And they begin to dis-
> cuss the character of a woman dead for nearly two hundred
> years. "And yet they say she was very happy with him."
>
> "A woman like that makes her own happiness. Besides, these
> were early times, you know - that vitality you get in her
> letters was everywhere. . . ." (p.180)

Julie's reading does not affect her any more than her drinking. This
Cary repeatedly makes clear by letting her appear in situations where,
manifestly enough, she is n o t reading the works which bear such
apparent relevance to her own story. Thus Wilcher finds "Stories Toto
Told Me" by Corvo, another "Yellow Book" contributor, lying unread on
a table for months.[49] No doubt Francis Thompson's religious mysticism
is meant to have held some appeal to her sweltering soul but, significantly, "The Hound of Heaven" lies on her floor "face downwards" (p.227)
In fact, Julie has lost all her zest for reading as the reader is given
to understand from her insusceptibility to anything new and from the
author's pun on the name of (George) Moore whose heroines also suffer
from restraint:

> The room was still kept neat and clean by Julie's devoted
> maid, but it had become revolting to me. I would say to Julie,
> "What, sitting in the dark, my dear - let me turn up the light.
> Oh, I see, you've been reading some Moore, "A Drama in Muslin."
>
> "No, I wasn't reading it - I know it by heart."

"Nothing new from the library."
"Nothing good - everything is so dull." (pp.303-04)

3) The indifferent god and unprincipled rebel pretending to "the Speaker's chair"

Julie's love for Edward makes a symbol of orthodox religion, i.e. the
believer's futile devotion to an indifferent god. At the same time as
their characters are alike enough to bring out the common denominator
of their "faithlessness", they must be contrasting enough to dramatize
the polarity of their relationship. Their basic affinity lies in the
fact that both are attractive, cultured, and talented, and, as a consequence, too spoilt with easy success to set any store by it. They are
too "free" because, to them, life makes as little sense as it makes a
challenge.

Contrary to Julie, whom Cary describes as "dark", Edward is "fair", and
throughout their polarity makes them differ in the same way as a developed photo and its negative plate evidence not only similarities but
also interrelated contrasts. Unlike Julie, the tragic actress and the
serious handmaiden of her ambiguous Lord, Edward is a light-hearted
dandy and irresponsible cynic. Whereas on her first appearance in the
novel Julie's life is already slowing down to a standstill, Edward is
still unmarked by his unlimited "freedom" albeit his meteor-like career
is soon to run into incandescence and spiritual combustion. In spite of
or, rather, because of all his cleverness Edward fails to identify himself with life. He is bound to be an outsider and whatever occupies his
mind is cursory and superficial:

> I was shocked and disgusted when Edward, after a meeting in
> which his eloquence had brought tears to our eyes, passed me
> this scrap of paper:
>
>> Let tyrannies all to free republics pass
>> The one by coppers ruled; the others, brass.
>
> The chairman was still on his feet, asking for a vote of thanks
> to our "gallant galahad of freedom." (p.154)

Edward is an inveterate waster spending his gifted self as well as
friends, women, money, and, significantly, "coals" with equal lack of
care.[50] Whatever he attempts is dissolved in the passing moment. This
also applies to his affections:

> Edward was at his best. He was not a man who gave one quality
> of entertainment to his friends and another to his family. We
> knew that he forgot us as soon as we were out of his sight.
> He never wrote to us, rarely knew anything about our family
> affairs. But we perceived that, when he was with us, his
> affection was real and quick. (p.123)

> Edward, as soon as the bedroom door closes, drops into a chair
> and takes a book out of the nearest shelf. In one minute his
> expression passes through affectionate earnestness with Julie,
> blank indifference as the door closes, and becomes attentive
> as he opens the book. (p.178)

This flightiness tends to give Edward's life a smack of affectation or
play-acting. Owing to its lack of substance it is the more vulnerable
to the freaks of chance. Announcing his plan to sum up his political
experience in a book he declares:

> ". . . I should like to do for politics what Tolstoy has done
> for war - show what a muddle and confusion it is, and that it
> must always be a muddle and confusion where good men are
> wasted and destroyed simply by luck as by a chance bullet."
> And then he said to me, "I'm not referring to myself." Edward
> was extremely quick to know another's mind and I had been
> thinking, "Poor Edward, he was knocked down by such a bullet."

> He smiled and said, "My case was rather different. I retired
> from the stage too soon, or too late, as you prefer. Like
> most circus performers and p r i m a d o n n a s . Like
> most people, in fact." (pp.268-69)

Superficiality is the curse of Edward's life, and owing to his intellec
sincerity he is unable to dodge the fact that he has been a true dilet-
tante throughout his life:[51]

> When I told him that he ought to be finishing his book, he
> would answer, "It's not worth finishing. Amateur stuff. I
> know enough to know that I don't know enough. Even the foun-
> dations have shifted. And I'm too old to begin a new education."
> (pp.274-75)

At the same time as Edward joins Julie in a polarity of symbolic significance, he implicitly matches his sister in a similar kind of relation by making a "faithless" version of her rebellious self. Thus, for
all the ultimate opposition of their symbolic functions, their portrait
have been given some common denominators to make the reader experience
a certain affinity. Like Lucy, Edward is possessed with a destructive
spirit, a "devil", even if the narrator fails to realize the fact. Thei
affinity above all manifests itself in the pronounced preference Lucy
shows for her brother and in the attraction unaccountable to himself
that Wilcher feels to them both. The two rebels' spiritual kinship has

also a physical correlate in the certainly not accidental fact that, contrary to Julie and John, Edward has a nose shaped like that of his "faithful" and beautiful sister, i.e. like a "beak".[52]

Edward shares his sister's egoism and courage and in so far both can be described as "free souls". Nevertheless they represent contrasting aspects of freedom. Early enough Lucy instinctively submits her unruly spirit to a rigorous rule of conduct by marrying Brown and turning herself into a "char" (p.76). For want of similar determination, however, Edward's promising life amounts to nothing. What in Lucy channels itself into fierce aggressiveness, becomes good-humoured cynicism or thoughtless wit in her brother. Thus, ironically his pungent attack on Lloyd George, his Liberal chief, first and foremost reflects on his own inability to check himself:

> Haul our great rebel's flag to Ritz's top
> The statesman's art is knowing where to stop. (p.204)

It appears that Edward's improvidence is to bring about his fall. When this Fortune's godless minion is on his way to crowning his brilliant career by deposing the Lords (!), an unexpected set-back saps all his enterprise and makes him turn his back on politics to start a leisured life exclusively dedicated to the enjoyment of literature, art, and beauty. Thus Edward's story equals that of the greatest of all fallen luminaries. Like Satan he has not conviction to match what he attempts. His fall is great because he falls in love which, in Cary's view, is liable to result in bondage.[53] By marrying a very young girl the aging Edward once again fails to live up to what he has irresponsibly pledged himself for. To him, the inveterate egoist, his beautiful wife is only a piece of art, an object for playful contemplation:

> Edward paid no attention to either of us. He had picked up his wife's hand, which was singularly small and of a perfect shape, unusual in very small hands, and while pretending to admire her rings, was admiring its beauty. She let it lie in his palm, but continued to discuss his affairs with me. "What I say is, he's got a duty to the people. Even if they have treated him badly."
>
> "Your rings need cleaning, Lotty dearest," Edward said. "What are diamonds without a drop of ammonia."
>
> "He told me there was going to be a revolution, and now it's come he's playing round here with all these fancy painters instead of taking his proper place at home."

> "Fancy painters," Edward said laughing, "she means some of
> the greatest in the history of art. . . ." (p.206)

When, at last, Lotty's waxing disappointment makes him break his untimely
"holiday" (or "unholy day") to attempt a come-back, it appears that his
"vital spark" is gone. What he apparently foresaw himself at an early
stage has now come true.[54] With the tragic candour of a Miltonic Satan
he makes it understood that there remains no other course for him to
follow that that of indiscriminate revenge and destruction:

> He spoke without his usual animation, but in Julie's melancholy
> tone, of one who accepts fate. "Plenty of people are ready to
> take any risk to themselves so long as they can get their
> revenge on somebody else - often some purely abstract enemy,
> like Germany or France, or England. See how the Irish nation-
> alists delight in hatred of England - which is a pure abstrac-
> tion."
> . . .
> "Another large group," Edward said, touching the poker but
> withdrawing his hand again. "Another large group," he resumed,
> "probably the largest of all, is the people who are dissatis-
> fied with their lot - the failures." He paused and I felt that
> he had plumped the word out in defiance of embarrassment. (pp.226-

Edward's words refer to the international situation of 1914, the deteri-
oration of which Cary emblematically couples with this public man's own
"corruption". On the Continent where, after his "rebellion", he withdrew
to enjoy his fatal "holiday", Edward has already scented what is to
develop into World War I, and he jumps at the prospect of a European
conflict to swing himself back into power or, at least, wage his own
Armageddon. At home he addresses meetings on the approaching danger and
appears even in uniform to make himself out as the leader whom he wants
to pass off on the nation but whom few are ready to follow. Thus he turns
himself into a puppet-like warmonger and to the narrator's mind "a clever
fool" (p.222) as, again, his conviction does not match his enterprise.
When Lotty realizes that her husband's days in politics are over she
leaves him. Although, as we have seen, Edward is perfectly well aware
of the inexorable finality of his fate, he only slowly gives way to
despair. Even when his life-long play-acting has at long last come to
an end and he lapses into a state of apathy, his adventurous spirit does
not, however, flicker out altogether; and as his life is quickly running
out, he seems to look forward to death as a redeemer of the spirit from
the bondage of old age which is quite in accordance with Cary's view of
"faith" as "the secret of youth".[55]

". . . And there's nothing so ageing as failure. Why, I can
hardly get round the lake; and look at my fingers, stiff and
swelling in every joint. Degommé. To come unstuck. The perfect
word." (p.275)

Therefore Edward is in excellent spirits when finally Cary gives him
"a mild influenza" (p.282) and with significant alacrity he makes the
best of this mild but, anyhow, passable excuse to slip his world.

In the chapter on the central theme and the vision variable[56] we saw how
by a shift of point of view Cary turned his objectified narrator into
an authorial commentator. For all this duality of vision, however,
Wilcher is unable to see how living "faith" is related to its orthodox
opposite until he is about to conclude his story. Therefore it has fallen
to Edward's lot to make it explicitly clear how any established order
bears the seed of its own "corruption". Like Julie's barren devotion it
is bound to melt to the blast of "the wrath to come" which, like "a bar
of heat", inaugurates a new age of restored vitality.[57] Edward's description of this process is of the utmost importance because it gives
the key to the author's view of human life and history, not to speak of
the significance of, for example, John's and Julie's degradation:

> "I don't think," I said to Edward, "that young men of sense
> (meaning, of course, John) are fairly represented in the
> newspapers - they're not so silly. It's only the half educated
> - the class that does swallow print, who talk about a futile
> world," etc.
>
> "A large class," Edward said, "perhaps the majority. Yes, it's
> interesting to see how revolutions actually come about - how
> they cast their shadow before them - no, not a shadow" -
> Edward visibly elaborated the material for a couplet - "a bar
> of heat. It's as if a furnace door has been opened - the furnace
> where new societies are forged, and the heat at once begins
> to melt everything, even a long way from it, things which will
> not be ready for the crucibles for a long time - ideas, insti-
> tutions, laws, political parties, they all begin to lose their
> firmness."
> . . .
> "I suppose it is simply expectation of a new order," Edward
> said. And I thought he was enjoying himself, as always in an
> abstract enquiry. "It is an intelligent anticipation of the
> wrath to come. But, of course, it affects people differently
> - Julie sentimentalizes, and John, it appears, marks time, or
> perhaps he has simply withdrawn gracefully. Every revolution
> has that handicap - that as soon as it starts a lot of the
> best brains in the country go out of commission - I mean those
> with independant judgment, the really scholarly and scientific
> brains, the ones that a revolution needs above every other."
> (pp.275-77)

It should, however, be pointed out that though Wilcher renders Edward's
view in scenic detail, he is not allowed to evidence any virtual understanding of what his brother's words imply. Thus the author lets him
see the very form of his simile but not its substance:

> "All that is very pretty," I said suddenly, in a voice so
> loud that I startled myself. "But it is only simile," and so
> on. "What exactly is this mysterious process of what-do-you-
> call-it, melting, softening?" (p.276)

Not even when an authorial cloudburst soaks Wilcher to the skin, does
he awake to the meaning of the simile, and by this practical joke Cary
makes the reader the more aware of the presence of his own autonomous
self.[58] In fact Edward acts as an extension of the narrator's consciousness and by virtue of his epigrammatic couplets Cary brings home his
views to the reader with a "cynic" succinctness which, for all the
variability of Wilcher's vision, has no response in the make-up of his
objectified self:

> Children forget their wrongs; a happy set
> Were we; or if we weren't, children forget.
>
> I thought this couplet in Edward's first book of epigrams, a
> typical piece of his cynicism; but now I see it's truth. (p.34)

As a rule these couplets are quoted by the privileged narrator who,
reasonably, should be conscious of their literal meaning. Whether this
is perfectly true seems somewhat uncertain, however. In the following
epigrams the author's spicy points hardly agree with the conscious
speaker's modesty:[59]

> Memento mori, spite of Keats and Kants,
> God strikes and strangers see your winter pants. (p.71)
>
> "The Foreign Office? All John Bull must know
> This writing on the outer door: F.O." (p.222)

To what extent Wilcher understands these couplets, is, of course, a
question of minor importance. What really matters is that they serve as
handy vehicles of the author's own ideas. Thus Cary declares his belief
in democracy despite the apparent duality of the view he takes:

> Tyrants hate Truth, death takes them by surprise,
> Hail Democrats, who love the larger lies. (p.235)

By conceiving his Edwardian politician as "too civilized" (p.202) a man
Cary gives himself ample opportunity to unfold a dual view of "civilization" that can be considered Hegelian in so far as it is always on

the move into its own antithesis. Like all Cary's dichotomies, in fact,
it can be reduced to a positive or negative manifestation of life or
"faith". This accounts for the confusion Wilcher experiences while he
and Ann are discussing the subject:

> "Yes, we may well have more wars of religion which would
> indeed destroy civilization."
>
> "Would that matter very much?"
>
> Now this is a question that always enrages me. And I told the
> young woman what I thought of her. . . . ". . . it's the
> young people like Robert and you who might bring about this
> awful misery simply by talking nonsense about our civilization
> having no value."
>
> She did not answer me, and I thought, "There now, we're
> quarrelling, And it's your fault, you old fool. You ought to
> be more careful. But what is one to do? Why must these children
> always talk rubbish? Why must they make everything more con-
> fused and more perplexing?"
>
> But Ann, after knitting half a round, answered only, "And,
> of course, there's the Maginot Line."
>
> "I agree with you, my dear. History will say that Maginot,
> that modest little soldier, was the greatest of all. He made
> civilization safe, by making European war a doubtful and
> dangerous enterprise."
>
> My own words filled me with wonder at the survival of civili-
> zation, by trifling strokes of luck, by the narrowest escapes.
> For what is it, a fabric hanging in the air - a construction
> of ideas, sympathies, habits, something so impalpable that
> you cannot grasp it. You look for its friends, and you find
> that it has none. Nobody cares for it any more than they care
> for the ground under their feet or the air they breathe. And
> it survives in spite of this mass of ignorance, selfishness,
> spite, folly, greed, hatred which makes up the ordinary polit-
> ical life of the world.
> . . .
> When Edward spoke of the secret and everlasting conflicts of
> life, I called him a cynic, and when Julie reminded me of the
> evil will, I was angry with her. But now I felt that evil will.
> It seemed to me that millions delighted in wickedness, a little
> wickedness, and that when all these little spites pushed the
> same way, war must come and civilization must fall.
>
> But what is strange, the moment war broke out all my terror
> and foreboding disappeared. I ran to the recruiting office.
> I was one of those who stood for fifteen hours in Whitehall,
> with thousands of my kind, men of all ages, of all classes,
> trying to enlist in the new armies. And I neither felt nor
> met despair. On the contrary, I felt an extraordinary gaiety
> and lightness of spirit, and round me I saw and heard the
> same gaiety, smiles, jokes. (pp.239-40)

When Wilcher volunteers for war service, he identifies himself with an
aspect of civilization that, contrary to Edward's, is a manifestation

of life itself. To Edward civilization does not justify his fighting
out his battle and, as a consequence, he "stands aside":

> We thought Edward would ruin himself with debts or women.
> We never imagined the real catastrophe, that he would retire
> from the battle to enjoy that civilization which he had given
> so much energy, so many years, to defend.
>
> "A bit too civilized." Robert's words. The very voice of his
> time in judgment on ours. I thought it nonsense, but now, as
> I stand in Edward's room, I feel not its truth but its
> meaning.
>
>> I knew Versailles, said Talleyrand; nor since
>> Such tolerant grace of life. True! traitor-prince
>
> What was Edward's charm; and Julie's and Mrs. Tirrit's; so
> different in character? A universal tolerance, based on a
> universal enjoyment. They were faithful to friendship, to
> kindness, to beauty; never to faith. (p.205)

The above authorial declaration implies that, after all, Wilcher is
possessed with a living "faith" which is strong enough to help him on
his wavering course through the polarities of life. This explains why
his sentimental "myopia" is constantly subject to inversion. Thus the
champion of democracy is "confused" at finding that he is about to slide
into the opposite camp:

> But now I was frightened by the privateness of such as Bill
> and Amy and John. I answered angrily, "And who is looking
> after the political people? Did you never hear of democracy
> or imagine that it had duties as well as rights?" etc., etc.
>
> "But I haven't got a vote, uncle."
>
> "What does that matter? Any sheep can vote. The thing you've
> got to do is agitate - agitate. Look at your Uncle Edward."
>
> And the boy with his peculiar detached tone of a sixth form
> boy murmured, "A scene of agitation."
>
> "Of course, what do you expect with people what they are -
> especially political people. Besides, that's the way democracy
> does work - the biggest agitator wins - it's a battle of noise
> and impudence and egotism." And, in fact, I found myself
> speaking of democracy with great bitterness. So that I stopped
> in some confusion.
> . . .
> "But, of course," I said, "it's the only government for us in
> England - in fact, it's the only reasonable government any-
> where, because people can agitate and make nuisances of them-
> selves when they feel like it. And if you don't let them,
> they'll get into worse mischief in revolutions and general
> throat-cutting." (p.235)

Some thirty pages later Cary authorizes this view of democracy as "agi-
tation" (i.e. in the dual sense of the word) by having Edward signally

dwell on its "confusion". Summing up his political experience he says:

> No one has written a real political novel - giving the real
> feel of politics. The French try to be funny or clever, and
> the English are too moral and abstract. You don't get the
> sense of real politics, of people feeling their way; of
> moles digging frantically about to dodge some unknown noise
> overhead; of worms all driving down simultaneously because of
> some change in the weather; or rising gaily up again because
> some scientific gardener has spread the right poison mixture;
> you don't get the sense of limitation and confusion, of
> walking on a slack wire over an unseen gulf by a succession
> of lightning flashes. Then the ambitious side is always done
> so badly. Plenty of men in politics have no political ambition;
> they want to defend something, to get some reform - it's as
> simple as that. But then they are simple people, too, and it
> is the simple men who complicate the situation. Yes, a real
> political novel would be worth doing. I should like to do for
> politics what Tolstoy has done for war - show what a muddle
> and confusion it is, and that it must always be a muddle and
> confusion . . . (pp.268-69)

As Cary makes it clear in Art and Reality, not only democracy but life
itself is, and has to be, confusion or "chaos". Confusion is man's
experience of life before he has been able to read into it a construction
that satisfies him. Being the progenitor of his own world he loves his
own creation and, like a jealous god, he does his best to preserve it
from change or as Edward's couplet has it:

> God loves democracy; the proof is plain
> It cannot die; tho' hopelessly insane. (p.198)

By relieving the narrator of some enlightened commentary Edward assumes
the role of the author's assistant mouthpiece. Although the story of
Julie's love may have been framed on the Duse-D'Annunzio affair and
Edward's character may thus have been moulded on this poet-politician,
we cannot get past the fact that Cary himself met with considerable
failure in life. As we have seen, he failed as a painter and scholar[60]
and, like his Edwardian hero, failure made him try his fortune in war.[61]
Therefore it is surely no accident that Cary, who was very particular
about his dress, describes Edward as a "dandy" and has him educated at
Clifton College, Bristol, his own public school.[62] Like this remarkable
politician the author entertained the idea of writing "a real political
novel", a plan that was carried into effect in his second trilogy.
Finally it should be pointed out that by describing her statesman son
as a pretender to the "Speaker's" chair, old Mrs. Wilcher delivers a
pun that only the author himself can be held responsible for:

"Do you want her to have the chair, Mama? What do you want?"

"Lucy was devoted to her father, and he to her."

"But about the chair; you understand it's Edward's chair, and
we're responsible for Edward's property."

"Our statesman doesn't concern himself with chairs, except
perhaps the Speaker's."[63] (p.161)

4) Dissolution as a waster of life in the post-war generation

The "universal tolerance" that in the narrator's view made Julie and
Edward waste their lives, is above all apparent in John who, like Gladys
represents the post-war generation but who, unlike her, acts out a
negative aspect of its "corruption". Wilcher's introduction of John
makes it implicitly clear that, contrary to Amy and Bill, he belongs to
the "faithless" category:

> John had grown into a tall fair boy, more like Edward than
> his own parents. I had taken to him at once, and, indeed, at
> this time began that warm friendship which gave me so much
> happiness and pain for many years. I would take occasion, even
> then, to talk with the boy about his studies, and I was glad
> to find that I could help him in some points of Latin syntax,
> etc. And I was charmed to see his devotion to his mother. A
> natural and proper thing, but always delightful. One would
> say that John, who had not seen Amy for five years, had
> fallen in love with this heavy plain woman. He would colour
> when she glanced at him; he would lie in wait for her; he
> would grow suddenly talkative and lively when they were going
> out together; he would secretly buy her presents and surprise
> her with them. (p.218)

John's physical likeness to Edward seems to blind the narrator to the
fact that, in character, he is a Julie whose gentle and devoted nature
he shares. To emphasize the significance of the boy's devotion Cary
facetiously extends it even to a millstone which his "faithless" conservatism forbids returning to practical use:

> "Perhaps a miller could find some use for it."
>
> "Oh, no, we must use it somewhere - after finding it like that,"
> as if he owed a duty to this foundling. (p.233)

As in the case of Julie and Edward, the author tries to keep the reader
in suspense as to John's spiritual status as long as his story has not
passed its inevitable climax. It is true that there is a heavy burden
of circumstances evidencing insufficient spirit, and that, on top of
everything, John seems bound to become a scholar, but ingeniously enough

Cary tries to couple his incessant reading and apparent introversion
with his love for sailing and thus intimate to the reader that there
may be in him an adventurer, a "Flying Dutchman", a "pilgrim" after all:

> Bill grumbled loudly, "Regular bookworm. Can't resist a bit
> of print. I don't know what's going to happen to him."
>
> But afterwards, when I asked John what he had found so inter-
> esting in the newspapers, he answered that it was an article
> about Captain Slocum.
>
> "Who was Captain Slocum?"
>
> "He sailed round the world in a twelve-ton yawl." The boy was
> surprised that I had never heard of this hero. And when I
> remarked that the European situation appeared very dangerous,
> he answered only, "I suppose it always is - at least rather."
>
> "Don't be so sleepy," I said. "A boy of your age should take
> an interest in things. And European politics are going to
> affect your whole life. Very much so."
>
> He reflected for a time, and then said, "But I suppose the
> political people are looking after this."
>
> It was as though I had heard again the voice of Amy saying
> that no doubt her insides knew how to look after her baby.
> John, too, appeared to be a private person. (pp.234-35)

What makes Wilcher describe John as "private" has, however, little in
common with the self-assurance of his parents. It rather equals the self-
centred absent-mindedness that is to be found at the bottom of Julie's
acquiescence and which, in John, Wilcher conceitedly enough mistakes for
a manifestation of congeniality:

> And I sought his sympathy. "You don't believe in war, John.
> Wars have never decided anything. They are the most useless
> kind of madness."
>
> The boy reflected thoughtfully, "War has never decided any-
> thing," and all the way to the house he seemed to reflect on
> my words. But as Amy came out to greet him, he said to her,
> in a heart-broken voice, "No wind, Mums, and the sail isn't
> big enough yet." (p.233)

In fact, John evidences a remarkable indifference to the impending war
and to his uncle's growing concern:

> John murmured, "The war is always with us."
>
> "Well," Bill said carelessly, "I suppose it's got to go on
> till we win - or they'd win," And he said to me, "John is a
> bit of a pacifist, you know; been listening to all this 'Stop
> the war stuff.'"
>
> "But you aren't a pacifist, John," Amy said, contradicting
> Bill.
>   . . .

> "I don't know what I am," John said, languidly raising a very
> small fragment of dry earth on his fork, and looking at it
> with a bored air. "But war doesn't seem to do very much good
> - not obviously." (p.244)

Like Julie's growing plumpness[64] John's apparent indifference to the war
acts as a suspender of the reader's judgment on his spiritual valence.
It is true that his self-preoccupation is largely due to the young
yachtsman's "Captain Slocum" dreams, but, at the same time, it testifies
to what the narrator, in Julie and Edward, describes as "cynicism":

> When Edward spoke of the secret and everlasting conflicts of
> life, I called him a cynic, and when Julie reminded me of the
> evil will, I was angry with her. (p.240)

The ambiguous significance of John's indifference cannot, in the long
run, blind the reader to the predominance of his "faithless" self. So
vast is indeed the young man's absent-minded acquiescence that he seems
utterly unable to take up any standpoints at all. In fact, the narrator'
fond inability to share the reader's view of John provides the narration
with some of its humorous highlights. Considering the nephew's gentle
indifference to his uncle's views we have, therefore, every reason to
believe that it was certainly not John who made Wilcher publish his
work on the devil:

> Of course when I say that, I allow for that grace of temper-
> ament in the boy, who was never, to my knowledge, rude to
> anyone in his life. It is possible, therefore, that I bored
> him with some of my middle-aged chatter, about old times, and
> the political situation, or even about theology. But it was
> John who urged me to publish my book on the need for a new
> statement of the Christian belief, which [sic] special regard
> to the positive power of evil; and the real existence of the
> devil. (p.262)

John's illicit enlistment for war service is certainly an act proper to
a "pilgrim" but, like Julie's attempted suicide and Edward's campaign
against the Lords, his decision is not primed with sufficient conviction
to let him follow up what he has in mind and so it seals his tragedy.
When he finally returns from his p.o.w. camp, he has become a perfect
incarnation of "the moral defeat" which Wilcher imputes to the young
generation but which, ironically enough, he observes in the wrong people
Thus his affection for John blinds him to the fact that the returning
soldier has grown into a copy of his uncle Edward whose improvident
egotism and volatile affection he seems to parody:

> We scarcely recognized the young man, who, laughing, limped
> up to us on the platform, and embraced us both. We had last
> seen John a school boy, clever, affectionate; but still a boy.
> We walked now, rather shyly, beside a man of the world. Even
> his conversation had changed. He no longer seemed, like a boy,
> to carry about secrets, from which, at unexpected moments,
> some cryptic speech unwound like a strange plant out of a
> wall. He spoke in lively tones, easy and self forgetful.
> . . .
> "Very hungry, Mums darling, and fearfully greedy. I want a
> really expensive lunch. And it's on me. I'm rich, you know.
> Or I shall be when the army pays up what it owes me."
> . . .
> ". . . I think we ought to have oysters, don't you? Don't be
> alarmed, Mums, I know you don't like oysters, but my plan is
> that you shall ask me to eat your share for you, and after a
> time, out of pure filial feeling, I shall give way." (p.258)

In the description of the above scene Cary lets his narrator unconsciously

make a highly significant use of the key-words "cynicism" and "cynical"

so as to bring home to the reader what is not yet clear to the blind-

folded Wilcher:

> And when I spoke to him at lunch about the cynicism, the moral
> defeat of the new generation, he answered "Our lot aren't
> worrying - life is too nice."
>
> "What do you think about this talk of a social revolution."
>
> "I don't know anything about anything. But I've a sort of
> feeling of earthquakes about. . . . ."
>
> And at the cottage, so far from being bored, cynical, he amused
> himself all day with the gramophone, his books and country
> walks. (p.258)

So strong is the narrator's affection for his nephew that when, at long

last, Edward and John appear in one and the same scene, he is led to take

a less biassed view of his brother's "cynicism":

> And he [Edward] began to flirt outrageously with the girl, who
> ended by sitting on his knee and ruffling his hair, etc.
> . . .
> John in fact was laughing at the scene. . . . And on Edward's
> face I saw the same smile, forty years older.
>
> But what was strange, neither was cynical. In both, so like
> each other except that Edward had the more regular features,
> one saw the same good-natured indulgence. And again in the
> midst of my impatience with Edward, I felt that sense of a
> disease, creeping through all veins, of every age and sex.
> And I brought up the subject of the corruption of the time. (p.271)

Certainly Cary has not given Edward "the more regular features" without

reason. This observation is probably meant to serve as an authorial

pointer to the indisputable fact that for all their common "cynicism"

John is a Julie in spirit. After all, the young man has very little of
his uncle's wit, enterprise, and independence. This becomes the more
apparent after he has become "stuck" in his weird devotion to Gladys
and has made Julie's acquaintance. The account of how this new relation
started is so hurried and matter-of-fact that their union seems to have
been the inevitable consequence of some innate affinity:

> I met him everywhere with Gladys, even at Julie's. I had not
> wished John to know Julie. He met her only by accident one
> day when I had taken her to the theatre. And I did not intro-
> duce them. But he asked me about her, and insisted on calling.
> And then it appeared that he knew very well in what relation
> she stood to me; that all the family were aware of it. He
> charmed Julie and he was charmed by her. (p.264)

After John has made Julie's acquaintance, their lives seem to run a
parallel course towards the consummation of their individual tragedies.
Both take to drinking but, contrary to Gladys, they are in such low
spirits that they cannot even get drunk (p.284).

John's assimilation to Julie is reflected in Wilcher's attitude to him,
which like his feelings for his mistress has a physical correlate and
which, immediately before the boy's enlistment, begins to herald a
significant change. Thus the originally "tall, fair boy" who "was more
like Edward than his parents" suddenly seems to have become somebody
else. Behind this new picture of John is the vexation Wilcher feels on
learning that the boy and his friends have spent a reading party on
Plato's Republic and not on the Bible which in the narrator's own youth
had been the object of a similar outing.[65] At the same time, however, we
must not forget that all portraits in the novel ultimately serve as
authorial statements of character. What Cary has drawn here is simply
a caricature of a "faithless" scholar:

> He had just returned from some reading party on the moors.
> At first sight I was disappointed in the boy. He had shot up
> into a tall, thin boy of seventeen, with his hair in his eyes
> and a stooping back. He had lost his looks. His forehead was
> too high, his nose too long, his eyes too small. He told me
> that he had been reading the Republic. (p.243)

As we have seen, Julie's corruption has a physical correlate in her
increasing "softness".[66] Cary does not let his narrator observe a similar
change in John, which, in view of his drinking, would have seemed
plausible indeed. Nevertheless the "softness" metaphor stands the author
in good stead when, at long last, he lets the young man's "faithlessness"

dawn on the narrator. Thus Wilcher's last conversation with John is set
in circumstances that make as telling an emblem of corrupt civilization
as his experience of similar "softness" in his mother's and his mistress's
seductive beds:[67]

> I did not feel horror at a speech which meant that John was
> indifferent to his wife's unfaithfulness; I felt only confused,
> and, as it were, out of my element. The car which enclosed us,
> like a drawing room on wheels, terrifying in its elaborate
> luxury; the seduction of the cushions, which seemed to draw
> me down into an attitude of defenceless acquiescence; the
> heavy air, scented with some perfume which also seemed to
> impregnate the leather, silk, carpets; their very dust which
> revolved in the pale sunshine, filtered to us through four
> layers of plate glass, all seemed to belong to a civilization,
> which, like John, found me superfluous. (p.287)

Although, in most of the characters, Cary's symbolism is determined by
temperamental properties, the fact remains that, in John's case, it is
heavily supported by certain factors which have little, if any, relevance
to his spiritual potency but, like Julie's recovery from her attempted
suicide, have to be ascribed to chance. Whereas Edward's defection from
his campaign against the Lords is the natural outcome of failing conviction, Cary lets an accidental wound and internment mark the extinction
of John's "faith" and loss of spiritual freedom. Similarly the young
man's death is apt to stir the reader's awareness of the author's
omnipotence. Whereas, quite in agreement with Cary's "Hegelian" view of
life,[68] Julie develops a "rage against the world" that eventually takes
her to an "asylum", John ends his days in a way that is as accidental
as his war injury and therefore smacks of authorial ministration:

> Strangely, it was with Gladys that I regained acquaintance;
> on our old terms of mutual forebearance. For when a few months
> later John lost his job, I helped her to support the house-
> hold. And when in the next year, he was run over by a car in
> Bond Street, we made arrangement together for his removal to
> a private ward of the hospital and for special treatment.
>
> In those days, I grew almost fond of Gladys. She seemed devoted
> to John. One would have said that his death would break her
> heart. He died, and she went at once to live with the man she
> called Doggie. (pp.287-88)

CHAPTER 6   THE AMBIGUOUS "I" NARRATOR

PHYSIQUE AND CHARACTER

As we have seen, the virtual speaker's anonymity allows the author to
shift his point of view with as little restraint as if he were oblivious
of the fact that his conception only holds one narrator. However true
it may be that his hero's mind pendulates between sentiment and spirit
or "faithlessness" and "faith", his objectified ego cannot, with impunity
make an unequivocal statement of each. Being unable to commute between
two contrasting identities on the stage of the fiction Wilcher acts a
tragi-comic puppet strained between the rivalling forces that alter-
natingly seduce his vision. He consciously describes himself as "subject
to anxiety" and "fussy" or, at other times, as liable to affectation,
i.e. "too serious or too jocular". Thus the comic character that Wilcher
is apt to cut, above all in his own eye, is a symbol of this conflict,
and he often finds an opportunity to represent himself as "a poor fool
and weakling" (p.156) or, simply, a "clown" (p.25):

> But though I was a scholar of my college, I had no quickness
> of mind; and I perceived already that these brilliant young
> men, like Edward, found me dull and foolish. I could never
> hit upon the right tone with them. For either I was too
> serious, or too jocular. (p.71)

> It was a common experience with him [Wilcher], to burst into
> rhapsodies over a view, a piece of music, a face, a poem,
> and find himself surrounded by discreet smiles. He would then
> become dignified, until, in another few minutes, he would
> once more forget that Nature had cast him for the droll and
> not for the poet. (p.138)[1]

> "I am converted," I say to myself, with that keen pleasure
> which comes from accomplishment. My excitement has acquired
> a meaning, and so I can understand it and respect myself as
> a reasonable being. What glory, for a small undignified
> person, at whom others were inclined to laugh, to be a mis-
> sionary. (p.141)

> It was true . . . that, at critical moments, I was apt to do
> foolish things, or the wrong thing, or nothing at all. I was,
> too, a bad speaker; and my voice, in moments of excitement,
> rose to a squeak. For this reason and because of my general
> appearance, I adopted usually a slow and rather pompous form
> of address; but forgot both my dignity and my measure, as
> soon as I became excited by my subject. (p.156)

This scenic character is far removed from the anonymous speaker whose unconfused intelligence makes him act as the reader's virtual guide through the narration. As we have often seen, Cary authorizes Wilcher's view of himself by letting him unconsciously dramatize himself as the comic figure he consciously describes, but although there is thus a "clown" in the focus of both the nominal narrator's vision and that of the implied author, they interpret the picture differently. Whereas Wilcher looks upon himself as a man of sentiment and, consequently bondage, Cary superimposes the implicit portrait of a man whose excess of spirit sets him free. Owing to his "blindness" Wilcher fails to realize that all the people who inhabit his world reflect facets of his own character. In fact, the attraction he feels to each makes a statement of this affinity. In him there is not only a devoted believer and a selfish dandy but also a born servant and reckless rebel who, in the reader's view, are rivals for the precedence. Being sponsored by the implied author Wilcher's "faithful" self has to lead, as it were, a periferal existence in the novel as his presence is largely left to the reader's inference.

Nevertheless it should be obvious to any reader who has become aware of Cary's typology that Wilcher's looks clearly manifest his affinity with the "faithful" characters. For all his lack of confidence his ugliness, round face, healthy colour, and snub nose intimate which of his rivalling egos is to come off victorious:

> . . . a small ugly child with a round red face, a snub nose,
> black hair growing out of his round head in tufts, like that
> of an old-fashioned clown, and iron spectacles. (p.25)

Apparently the "iron spectacles" are meant to act as a reminder of his "short-sightedness" or inability to view himself in a proper perspective. At the same time, however, the failing vision of this "Roundhead" seems to symbolize the Nonconformist's intimate communion with God which, in the view of the established Church, equals "nonsense" but which, in the facetious author's view, apparently makes it impossible for the orthodox Christian to "pull his nose".[2]

The portrait of Wilcher as a grown-up man in his twenties bears a remarkable resemblance to the "old-fashioned clown" of his childhood:

> . . . he was very plain, with an absurd ugliness. His red
> face, his snub nose, his stiff black hair, his round specta-
> cles and peering startled eyes, were comic in themselves. And

when he forgot them and began to chatter, to wave his hands,
he became at once grotesque. (p.138)

The striking similarity of these two descriptions, which are the clearest
portraits Cary lets his hero draw of himself, tends, of course, to vouch
for their validity. By stressing Wilcher's comic appearance in both cases
the author apparently wants to make it understood that the face of the
"old-fashioned clown" is an essential part of the comic sight that the
narrator has been unfortunate to offer throughout his life and accordingly it maintains its relevance to him irrespective of age. This is in
fact what can be inferred from his comment on the above portrait of
himself as a young man. Thus the narrator's repudiation of this forty-
year-old vision resounds with so striking an emphasis that the observant
reader cannot but sense the presence of the author with his tongue in
his cheek:

> The alpenstock makes me smile, and yet I can enjoy my own
> affectation. For that young man has gone from earth even more
> completely than if he had died; . . . (p.138)

Since in the frame-story Wilcher makes no attempt to visualize his
present self except restating his comicalness by occasional descriptions
of his amusing fashions, the "old-fashioned (!) clown" of his childhood
seems to equal the queerly clad invalid who has returned to his Tolbrook
nursery to close the cycle of his life where it once began.

As we have seen in the narrator's descriptions of Julie and John,[3] his
portraits are implicit statements of his intuitive response to their
spiritual valence. This also applies to himself. In a passing fit of
"faith", he sees in the face of the "old-fashioned clown" no "shy little
boy" but a "devil":

> The shy serious little boy, making his anxious and careful
> way through a world full of older brothers and sisters all
> capable at any moment of the most unpredictable fits of
> violence or mockery, gives place, like a magic-lantern slide,
> to a stranger. I see the serious face split by an enormous
> demoniac grin; the tufted hair speaks no longer of disability
> and ugliness, but of an unruly coarseness. I am full of
> violence and rebellion. (p.47)

To make up for the implied "pilgrim's" inability to describe himself
explicitly, Cary uses what may be called a "split-self reflector". This
function is served by Jaffery who seems to serve the reasonably redundant role of the old solicitor's legal adviser and business manager over

the years. Jaffery seems to be a true hypocrite because Cary makes us
infer that the firm "Pamplin, Jaffery and Jaffery" was started for the
sole purpose of discreetly cheating Edward out of his money[4] and that,
on the outskirts of the author's vision, Jaffery is no other person
than Wilcher himself. Like Rozzie in Herself Surprised who serves as
Sara's "reflector", Jaffery is older than the narrator except in spirit
where he seems to be vital enough. Both are joined in so splendid a
polarity that Jaffery has to appear in "baggy" trousers because Wilcher's
have been cut to "show the limb".[5] As a result the very presence of
"young Jaffery" inspires the old lawyer of a conservative turn with
resentment:

> Jaffery is older than I am, but he affects the young man,
> wears a light suit, and probably a body belt. I have even
> seen him in an open-necked shirt, without a tie, a ridiculous
> object, like a beadle in fancy dress. He does not understand
> that an old man belongs to his own age and should not ape the
> dress and manners of another, where he appears like a foreigner.
> . . .
> Jaffery has an expression of absurd self-confidence on his
> old red face, wrinkled like a fried tomato. He speaks to me
> as to an invalid, gazing with discreet but sharp curiosity,
> as if asking, "Is he really as mad as they say? Did he burn
> his house down? Does he want to marry his cook?" (p.32)

In this way Cary objectifies what is going on in his hero's head. In
"Pamplin, Jaffery and Jaffery", i.e. Wilcher's obscure firm, "old Pamplin"
acts as "the senior partner". He represents the narrator's conservative
self and, possibly, also his own orthodox God.[6] Anyhow, when the narrator
on one occasion accounts for what he thinks of Pamplin, it is the "faithful" Jaffery-Wilcher who rebels against Pamplin-Wilcher, his "faithless"
senior self:

> . . . now I delighted in opposing a suggestion in the firm,
> that soft collars should be permitted in office hours; not,
> as formerly, out of loyalty to the old Westminster collar,
> which I wore myself, but because the senior partner, old
> Pamplin, was inclined to give way on the point. I enjoyed
> telling Pamplin that he was growing slack in his ideas. For
> he was a great upholder of duty; Church and State. And the
> times appalled him. Every week, with his beaked nose and
> round blank eyes surrounded by wrinkles, he seemed to grow
> more like an owl; startled by the collapse of its barn and
> the intrusion of daylight.
>
> The old man, in his gloomy slow voice, would say to me "England
> is finished - no sense of duty anywhere - no honesty - the
> only question anyone asks, what can I get out of it?" And I
> would answer, that on the contrary, I thought the country was
> doing very well.

. . .
Pamplin was the kind of Tory of whom Edward wrote:

> Leave politics to us, the tories cry,
> For politicians cheat and rob and lie. (p.307)

What throughout alerts and sustains the reader's awareness of the narrator's insufficient vision are the implied author's recurrent reminders of the ambiguity of his ultimate view with which the myopic "clown" is unable to grapple. Wilcher often indulges in the view of himself as a humble and dutiful servant to his family. Indeed he makes himself rank with those who, in Charlotte M. Younge's world, are the "Pillars of the House":[7]

> . . . when I was condemned to be a lawyer and money-manager,
> I was put in the position of that heart which in a man's body
> does all the work and gets no attention or thanks whatever.
> The brain, the will, the passions, what do they care about
> that poor humble creature, pounding away for ever in his dark
> prison, on the everlasting treadmill which gives to brain,
> will, etc., their light, and their life. (p.182)

From the fictitious narrator's point of view his description of his life-long service, or "duty", or "responsibility" to the Wilcher family is certainly not untrue. In his voice, however, there is a self-righteou tone that tells of the existence of a complementary aspect. In fact Wilcher is sometimes able to see himself in this dual perspective. In a passing moment of waning bias he describes his financial and amorous affairs in their proper dubiety although self-pity soon enough manifests his inability to retain the author's dual vision:

> It would flash upon me, "It's true. I have got Tolbrook from
> Edward and now the London house as well. It's true I carried
> out the separation between Edward and Julie. If I had not
> done so they would almost certainly have drifted together
> again. And Julie did always encourage Edward and help him in
> his career. She gave him a refuge; she gave him absolute
> loyalty. Yet, if I had not arranged the separation, Edward
> would have probably been ruined, and if I had not saved
> Tolbrook it would have been lost to the family."

> And my reward for years of heavy soul-destroying worries is
> to be thought and called a usurer. (p.219)

As we have seen in our examination of the epic narration,[8] the speaker sometimes gives summaries where he acts as the reader's dependable guide On these occasions the narrator evidences the detachment of a judicious scholar interested only in facts. Wilcher's terse account of his war experience is a clear instance of narration where the author suspends

his speaker's judgment, thus letting the facts speak for themselves.
When, despite his sense of inferiority, "the life-battered gnome" refuses
a commission and voluntarily joins the army as a "stretcher-bearer", he
bears the hardships of this racking service with perfect ease. Nevertheless, when the unhappy narrator looks back on this time of astounding
happiness, he lets it pass as a matter of course. What furthermore
heightens the significance of the diffident "clown's" transformation
into a confident ranker is the fact that he still views himself as the
butt of everybody's mirth:

> I had been happy in the army at war. I had lived among grum-
> bling and that private soldier's wit which makes of all life,
> its glories, as well as its miseries, something obscene or
> contemptible. I, too, had spoken of a dead comrade as a stiff
> or a landowner, and called the cemetery the rest camp. I
> enjoyed being called Pink-eye, Little Tich, or Shorty, and
> told that I had the duck disease because of my short legs. (p.241)

Above, the narrator unconsciously verifies a view of himself that he
repudiates consciously. Thus he resents the idea of being a "ranker":

> They are the private soldiers who do the hard fighting, while
> the generals take the glory.

> Bill used that very image to me on the evening of Edward's
> party. "You and I are rankers to Edward."

> But to Bill, of course, that was a natural and proper relation.
> He had no envy, no grudge, in his composition, and no idea of
> justice either. Bill, as he grew older, became simpler, and
> also less consistent. Just as he surprised me by his respect-
> ful attitude to the pacifist, he now threw me into a fury by
> taking it for granted that I should continue in the agency. (p.176)

In addition to the silent commentary that is the ultimate effect of the
author's suspension of his hero's judgment of his own words, Cary controls
his reader's vision by inviting him to implicit comparisons. Wilcher's
disdain of his own role in life lays him open to the reader's doubt
because, throughout the novel, he pays homage to women who without
exception do far more menial and unrewarding work than he. Thus, for all
her pride, Lucy is represented as a floor-scrubbing char.[9]

This fallibility is, however, made up for by other speakers. Apart from
the author's anonymous, privileged "I", a number of secondary voices
help to correct and control the reader's vision. This function is above
all served by Edward whose brilliant intellect makes him particularly
eligible to speak on the omniscient author's behalf.[10] He proves a
reliable judge of ulterior motives:

> Forty years ago, when I complained to Edward of my lost career,
> he smiled and said, "You've got what you wanted. You always
> meant to live at home. It's a shame the place wasn't left
> to you." (p.175)

When Julie learns that Wilcher is determined to rid himself of his
"bondage" to become a missionary, she gives utterance to an ambiguity:

> "No, no, a missionary, that's absurd. When your duty is so
> plain." (p.146)

CONFORMITY AND DISSENT

1) The ambiguous concepts of "responsibility" and "duty"

At the same time as Wilcher, the "faithless" conformist, is burdened by
insufficient knowledge of himself, he is engaged in what can be describ
as an implicit discussion on "duty" and "responsibility" with his "fait
ful", dissenting self. In the former's experience "duty" lays a burden
on man's soul:

> As I sought the joy of the Lord, so I could seek that joy of
> the devil. As I was drawn to Julie, not only by her gentleness
> and beauty but by the idea of her corruption, so I could have
> embraced the fury, the lust, the cruelty of Marianne. Drawn
> to filth by its filthiness, to villainy by its wickedness.
> Not to have any scruples, any responsibility, any duties. (pp.203-

> . . . when in my new responsibilities to the estate I was
> asked any question about business to which I did not know the
> answer, I looked resigned like a grown-up pestered by children,
> and said, "Well, it's rather complicated." (p.159)

On other occasions, in particular before Ann, Wilcher takes a dissenter
view of "duty" and "responsibility" as the only way out of spiritual
bondage. In this sense it equals "an object in life" as he tries to mak
clear to her:

> "Well, uncle, Aunt Lucy wasn't happy with her butcher, but
> she fell for him."

> "No, she did not fall for anybody. She would not even have
> understood that horrible phrase. She made her own life."

> "Then why didn't she make it happy?"

> "It was a happy life, though I suppose you can't imagine it
> - neither could I. But then I was a young fool myself at that
> time. I didn't know how to be happy."

> "How is it done?"

> "You must have an object in life - something big enough to

make you forget yourself." (p.52)

"To forget oneself", however, is, in Cary's use, an ambiguous expression
which becomes apparent enough when he maintains that Robert has "a sense
of duty" despite the fact that he has run away from his wife in the
company of his young mistress, and so "forgotten himself" indeed:

> "Robert has behaved badly, but so have you - I can't think
> how you could be so stupid - throwing away a good husband
> like that."
>
> "A good husband?"
>
> "He might have been a very good husband. He had a sense of duty
> - that's the main thing. But of course you don't believe in
> nonsense like a sense of duty. . . ." (p.274)

In the "faithful" Wilcher's view, "duty" or "responsibility" implies no
limitation of man's free will but rather "a great opportunity". It is
also the author's view as we are given to infer from his insertion of a
"perhaps" which, as we have seen, sometimes serves as a warrant of
authorial agreement:[11]

> The nurse's amens, so charged with ardour, and Ann's silence,
> appeared to me to show an equal emotion, and I felt it a duty
> and perhaps a great opportunity, to speak to the young mother,
> a few words such as might bring to her confused feelings a
> clear idea of the privilege granted to her by God and the
> solemn responsibility laid upon her, etc. (p.127)

It is true that the author lets Wilcher look at "responsibility" and
"duty" in a religious aspect but, in the author's perspective, "religion"
is not a matter of confession: it is instead tantamount to spiritual
freedom. For all the protection Wilcher enjoyed in his strictly religious
home, he is liable to confuse the reader by using "religion" in the sense
of "unqualified freedom" which in Nonconformity implies "individual
responsibility for sin":[12]

> But none of us was encouraged to self-pity, the disease of
> the egotist. Religion was not our comforter. How could we be
> comforted by hell fire; and individual responsibility for sin?
> (p.46)

This flagrant confusion is apparently designed to call the reader's
attention to the question of responsibility which in English religious
life has proved a true divider of the nation and which, consequently,
is a point of crucial importance to the man who in the novel has to
represent all the division his people always has been heir to. Thus
Cary's implicit discussion on "duty" and "responsibility" largely acts

as an analysis of religious conformity and dissent.[13]

When the narrator uses the word "duty" in the sense of "a great opportunity", he voices the Nonconformist belief that God has given man
perfect freedom of will and that, in return, man has to assume "individual responsibility for sin". This implies a most intimate relation
between God and man. Their intimacy is, in fact, so close that it allows
of no room for either Church, or State, or any other intermediary.
Therefore, the burden of the dissenter's responsibility or duty is heavy
indeed. It is, however, the toll taken of every "pilgrim" on his progress
towards heaven. It cannot be shirked. It is "the only way out", the only
escape from the gaping gates of hell:

> "My dear child," I said, "your marriage has hardly begun - it
> hasn't had time to fail. And if you break it, perhaps you will
> break your heart, too. The only thing we can rely on in a tight
> corner is our duty. That's the only way out. Duty, duty, that's
> the salvation of poor humanity. Do your duty and then if every-
> thing goes to the devil, you won't have to blame yourself for
> your own misery, which is the worst misery of all. I think it
> is really what is meant by Hell." (p.163)

Occupying "the Speaker's chair" Edward has at a very early stage pointed
out that this view of duty as "individual responsibility" is the only
road to salvation. What Edward is reported as saying for the reader's
benefit actually makes a restatement of Wilcher's view as quoted above:

> Edward used to say that the effect of a Protestant education
> was to make people a little mad. "It throws upon everyone the
> responsibility for the whole world's sins, and it doesn't
> provide any escape - not even a confession box." (p.22)

In the dissenter's eye, the conformist's idea of responsibility must
equal irresponsibility. In the narrator's use, therefore, this word
proves as ambiguous as "responsibility":

> Certainly my father's battles with Lucy were often terrible
> to them both. For though my father by sticking to the regula-
> tions erected between himself and conscience a wall of irre-
> sponsibility, yet he loved Lucy, and hated to punish her, and
> feared the consequences. (p.41)

This "wall of irresponsibility" is a typical instance of authorial irony
While in the conformist's view Wilcher's father discharges his responsibility by maintaining some general rules very strictly, the ambiguity
of "irresponsibility" also suggests the presence of the narrator's
dissenting demon in whose perspective the inflexibility of the Colonel's

conduct testifies to inability to answer for his own acts. This conflict
of vision is above all apparent in Wilcher's account of his happy childhood. Thus his facetious antagonist successfully deflates all his serious attempts at soaring eloquence:

> How could we be comforted by hell fire; and individual respon-
> sibility for sin? We lived in the law, that ark of freedom. A
> ship well founded, well braced to carry us over the most
> frightful rocks, and quicksands. And on those nursery decks
> we knew where we were, we were as careless and lively as all
> sailors under discipline. (p.46)

The ambiguity of the above passage does not, in the first place, affect
the reader's belief in the narrator's veracity as far as his story goes,
but it is nevertheless intended to shed a dubious light on his idea of
"freedom". The author does not let his hero describe himself as "free"
but "careless" which implies that, "under discipline", these "sailors"
could not care less about "individual responsibility". Besides, an "ark"
is not a ship designed to win the reader's confidence however "well
founded" it may have been but bound to founder on the rock of some
implacable covenant!

Being in duty bound to justify his own mirth, the author eventually lets
the grand "ark" go down leaving the narrator in a sea of troubling
responsibilities:

> . . . I was distracted with worry. Responsibility is an idea.
> For three years I had made all decisions. But because I had
> acted in my father's name, I felt no burden. Now when I was
> asked to decide this or that, I hesitated. I lay awake at
> night under the burden of this thought, "Destiny, the happiness
> of others, depends on me." For the first time I understood
> that heavy word - "duty." (p.160)

By letting scales fall from his hero's eyes in this way, the author
makes it perfectly clear to the reader that the faith that gave the
young Wilcher confidence enough to act "in his father's name" (!) has
proved an illusion. Here again, however, Cary suspends his narrator's
judgment and leaves it to the reader to conclude that old Wilcher's
departure means the death of his son's orthodox faith.

2) Hypocrisy and the ambiguous concept of "grace"

In Wilcher's life-long tug of civil war, the conformist's "myopia" makes
him obliquely support the dissenter's view. This does not mean that the

author unequivocally sides with the latter's acting self. In fact, Cary
is anxious to do justice to both or, rather, sustain the ambiguity of
his vision throughout the narration. This becomes apparent enough if
we give our attention to the concept of "grace" which offers an importar
aspect of the author's exposition of consent versus dissent. In
Nonconformity, "grace" is a feeling of having been chosen by God for
salvation.[14] In consequence of the private nature of the Nonconformist's
communion with his Lord, it is by no means a matter of established conduct. Thus it is no militant "pilgrim" who is speaking below:

> Even as a child I had a passionate love of home, of peace, of
> that grace and order which alone can give beauty to the lives
> of men living together, eating, chattering, being sick, foolish
> and wicked, getting old and ugly. I hated a break of that order.
> I feared all violence. (p.78)

In Edward, "grace" seems to be a matter of form or behaviour and as a
child Ann does her best to acquire her father's elegance:

> . . . during the daytime, at least, he seemed to work with
> purpose, and affected a strict routine.

> Breakfast at nine, correspondence till eleven, with a secretary
> from Queensport, work afterwards. At half-past four Ann, dressed
> in her smartest frock, was brought down to his room for tea.
> And he would receive her with that affectionate grace which he
> always showed to women until he knew them too well. He placed
> a chair for her, stood till she was seated, and adjusted her
> cushions.

> It was her duty to preside, to pour out the tea. When I was of
> the party, I could not bear to see the child's nervous anxiety,
> . . . (p.269)

Of course, Wilcher's mother tends to incarnate the very essence of this
idea of "grace":

> I seemed in that room to be existing within my mother's being,
> an essential quality, indescribable to me then, and not easy
> to describe now; something that was more grace than happiness,
> more beauty than joy, more patience than rest, a dignity without
> pride, a peace both withdrawn and sensitive. But for me, as a
> child, beauty, grace and distinction. (p.31)

Describing his mother's "faithless" refinement Wilcher distinguishes
between "happiness" and "grace". This distinction seems not to exist whe
a few pages further on, he explains what Tolbrook means to him. Now "gra
equals the "faith" it restores him to:

> Sara had renewed to me that joy which is the life of faith.
> And in those days, while she cleaned the house and set it
> to rights, after many years of lazy and careless maids, I
> came again to feel its value, to enjoy its grace. (p. 36)

Wilcher's anxiety to hush up some of his dealings has a smack of hypocrisy. Often enough, in fact, he proves a great hypocrite and then the
Nonconformist view of "grace" stands him in good stead. This is particularly apparent in the passage below where the narrator tries to make
the reader believe that it was by divine revelation that he learnt that
Ann's first-born should be christened "John".[15] His confusing grammar
seems not to be due to any confusion of mind:

> Now though I had begun to read in a spirit of formal duty, to
> improve the occasion, the words took hold of me and carried
> me into grace. (p.127)[16]

By suspending the speaker's judgment Cary time and again lets him blunder
into confessions of gross double-dealing. Thus, for all his explicit
complaining of the ingratitude he met with as his eldest brother's
business manager, his work seems, after all, to have been not completely
unrewarding:

> The next day I wrote to Edward, proposing to accept the agency,
> on proper conditions of pay, etc., and a proper security for
> the house. I lent him a thousand pounds, secured on the timber,
> in order to pay off Bill; and obtained a promise, for what it
> was worth, that he would borrow nothing more except through me
> or the firm. I joined the firm at once. It was still called
> Wilcher and Wilcher, although the actual partners were Pamplin,
> Jaffery and Jaffery. (p.180)

In fact, Edward's improvidence makes him an easy victim in his inferiority-
ridden brother's covetous hands, and the various names of his partners
actually seem to serve the only function of a virtuous screen hiding the
fact that, in reality, there is only one creditor whose anxiety to secure
Edward's fortune as well as his mistress makes him "fuss" and "buzz" at
her:

> Within a week I began to read for my articles as a solicitor.
> And all my reward for this sacrifice was a new heap of bills
> from Edward's creditors, and the remark, in passing, from
> Julie, "You were born to fuss, Tommy. You buzz at me like a
> fly. But I suppose somebody must buzz." (p.180)

On top of everything Wilcher justifies his dealings with arguments that
testify to his self-deception and irresponsibility. Here Cary's irony
comes into full play and for this end Lucy's slanderous tongue stands
the author in good stead. In the passage below Wilcher, the solicitor,
accounts for his negotiations with Wilcher, Edward's sole creditor:

> And Edward's financial position, at a critical moment in his
> fortunes, enabled me, or rather the firm, to impose terms. The

first clause in our agreement, a clause not put into writing,
was that he [Edward] should leave Julie and marry Mrs. Tirrit.

We insisted on this. For only Mrs. Tirrit could satisfy the
creditors, who were prepared to accept, on her verbal assur-
ance alone, a delay of proceedings, and afterwards twelve and
sixpence in the pound. They wanted fifteen shillings, but the
lady refused them. Mrs. Tirrit was rich, but she was also a
woman of business. She did not mean to pay for Edward more
than was absolutely necessary.

This agreement gave the firm and especially me, much satisfaction. Should I say that we felt a real pleasure in humili-
ating the glorious Edward? Lucy thought so. But I should be
wrong and Lucy was wrong. We were not vindictive. We were
only in revolt against the self-deception, the irresponsibility
of our hero and master. (p.184)

As we have already seen, the firm of "Wilcher and Wilcher" or "Pamplin,
Jaffery, and Jaffery" seems to serve as an allegorical representation
of the dissenting narrator's relation to his Lord or "senior partner".
Wilcher's double-dealings may consequently dramatize a crucial point in
Nonconformity that has often laid the dissenter open to distrust and
ridicule.[17]

Like Brown, the evangelist, the narrator is too apt to mistake the voice
of his egotist self for that of his "senior partner". In Wilcher, both
the solicitor and the dissenter often enough shirk their responsibility
by usurping the "partner's" role. Looking down upon him he has the face
to say:

We were the heart and stomach, saying finally to the poetic
genius in the upper story, "Come now, please to remember that
you also are human." (p.184)

The dissenting Wilcher's hypocrisy is not, however, only subject to
implied ridicule. At a fairly early stage of the narration Cary is
anxious to give the reader an unbiassed view of what in Nonconformity
equals "grace". He introduces "an American evangelist" for the sole
purpose of giving an explicit definition of the word.

"Grace is a feeling inside you that God is there all the time,
to help. So all you've got to do is tell these poor sinners
that they've got the feeling, and they always believe it. Why,
if you told them they'd got a pain, they'd soon find it for
you, show you the exact place. So when you tell 'em they've
got a feeling, they soon find one. And then you only got to
tell 'em what it's saying to them. And they're yours."

"What do you tell them that it says?"

"That they got to stop worrying about themselves and their

troubles and hearken to the voice of the Lord."

"And do they forget their domestic anxieties and responsibilities so easily?"

"They just do. Why, the most of men are just about half mad with worrying. They're just delighted to hear there's anyone to tell 'em what to do." (pp.60-61)

Soon after, Cary gives a little scene that objectifies the evangelist's view of "grace":

But when I came to the kitchen, I found Lucy holding Mrs. Jones with one hand and Mr. Jones with the other. They were gazing at her with round foolish eyes, like sheep at a sudden fire, and Lucy was saying, "A great and wonderful day for us all when the master comes - when we hear the call of grace in our hearts. Do you not feel it?" She spoke to Mrs. Jones. "Ask of your heart - don't you find it there - something which says to you, 'A wonderful and strange thing has happened to me' - there, I see you do feel it. . . ."

. . .

Lucy and the Jones' suddenly knelt down together on the kitchen floor. Mrs. Jones was weeping and singing at once. She raised her face to the ceiling in a mournful expression, like one defeated. The old man was not singing, and he looked from Lucy to his wife, with pursed lips, and raised eyebrows, surprised at what he was doing. (p.68)

Although this scenic verification of the power of "grace" does not, of course, imply any authorial subscription to Nonconformity, it acts as a corrector of the reader's experience. To that end Cary even goes so far as to let young Wilcher make a fool of his "faithless" self before the author's "evangelist" mouthpiece, whose parable of "the too clever ass" aptly illustrates his spiritual dilemma:

"And what does the Lord, that is, what do you, tell them to do?"

"Young man, I tell 'em to do the Lord's work in love and charity."

"It is not always very easy to know what is the Lord's work."

"No, young man, it is not. They got to wrastle and pray for it. And they do wrastle -"

"So they're just where they were at the beginning."

"Not so my young friend, for now they wrastle for the Lord, and so they get grace - that makes a difference, believe me."

But like a young man I had always an answer to one who would teach me. I quoted Edward to him.

"Grace, Lord, I crave. Answer thy servant's question:
Is this Thy grace I feel, or indigestion?"

Then the American evangelist looked at me and answered, "I

> pity you, young man, you are like the ass who was too clever
> to walk upon the beaten path."
>
> "What happened to that ass?"
>
> "He stuck among the thorns and no one listened to his bray.
> For he was a useless ass." (p.61)

For all the dubious "grace" of the dissenting Wilcher and his conformist
self's unqualified contempt of this "feeling", the speaker does not seem
quite unequal to an unadulterated experience of it. Anyhow, in a passage
which seems to be little short of an interior monologue, we are given
to understand that, like any honest believer in religious dissent, he
is painfully conscious of the transitoriness of "grace". Like the
"American evangelist" and Brown[18] he prays desperately for the sustenance
of his experience:

> The feeling. What is this feeling that I talk about to Ann,
> and how can she know what I mean, when I barely know it my-
> self. When I, with all my church-going, my prayers, lose it
> so easily. One would say I was a dead frog, which shows
> animation only at the electric spark from such as Lucy. The
> touch of genius; of the world's genius. And when that contact
> was withdrawn, I became once more a preserved mummy. (p.84)

WILCHER, THE REVELATIONIST

As Wilcher tries to make it clear throughout his narrative "faith" or,
what virtually amounts to the same thing, "grace", is no matter of
established religion. Therefore the road to "grace" is not through
religious subservience. Amy's "religion" is "simply regimental" (p.340)
and so is Sara's. To them religion means only a material to be reshaped
or reinterpreted so as to fit into the general view of life that each
has conceived for herself:

> Amy and Sara, countrywomen both. They didn't submit themselves
> to any belief. They used it. They made it. (p.339)

Wilcher's family look upon Sara as a hypocrite but, in the privileged
speaker's unprejudiced eye, she is an incarnation of true "grace" and
therefore in possession of profound experience:

> From the beginning, I had noticed one good quality in Sara,
> her regularity at prayers and church. But I knew she had
> been well brought up by a god-fearing mother and thought her
> piety merely habitual. I came to discover how strong and rich
> a fountain of grace played not only in the energy of her
> religious observance, but in everything she did, and in her

most casual remark. All was coloured by these country maxims,
so often in her mouth, which rise from a wisdom so deep in
tradition that it is like the spirit of a race. Never sigh
but send. Hot needle and a burnt thread. Give me to-day and
I'll sell you to-morrow. (p.320)

A "fountain of grace" is a "fount of revelation". This Cary makes
explicitly clear in the following conversation where Wilcher is anxious
to make Ann get his view of Brown right:

"What do you know about him?" I said, startled to think I had
prejudiced her already against Brown. "He was a great man, a
great Englishman, in the line of Bunyan, Wesley, Booth. What
a preacher." And I began to explain to her the absolute necessity, to a living faith, of the new revelation. That such as
Brown and Lucy, who can give the experience of grace, are the
very founts of God's revelation, etc., and so on. (p.100)

In Wilcher, too, there is a revelationist to whom nature, as it did to
Blake, appears informed with divine intelligence. This we are given to
understand from the variations of the "fountain" motif that his depictions
of the Tolbrook scenery amount to. Below, he himself seems to be bathing
in an abundance of "grace" and the sanctity of the scene is enhanced by
its resemblance to Milton's Eden. Thus, "the great lime" and the "water-
fall" correspond very well with "the Tree of Life" and the "fountain"
on the mountain in Paradise Lost:[19]

Sunlight falls upon a lime as upon no other tree. It pierces
the oak as with red-hot arrows; it glances aside from the elm
as from a cliff; it shrinks from the yew as from a piece of
darkness; it tangles itself in the willow and seems to lie
there half asleep; among the crooked apple branches it hangs
like fruit. But over a lime it falls like a water made of
light, the topaz colour of the moor streams, and full like
them of reflected rays, green and sparkling.

Only to stand beneath the lime was such a delight to me that
often I turned aside to avoid that strong feeling. Especially
in summer, when the tree was in flower, pouring out that sweet
scent which seemed to float on the falling light like pollen
dust on the moor waterfalls, and every crevice was full of
sailing bees; I shrank from an excitement so overwhelming to
my senses. The organ noise of bees, like vox angelica, the
scent which made the blood race, the slow smooth fall of light
in its thousand rills, over the living flesh of this beautiful
and secret creature, enticed at once the eyes and the imagination.
Within that burning tree I felt God's presence. And there I
bathed in an essence of eternity. My very consciousness was
dissolved in sensation, and I stood less entranced than myself the trance; the experience of that moment and that place,
in the living spirit. (pp.220-21)

In Wilcher's revelationist pictures, the sky is reflected in running water which bears its heavenly significance:

> The weather was mild for February. In the morning it had
> rained, and the yards were flowing with pools and rivulets
> between the stones. But now the sun had come out and filled
> the sky with a dark blue-green radiance. It was like sea
> water in an aquarium lighted from some hidden source, and
> the big ragged clouds, which floated in it, seemed to be
> dissolving at the edges like gouts of yellow foam, after a
> storm. The pools reflecting this sky were darker still, like
> great table sapphires, and the noise of water running from
> spouts and wall drains, had the gaiety of fountains, so that
> one could not help smiling with pleasure. (p.191)

Cary's landscapes have a transparent quality in so far as they celebrate
a close correspondence between heaven and earth and, like the river
motif below, ultimately point to a common identity:[20]

> March weather like this was Lucy's delight; with all the moor
> streams full and roaring down the stones, and winds blowing
> up the clouds and the rain together, so that the clouds pour
> along the sky, and the rain showers sail along in mid air,
> like enormous cobwebs, at the same pace. The sky and Tolbrook
> river flow the same way, and you seem to stand between two
> rivers, one above and one below, whirling foam and glittering
> bubbles to the east; till they fall over the horizon together.
> (p.93)

As can be inferred from the above passages, expressions of motion make
a central element in Cary's "living spirit" imagery. The wind, the west-
bound clouds, water gushing out of rain-spouts, rivulets and rivers, the
waves of the sea and the rollers of the ocean manifest the "spirit" that
is always on the move through time:

> All about Tolbrook in this south-west country, March has always
> smelt of salt. Its sky has the translucency of an ocean sky
> where there is no dust, and all the birds are as white as foam.
> Gulls fly over our furrows all the year, but especially now,
> when the winds roll them about in the air like small boats in
> an offing.
>
> When I look back again at the window the three clouds have
> jumped up towards the left-hand bow of the frame and the house
> seems to rock beneath me like a ship. I, eating breakfast in
> bed, and always the worst of sailors, feel as if I were at
> sea, as if England itself were afloat beneath me on its four
> waves, and making the voyage of its history through a perpetual
> sea spring. (pp.108-09)

Thus the wakes of the "pilgrim's" voyage run parallel with the furrows
of the Tolbrook fields and by letting the gulls of the "ocean sky" follow
both, Cary makes them trace the invariably "Protestant" course of both
his ancestors and heirs:

> Robert, I suspect, is more Brown than Wilcher, a peasant in
> grain. But he does not destroy Tolbrook, he takes it back
> into history, which changed it once before from priory into
> farm, from farm into manor, from manor, the workshop and court
> of a feudal dictator, into a country house where young ladies
> danced and hunting men played billiards; where at last, a new
> rich gentleman spent his week-ends from his office. . . .
> Robert has brought it back into the English stream and he him-
> self has come with it; to the soft corn, good for home-made
> bread; the mixed farm, so good for men, to the old church
> religion which is so twined with English life, that the very
> prayers seem to breathe of fields after rain and skies whose
> light is falling between clouds. (p.328)

Being a site of cultivation from time immemorial, Tolbrook acts as a
symbol not only of England but of "the living spirit" of man. This is
what Cary wants to say when he makes his hero blurt out:

> "But damn it all, . . . you old fool, you know there is love,
> there is hope, there is faith. Does not everything in this
> house say to you 'God is.'" (p.106)

What above all testifies to the immanence of this spirit is Cary's
conception of Wilcher's world as a "garden".[21] In Herself Surprised a
"kitchen garden" provides the heroine with a most significant setting,
and in To be a Pilgrim the ancient trees of Tolbrook Manor to whose
preservation Wilcher strongly commits himself, make a similar statement.
In Cary's use, a "garden" implies man's view of life. To all appearance,
his brother Bill's idea of life equals the little garden into the creation of which he puts all his heart. For all its modesty, the declaration
he gives shortly before his death is full of significance:

> "Oh, well, I'm not a gardener. Not a real expert. I just had
> an idea about the place." (p.261)[22]

As the speaker points out in a spell of privileged vision generations of
similar gardeners have left their marks all over the English countryside:

> It is as if a thousand years of cultivation have brought to all,
> trees, grass, crops, even the sky and the sun, a special quality
> belonging only to very old countries. A quality not of matter
> only, but of thought; as if the hand that planted the trees in
> their chosen places had imposed upon them the dignity of beauty
> appointed; but taken from them, at the same time, the innocence
> of natural freedom. As if the young farmer who set the hedge,
> to divide off his inheritance, wrote with its crooked line the
> history of human growth, of responsibility not belonging to the
> wild hawthorn, but to human love and fatherhood; as if upon
> the wheat lay the colour of harvests since Alfred, and its
> ears grew plump with the hopes and anxieties of all those gen-
> erations that sowed with Beowolf and ploughed with Piers and

> reaped with Cobbett. Even at my own last harvest at Tolbrook,
> nine years ago, the gardeners' boy brought me from the field
> a little plait of straw. He did not know what it was or why
> he brought it, or that he was repeating a sacrifice to the
> corn god made so long ago that it was thousands of years old
> when Alfred was the modern man in a changing world. (p.135)

The appearance of "the gardeners' boy" is not accidental. In Herself
Surprised the reader is given to conclude that Sara suffered herself to
be seduced by a "garden-boy" though, in fact, there is no room for him
in the several affairs she accounts for or hints at. In To be a Pilgrim
there is a similar boy who is often mentioned but who never appears on
the stage of action. He runs his master's secret errands into the outer
world. As he leads his existence on the fringe of the fiction proper, he
is liable to mystify and assume the spiritual quality of a useful but
self-willed Ariel.[23] In the "revelationist's" view, a "gardener" actual
seems to imply nothing less than a god. When Lucy tries to drown
herself out of spite, she is rescued by a providential gardener who, as
the author gives the reader to understand, may have been the "Senior
Gardener Himself" enjoying his day of rest from creation:

> Luckily, when I screamed, a gardener was near, and he came
> running. He was in his Sunday clothes, a dark blue suit and
> a bowler hat; I suppose he had been strolling in the garden,
> as gardeners do on Sundays, to admire his own work. (pp.44-45)

Like Milton's Eden, however, Tolbrook is a "rural seat of various view".
Among all its neglected trees there appears to be, somewhat surprisingly
"a small topiary garden, called Jacobean" (p.11). No doubt it has been
designed by the author to make the orthodox believer in Wilcher find
proper solace among well-trimmed trees and shrubberies and thus give
his speaker's setting a complexity that meets the demands of his character.[25]

At Tolbrook, there is also a "rose-garden". The word sounds like a
reference to T.S. Eliot's Four Quartets which appeared in 1939 - 1942
when To be a Pilgrim was in gestation.[26] Apparently Cary was highly
familiar with this poet's view of time,

> Only through time, time is conquered.[27]

and his view of human experience,

> The knowledge imposes a pattern, and falsifies,
> For the pattern is new in every moment
> And every moment is a new and shocking
> Valuation of all we have been.[28]

Above all, Eliot's treatment of the past and man's reconciliation to change in East Coker to which the manor of the poet's own "pilgrim fathers" has lent its name, proves an obvious parallel to Cary's novel. In fact, Wilcher's story acts as a dramatization of Eliot's theme. The final words of East Coker excellently epitomize the revelation of Cary's "pilgrim" protagonist:

> Old men ought to be explorers
> Here and there does not matter
> We must be still and still moving
> Into another intensity
> For a further union, a deeper communion
> Through the dark cold and the empty desolation,
> The wave cry, the wind cry, the vast waters
> Of the petrel and the porpoise. In my end is my beginning.[29]

It is the great paradox of Wilcher's life that when its cycle is going to close, it is entering on a new beginning.

THE UNCERTAINTY OF WILCHER'S MENTAL HEALTH

At the beginning of the novel, the frame story implicitly raises the question of the narrator's mental health, i.e. whether or not he can be held responsible for his conduct. As far as the fiction goes, Cary seems anxious to sustain the uncertainty of his condition rather than help the reader to a definite conclusion. It is true that Wilcher's exhibitionism, his fits of distraction, his dependence on Sara, not to mention the mysterious circumstances under which his London house burnt down are facts that give his family reason to doubt his sanity, but whether they really do so is uncertain. The only thing that the reader can be convinced of is that the narrator entertains the not unjustified suspicion that his heirs want to have him legally declared incapacitated to manage his own affairs before Sara is out of jail and can set her cap at him again, By letting evidence and counter-evidence suspend the reader's judgment and by letting the narrator's initial anxiety on this point soon ebb out, the author makes the question of Wilcher's sanity come out the more clearly as an illustration of the ambiguity of "faith". Thus, whether Wilcher should be held responsible for fire-raising in the same way as he was held responsible for indecent behaviour is a question that, in the author's perspective, is of little consequence. As a matter of fact the author consistently refuses the reader any clues to the solution of the fire mystery. It is true that the narrator takes obvious

delight in frightening his family with the possibility of guilt, but he
never traps himself in what can be considered a binding confession.[30]
In fact, the relative-clause interpolation in the sentence below seems
to verify the author's determination not to settle the question:

> How on earth, I thought, did that chair come to be transported
> from Craven Gardens, which was, in any case, burnt out, four
> years ago, to a cottage in Lewisham. (p.315)

In a figurative sense, however, the dissenting Wilcher is undoubtedly a
fire-raiser as, by identifying himself with the French revolutionaries
of 1789, he consciously admits:

> I see again the horde of savage brutes pouring out of St.
> Antony's ward to loot Versailles, and to insult that king
> whose only fault was his gentleness, his hatred of violence,
> his civilized distrust of everything extreme, ostentatious,
> vulgar; from Mirabeau's style of dress to his own state bed-
> room. And what is worse, more terrifying, I feel that I too
> could have served in that mob. As I sought the joy of the
> Lord, so I could seek that joy of the devil. (p.203)

Being a manifestation of "the living spirit" Wilcher's "madness" springs
from the same source as the continuous rebellion of youth against the
inflexible norms of age. In the novel, this youth-age opposition apparent
afflicts any "partnership", e.g. Lucy-Brown, Ann-Robert, not to mention
Wilcher's own relation to Jaffery, his spirited partner-ego, who is
described as both young and old.[31] Even a psychiatrist whom his family
sends for seems to incarnate the conflict that has resulted in his
patient's "insanity" and, consequently, the very appearance of this
"pathologist" vouches for Wilcher's normality. The doctor looks like a
disillusioned "scholar" who, like the narrator, nourishes a distant
dream of a life with a buxom Sara among cows and crops:

> Blanche's favourite was a little young old man with a face
> like a Manchester terrier. His hair was flaxen, his huge eyes
> were water coloured; his sharp nose was as pale as if powdered;
> his hollow cheeks were pale green. He was dressed also in a
> suit of pale yellow tweed; with pale lemon-coloured boots; and
> he talked to me about his farm in Surrey, his Guernseys, his
> Punches. But all in a little pale voice; and looking all the
> time into the air as if he were thinking of something else;
> a sad memory. (p.309)

When, in a fit of abounding "grace", Wilcher feels tempted to pull the
doctor's nose which, significantly enough, is neither "long" nor "snub"
but "sharp",[32] he is surprised to find that his vis-à-vis is not foreign
to his own feelings:

"Yes, exactly. I know the feeling. It's quite natural. Quite
a lot of people get into prison for no other reason. They
even confess to murders they haven't done, you know."

"Oh, I've heard of that."

"Anything to break the pattern," he said. "Personally, I go
in for rock climbing."

"Rock climbing?"

"Yes, it keeps the nerves on the stretch. It acts as a safety
valve for all that superfluous energy - and it breaks the
pattern. Asylums, you know, have plain walls." (p.310)

Thus, as the author facetiously gives us to understand, the doctor
considers his own mental health to be on a par with Wilcher's but rather
than have himself certified he prefers being at large climbing mountains
whose rocks undoubtedly give better foothold than plain asylum walls.
He accordingly acts as the author's mouthpiece explaining the significance of Wilcher's "irresponsible" conduct. To make his point still
clearer Cary even goes so far as to have this conversation scene suc-
ceeded by a monologue where the speaker is allowed so privileged a view
of his exhibitionism that he consciously identifies himself with the
"Protestant" humanity he has to represent:

To change the pattern. To get into prison, into an asylum.
You would say whole nations grow suddenly bored at the same
moment; and tear off their clothes to dive into vice; (p.311)

ANN, WILCHER'S DAUGHTER

Like all the other figures of the memoir narration the "young old"
psychiatrist serves as a projection of Wilcher's character. In the frame
story a similar function is served by Ann who acts as the speaker's
principal self-reflector throughout the novel. Like the disillusioned
doctor above, she is a "pathologist" or she has, at least, intended to
qualify as one.[33] Like him she is an exponent of the youth-age conflict
as can be inferred from Cary's description of her as "one of the Velasquez
infantas" (p.13).

Ann is the daughter of Edward to whom, in the narrator's view, she bears
some distant resemblance:

Now that I begin to get used to this girl, I see that she is
like Edward in many ways, even in looks. Her plainness is
merely a veil drawn over Edward's handsomeness. You can see
his features beneath. Her eyes are not blue like his, but

> smoke grey; that is, a shaded blue. Her nose is not fine but
> flattened and broad, like Edward's delicate beak pressed down
> and coarsened. Her hair is a dark yellow, old straw to Edward's
> bright new straw. (p.13)

The narrator is, however, blind to the apparent fact that, on some signal
points, he and Ann are strikingly alike. She has about the same nose and
hair as he and, like him, she wears "round spectacles" (p.13) to manifest insufficiency of vision.[34] What furthermore testifies to their
affinity is the author's recurrent use of "fussy" in his descriptions of
both.[35] Like her uncle, she is engaged on a biography (her father's!),
and she tries to restore Tolbrook to her romantic idea of its past:

> Ann came in with a step-ladder, and a paint pot, etc. She was
> about to paint the upper cupboards. She stood beside Robert
> during his last speech while he continued in the same voice,
> as if it did not matter if she heard it.
>
> "You were pleased when I grew my hair." Ann said, whose hair
> was now in a neat bun. She showed me the paint. "Is this the
> colour, uncle. Georgian green they called it."
>
> I said that the colour, in Edward's time, had been a little
> paler.
>
> "I'll thin it," Ann said.
>
> "I was pleased when you grew your hair," Robert said, "but I
> thought you were growing it from sense and not from some
> nonsense."
>
> Ann climbed up her ladder and began to paint. She asked from
> above, "What sense and what nonsense?"
>
> "Well, I should say it's sense for a woman to be a woman. And
> I should say it's getting on for nonsense for anyone to play-
> act at being their own grandmother." (pp.174-75)

Ann even goes so far as to attend her uncle's morning prayers although
her Christian belief seems too uncertain to justify her regular observance of this old custom.[36]

It is true that, with her "stooping" back, Ann tends to make as striking
a caricature of a "faithless" scholar as John[37] but at the same time
she is as "faithful" an exponent of the modern generation as Gladys
whose "disproportionately large and round face" and "large blue eyes"
(p.264) apparently make her, too, resemble "the Velasquez infantas".
What, however, particularly testifies to Ann's affinity with Gladys is
the sexual freedom they both enjoy and their lavish make-up which seems
to make a statement of their independence:

I asked Ann afterwards what she thought of Gladys, meaning to
warn the child against so bad an example. But Ann said only,
"She's from London, isn't she?" She seemed, as usual, to be
storing knowledge for use.

"I hope you will never paint yourself like that."

"I wonder where she gets it?"

And I dared say no more. (p.272)

In the implied author's view, Ann's make-up actually corresponds to
Wilcher's exhibitionism as can be inferred from the offence he recur-
rently takes at his niece's as well as other women's lack of what he
believes to be his own shame-facedness:

"My face, uncle - isn't it all right?"

"No, it is not - it looks like a chamber pot crudely daubed
with raspberry jam. I cannot conceive how you can make such
a fearful object of yourself. . . ." (p.19)[38]

Whereas Wilcher's spirited self (including, of course, the exhibitionist)
has to lead a repressed and mostly implicit existence, Ann can, before
his eyes, incarnate both his natures. Like her fellow-pathologist Ann
acts as a justifier of her uncle's deviation from the accepted standard
of society.

By conceiving Ann as Edward's daughter and at the same time making her,
in the first place, resemble her uncle, Cary points to the latter's
affinity with his brother. In practice, she therefore acts as the daughter
of both. She is not only, like Wilcher, a "fusspot" but also, like
Edward, one who does not "know things thoroughly" and by describing herself as both she actually gives a full statement of her dual parentage:

"I may be a fusspot, but that's not the trouble. I just don't
know things thoroughly." (p.254)[39]

When on one occasion Wilcher finds that Ann has become "more like a
daughter", there is undoubtedly some truth in what he says.[40]

THE WILCHER-CARY "PARTNERSHIP"

At the same time as various facets of the narrator's character are
reflected in the hall of mirrors of his surroundings, his affinity with
all these people puts him in the centre of his own world and, acting as
its crucible, he dramatizes the presence and the absence of the "living
faith" or "grace" that he and his family have been given to incarnate:

> Our grandfather was a Plymouth brother; . . . and there are
> Quakers, Shakers, fifth monarchy men, even Anabaptists, on
> the maternal side. I did not know it then because I knew
> nothing and nobody real, only knowledge about things. I knew
> no living soul, not even Lucy, until I knew Sara, and found
> in her the key of my own soul. A key forged in English metal
> for an English lock. At that time my own English spirit, like
> Lucy's, was a mystery to me. (p.21)

Only late in life does Wilcher realize that "the key to his own soul"
lies in the release from legalistic obedience to the Mosaic Law that
these sects had helped his forebears to achieve. His life-long misery
is accordingly due to his own "pig-headed" and "senseless" disdain of
the antinomianism[41] that, implicitly, his story celebrates:

> When I asked some women if they realized that they were throwing
> away the lives of young men yet unborn, perhaps their own grand-
> children, etc., by their pig-headed unreason, and senseless
> Antinomianism, I was actually assaulted, etc. (p.247)

Wilcher's confusion turns him into an unconscious propagandist of the
author's ideas. In this way Cary even makes him expound Blake's view of
the "One-ness of the Human and the Divine" which, as we saw,[42] is the
basis on which the author has conceived his book:

> . . . it proved useless to argue with the fellow [the curate].
> He answered, according to rule, that goodwill was a principle
> of unity, superior to individuals and pointing, therefore, to
> a Power superior to all individuals; whereas, spite and hatred,
> etc., were self-regarding vices in the individual, factors of
> disunity requiring no higher power beyond . . . (p.248)

When, as we have seen, Wilcher tries to refute his antagonist, his mis-
guided spirit makes him prove more than he has bargained for. Here he
evidences the "disunity" of his own fallen state:

> "Excuse me," I said, "but I heard you argue, from the pulpit,
> that the best proof of a personal god is the existence of the
> good will in man, of love, charity," etc., and so on. "The
> usual thing, and quite right, too, nothing could be better."
> For I wished to do him justice and to show that I was not
> prejudiced against him. "But if so, surely the evil will in
> man, his lust, spite and cruelty, his love of supporting a
> bad case by mere argument, out of pure conceit" (for I thought
> I might touch his conscience here) "are proofs of the devil's
> real existence - and a pretty devilish existence, too, at
> the present moment of the world's history." (pp.247-48)

We have every reason to believe that Cary considered himself the victim
of the very same tension between "disunity" and "unity" that racks his
speaker's soul. The poet of _Paradise Lost_ has been described as the hero

of his own poem and a similar view of the author of To be a Pilgrim is
by no means unjustified.[43] However much fun Cary makes of his blind-
folded "pilgrim", the fact remains that they have very much in common.
For all the resemblance that Edward bears to his spiritual father,
Wilcher's portrait and story offer a wealth of parallels to Cary's
character and life. Like his hero, Cary was short of stature and delicate in constitution. Wilcher was invalided out of the army with "pneu-
monia" and "a damaged heart" and Cary who suffered from asthma had to
leave Colonial Service on similar grounds. Last but not least, his eyesight seems to have been as poor as his speaker's.

The stories of both include a murky Oxford past. Although too old, both
had volunteered for war service but whereas, in 1939, Cary was refused
enlistment, Wilcher, in 1916, was admitted as a "stretcher-bearer" which
means that he was allowed to do the same kind of work as the author did
in the Balkan war of 1912-1913. The narrator's peace-time travelling is
limited to visits to Paris, Edinburgh, and Cardiff. Apparently these
names are no random choices. In the first two cities the young Cary
studied art and although the role that the Welsh port may have played
in his life is unknown, it should be observed that it is within easy
reach of Clifton College, the author's (and Edward's!) public school on
the opposite side of the Bristol Channel.[44]

Contrary to Wilcher, however, Cary sported a nose that seems to have
been somewhat aquiline in shape and like Edward's "beak" it was certainly
"delicate" in structure. In fact, it ran into several accidents and at
times it may have been flattened enough to conform to his hero's "faithful" somatype.[45]

Thus the "partnership" between Wilcher and Edward and the fallible
speaker's relation to his anonymous privileged self as well as the implied author apparently dramatize a similar age-youth conflict in Cary
himself. Perhaps he had this division of his own soul in mind when, in
the first chapter of his novel, he made his narrator say:

> My hatter tells me that there is only one man in England beside
> myself, who still wears a curly-brimmed bowler. But he agrees
> with me that there has never been a better hat, that hats, in
> fact, since the last war, have gone to the devil. (p.10)

Quite possibly the other man is Cary, the conformist, and quite possibly the hatter who like Wilcher, looks upon a modern felt hat as a devil's contraption, is no other than the author's dissenting self. Anyhow, he seems to have been a snub-nosed "evangelist", for hatters are mad, aren't they?[46]

CONCLUSION

In Art and Reality Joyce Cary distinguishes between an artist's intuition
of truth and the finished work of art. He does so in opposition to
Benedetto Croce who maintains that an artist's inspiration cannot be
known until he has given it an adequate expression. Cary objects to this
monistic view of art because it ignores the "hard conceptual labour"
that, in his experience, the composition of a novel amounts to. The
author claims, in other words, that justice should be done to the long
and laborious process of trial and error that the conception of an appropriate form means to a writer. Cary describes form as the organization
of "facts and feelings" into a "total symbol", but he is very vague
about the means by which his theory should be put into practice.

In Cary's view the casting about for a felicitous form is a struggle
that there is "no end" to. As far as his own fiction goes, this seems
true enough and it particularly applies to To be a Pilgrim where we are
faced with a dualism in whatever aspect the author considers man and
life. This certainly seems to support Robert Bloom's verdict on Cary's
view of the world as "endlessly divided". In addition to this, however,
the author's characteristic mode of vision and thought also affects his
use of a fictitious first-person narrator as objectifier of his own
subjectivity. The consistency with which Cary applies his divided vision
makes a detailed analysis of form a rewarding undertaking. It makes it
tempting to believe in the author's dependence on a simple creative
formula which may have helped him to fathom his ambivalent world in its
entirety, without making the reader unduly conscious of all its conflicting elements.

As the title of the novel suggests, To be a Pilgrim describes a
"pilgrim's progress" and it does so in the form of a fictitious autobiography. It has a frame-story where the narrating "I" introduces his
present ego to the reader and gives odd bits of information which invite
us to imagine an epic situation of some, although insufficient, plausi-
bility. We are tempted to believe that we are reading a private journal
written by the narrator with a view to maintaining his uncertain sanity.
His experiences in the present touch off memories of the past. The memoir
part which constitutes the bulk of the narration is hardly capable of

supporting the reader's epic illusion but it hardly detracts from it either. This is due to the fact that the speaker, who is in virtual charge of the narration, seldom identifies himself completely with his fictitious self. Besides a virtual epic situation soon establishes itself by virtue of the speaker's implied awareness of a reading vis-à-vis as well as his equally implied control of a central theme. Wilcher's book is not only an individual record. His exposition of the forces that are rivals for his soul makes it at the same time apparent that his conflict is a human dilemma of universal applicability.

There are many sides to Wilcher's problem. Primarily it manifests itself as a spiritual dilemma created by man's need of faith in both himself and God. "Faith" appears to be an ambiguous concept and the speaker' changing spiritual need makes him use the word with unconscious inconsistency. The dilemma can also be described as a conflict between man's need of freedom to create his own world and his need of preserving his creation. The conflict also manifests itself in Wilcher's inconsistent use of other key-words. Thus "duty" and "responsibility" sometimes imply predictable behaviour in agreement with established norms whereas on other occasions the words imply unpredictable action, i.e. freedom to act up to individual principle. Therefore Wilcher's problem can also be considered a conflict between the demands of society and the needs of his own creative individuality. As a consequence his life holds both comedy and tragedy. His attempts to live up to the norms of established society make him a "comic clown" whereas his inability to identify himself with these completely makes him a tragically isolated character.

In Cary's view life means change. To any individual the world will make no sense but remain "confusion" until he has learnt to read into its chaos of possibilities a cosmos to his own liking. Therefore man must take his own pilgrim's course through life. Wilcher's "progress" is a journey through a world of bewildering contrasts and it does not make any sense until, on the verge of death, he becomes aware of its transparency and, like Blake, is given a vision of perfect unity.

Long before the narrator arrives at his final and explicitly stated revelation, it gradually appears that the confusingly conflicting elements of Wilcher's world fall into a neat pattern of polarities. It

appears that the author's ambivalent mode of thinking affects not only
his speaker's vision but also the very narration in so far as it often
implies more than we are apt to believe at first sight. Often the narration offers instances of ambiguity that suggest a perfect inversion
of the surface narration. This undercutting of the narrator's explicit
self-portrayal suggests that Wilcher, the agonist, has an antagonist
ego, an unscrupulous character whose double-dealings give the narration
a picaresque smack.

The ambiguity or inclusiveness of Wilcher's self-portrayal is apparently
consequent on the influence that Blake's philosophy had on Cary. The
latter's representation of life as both disunity and unity is also in
agreement with his literary theory which, like Blake's, describes reading
as a process that is both conscious and subconscious. This does not, of
course, allow us to conclude that Cary's idea of symbolic form simply
amounts to the undercutting of explicit narration. It seems, however,
fair to assume that by implicit means the author meant to suggest the
existence of an alternative reality as a complement to his materialized
world. As a consequence he may have expected the reader to become subconsciously susceptible to the complexity of his art without detriment
to his belief in the surface narration. This does not mean that Wilcher's
character is not divided enough to allow of the rogueries implied. In a
type-written manuscript of To be a Pilgrim, apparently the one sent to
the printer, the following two sentences have been crossed out in the
first chapter:

> It was she [Sara] who was foolish, in their sense of the word
> and I who schemed. I schemed to take care of myself and my
> possessions.[1]

Cary was certainly right in not making his speaker give the above self-
confession. The narrator's character, as it is objectified by his own
narration, hardly allows of such unqualified awareness of guilt. Nor
does the author take such an unambiguous view. Wilcher is a sinner as
well as a saint and the one cannot be distinguished from the other,
whether he suffers the bondage of sentiment or acts as a man of free
spirit. In this fact lies both the comedy and tragedy of his life. If
Wilcher had been made enough conscious of his double-dealings to describe
himself as a "schemer" he might not only have given the reader too explicit a clue to the implied narration but also have made him unduly

aware of the speaker's ambiguous identity, not to mention what might
be taken for the ambiguity of his motive.

Cary's divided vision, of course, has an ironic implication. No critic
has so far commented on the author's use of verbal irony, i.e. his undercutting of the surface narration and inconsistent use of certain
signal words. Whether or not this fact speaks well for his craftsmanship and supports the validity of his literary theory is uncertain.
However that may be, it takes no close reading to find that throughout
the narration there runs a vein of dramatic or tragic irony. It is due
to Cary's use of scenic contrast and Wilcher's inability to see or
accept that life has to be subject to change. The experiences that are
related on both narrative levels imply a comparison of the present with
the past and make the narrator too apt to declare the young generation
destitute of the virtues that he flatters himself to champion. Thus he
mistakes similarity for difference and conversely.

In Wilcher's world youth is not simply a matter of age. It is also a
matter of spiritual freedom. This explains why some characters are
described as both young and old. Thus Mr. Jaffery, Wilcher's unscrupulous
solicitor, who is a minutely drawn inversion of the speaker's fictitious
self, is superior to him in vitality though he is his senior. In this
spiritual sense most of the characters in Wilcher's world are decidedly
young or old. They dramatize the division of his mind by representing
either aspect of the dualities of "faith", "duty", "grace", etc. These
characters give an exploded view of the protagonist and in this way
they seem to justify Cary's paradoxical use of "character" in which the
word refers to both individual man and the world as experienced by him.
Physically these groups are easy to identify because their members have
been moulded on either of two somatypes which bear a striking resemblance
to the leptosomes and pycnics of Kretschmer's well-known typology. Wilcher
is unconscious of this basis of division as well as the fact that his
own physical mould clearly shows that, for all his attachment to the
past, he is still a man of living spirit.

Wilcher is not only a divided character but also his function as speaker
is subject to division. In strict agreement with his explicit description
of his present ego the narrator sometimes appears to lack sufficient

control of his narration and consequently offer the reader one of the
chief pleasures of the first person narrative method. On other occasions
the speaker's grasp of what he narrates is firmer. Then he acts as the
reader's obliging guide by delivering facts with the unquestionable
reliability of a reference-book or camera-eye. At times, however, he is
not only in control of the fiction but he seems also to be in full
command of the author's underlying message. Such authorial views are
presented either as eloquent soliloquy or with an obvious intention to
edify a vis-à-vis. The speaker's reliability and the motive behind his
narration are thus subject to considerable variation. They are variables
that in principle seem to be independent of each other but the fact
remains that reliability as a rule goes with a need to inform a listening
or reading recipient.

Wilcher's unsettled character and the variation that, in some respects,
the narration is subject to makes it impossible to establish the speaker's
identity or, rather, distinguish between his several identities. This
uncertainty, however, hardly affects the reader's confidence in the
voice that ultimately is in virtual charge of the narration. It rather
seems to suspend his judgment on this point in particular as the narration, despite its variability, testifies to the existence of a major
perspective in the light of which everything appears to be under unre-
mitting control.

Wilcher is not the only character to whom Cary ascribes the author's
own words. Edward, the speaker's elder brother, is also equal to views
that are as detached as Wilcher's. He even enjoys greater freedom to
speak in this way because his Liberalism, unlike the narrator's, is not
intermittently paralysed by Conservative sentiment. Not only Wilcher and
Edward, however, can speak on Cary's behalf. In principle any character
seems to be eligible for this function or, at least, for inserting an
authorial pointer. At times Cary introduces even new characters for the
sole purpose of having a certain view voiced by somebody who is experienced enough to give it a proper underpinning of authority.

To be a Pilgrim can be described as a fictitious autobiography. As usual
such a definite statement holds only half the truth because, as far as
the narrator's spiritual conflict goes, Cary's novel equals a most per-

sonal statement. The author's close identification with his hero certainly explains why on different odd points their characters and lives
bear such a striking resemblance to each other. In the same way the
author seems to verify Wilcher's identification and his own with Edward.

In Art and Reality Cary opposes allegory to symbolism. In his view allegory ignores the complexity of "real truth" by laying down "copy-book
maxims". To anyone who has become conscious of the strict pattern of
parallels and antitheses on which the novel has been moulded it may read
an allegory. In fact all the secondary characters can be described as
substitutes for easily definable abstractions. The remarkable stubbornness of some people and the equally remarkable indifference of others,
the suddenness of their appearances and exits testify to authorial
puppeteering. According to Cary the greatest literary triumphs are to
be won "in that narrow space between allegory and the dramatic scene".
As a rule the narration is conducted on the borderline between these
narrative modes. However true it may be that sometimes the secondary
characters seem to lack inner motivation, the fact remains that on other
occasions they evidence touches of verisimilitude that make them
convincing. As a consequence it often appears most difficult to say
whether a character unequivocally represents something else and thus has
an allegorical function or whether it is part of a greater unit that
gives it symbolic significance.

In To be a Pilgrim all the secondary characters seem to reflect aspects
of the narrator's split personality. In this way they dramatize the
author's view of the world as "character". The speaker's relation to his
surroundings gives us a clear idea of Cary's application of form and,
I believe, a rewarding approach to the "total symbol" that, in his literary theory, a successful work of art amounts to. However that may be,
the fact remains that the objectification of the author's ambiguous view
of "character" gives his speaker's endlessly divided vision a remarkable
unity. At the same time as the author-narrator creates a material world
out of the protagonist's chaotic mind, the latter's relation to his
surroundings gives his experience a quality of ulterior significance.

From the narration the reader is often given to understand that Tolbrook
Wilcher's family estate, incarnates England. It represents change in the

same way as Wilcher represents not only his own seafaring people but man, the eternal pilgrim who, willing or unwilling, is carried on by the wave of time. The flux of life is suggested by pictures of running water. These water images are often coupled with descriptions of the sky. By making water and sky reflect each other the author visualizes a correspondence between the material and the immaterial that in this novel amounts to both meaning and form.

NOTES

All references to Cary's novels are to the Carfax edition published in London by Michael Joseph.

Abbreviations: TP identifies To be a Pilgrim.
HS " Herself Surprised.
AR " Art and Reality, 1958.
PM " Power in Men, 1963.

PREFACE:

1 Mitchell, 1971, p.20

2 Ryan, 1958, p.30

PART ONE

CHAPTER 1:

1 For biographical information given here and elsewhere in this thesis I am, in the first place, indebted to Foster, Joyce Cary, a Biography 1968. To some extent I also depend on Wright, Joyce Cary: A Preface to his Novels, 1958. I have also been fortunate to see Mrs. Winifred Davin, one of the author's closest friends who now acts as the literary executrix of the Joyce Cary Estate. Apart from permitting me to see his manuscripts and notebooks, deposited in the Bodleian Library, she readily answered my questions and took me to 12 Parks Road, his Oxford home. The house now belongs to the Department of Theoretical Physics in Oxford University and, according to Mrs. Davin is soon to be demolished.

To some extent the Cary family subsisted on the generosity of Mr. William Maxwell Ogilvie, Mrs. Cary's father. (See Foster, p.262 ff.)

2 Wright, 1958, p.26

3 ibid., p.13

4 ibid., p.14

5 Allen, 1963, p.13

6 Foster, 1968, p.452; Wright, 1958, pp.7-8

7 Foster, 1968, p.278

8 AR, p.155

9 An excellent summary of Cary's liberalism is to be found at the end of his Power in Men, 1963, pp.244-51. In an essay published in Preuves, XLII (August, 1954) Cary distinguishes between "freedom" ("liberté personelle") and "liberty" ("le concept juridique des droits"). As Wolkenfeld points out, Cary tries to maintain this distinction in Power in Men. As in the case of "real", "character" and other terms Cary's usage is not very strict. Cf. Wolkenfeld, 1968, p.187, note 7.

10 Foster, 1968, p.330

11 ibid., pp.333, 336-37

12   Allen, 1963, p.10; Wright, 1958, p.108

13   PM, pp.194-95, 230

14   AR, p.5

15   Cary, "The Way a Novel Gets Written", p.91

16   PM, p.7

17   ibid., pp.3-8

18   ibid., pp.28-31

19   Foster, 1968, p.281

20   PM, p.193

21   Foster, 1968, p.455

22   ibid., pp.277-86

23   Wright, 1958, p.108

24   "Art and Reality" is Cary's "Dichtung und Wahrheit". It is the title under which his six Clark Lectures were published in 1958. See Foster, 1968, p.513.

25   Foster, 1968, pp.513-15, 517-18

26   Averitt, 1963, pp.29-30; Wright, 1958, p.22

27   AR, pp.1-2; Mitchell, 1971, pp.9-22

28   Wellek, 1963, p.179

29   AR, pp.57-58

30   ibid., p.138

31   Baugh, 1967, pp.1134; Raine, 1969, p.30

32   AR, pp.9-10

33   ibid., pp.57-58

34   ibid., p.174

35   Barnet, Berman, and Burto, 1960, p.8; Encyclopaedia Britannica, 1965, vol. 13, p.135; Jacobi, 1943, pp.3-7

36   Barnet, Berman, and Burto, 1960, p.8

37   AR, pp.174-75, 119-20, 164-65

38   ibid., pp.162-63; cf. Cary, "The Way a Novel Gets Written", p.90

39   See Cary's letter to M. Schorer quoted in Foster, 1968, p.451.

40   AR, p.166

41   ibid., p.163

42   ibid., p.26

43   ibid., pp.26-30

44   ibid., p.86

45   ibid.

46   ibid., p.103

47   Baugh, 1967, p.1133

48 Schorer, 1946, pp.182-85

49 AR, p.174

50 No doubt this unwillingness was due to the author's fear of "killing" his books by drawing the reader's attention to the "propagandist" novelist's presence in his own fiction.

51 Barnet, Berman, and Burto, 1960, p.84

52 AR, p.103

53 It is true that, to some extent, Cary's critics are observant of his use of irony but owing to their failure to map its consistency they fail to consider its full bearing on his form-making and, consequently, to do full justice to his craftsmanship.

54 Bloom, 1962, preface and pp.1-43

55 ibid., preface: p.viii

56 AR, pp.29-30, 112

57 Hardy, 1954, pp.182-83

58 AR, p.116

59 ibid., p.114

60 Foster, 1968, pp.449, 451-52

61 ibid., p.451

62 AR, p.120

63 ibid., p.120

64 ibid., p.30

65 ibid., p.14

66 For "suspension of disbelief" see Booth, 1961, p.112.

67 Hoffman, 1964, p.67

68 Allen, 1963, p.5

69 AR, pp.163-64

70 Cf. Blake's view of allegory (p.35).

71 AR, p.155

72 Lewis, 1953, p.44

73 AR, pp.162-63

74 ibid., p.158

75 See p.12.

76 Foster, 1968, p.450

77 Cary, "The Way a Novel Gets Written", p.90

78 Hardy, 1954, p.182

79 Wright, 1958, pp.72-73

80 Cary, "My First Novel", p.637

81 HS, p.7 (from the prefatory essay specially written for the Carfax edition of Herself Surprised)

82   Barnet, Berman, and Burto, 1960, p.85. In Schorer's view myths
     are "the instruments by which we continually struggle to make our
     experience intelligible to ourselves." (Schorer, 1946, p.27)

83   Barnet, Berman, and Burto, 1960, pp.57-59 ("myth")

84   AR, p.120

85   ibid., pp.153-54

86   ibid., pp.174-75

87   Wellek, 1967, p.335

88   ibid., p.335

89   Schorer, 1946, p.27

90   Poetry and Prose of William Blake, ed. G. Keynes, 1948, p.869

CHAPTER 3:

1   About the narrator Allen writes, "Wilcher is a true original: there
     is no other character like him in the range of our fiction." (Allen,
     1963, p.22)

2   In my opinion, most of the disagreement among Cary's critics is due
     to their varying "suspension of disbelief" or varying susceptibility
     to the single myth that invariably manifests itself in all his novels.

3   Wright, 1958, p.109

4   Averitt, 1963, preface: p.iii

5   Allen, 1963, p.13

6   Adams, Joyce Cary's Three Speaker's, 1959, p.109

7   Barnet, Berman, and Burto, 1960, p.62

8   For a definition of "epic situation" see p.ii. Cf. Romberg, 162, p.33

9   Reed, 1965, p.106

10   For a definition of "dramatic monologue" see Barnet, Berman, and
     Burto, 1960, p.33.

11   See, in the first place, pp.44-46.

12   Allen, 1963, p.22

13   Adams, Joyce Cary's Three Speakers, 1959, pp.109-10

14   See p.51.

15   Stockholder, 1963, p.233

16   See pp.52-56, 128-54.

17   Cary, "The Way a Novel Gets Written", p.92

18   ibid.

19   James, 1934, p.320

20   See chapter 3, pp.52-56.

21   For a definition of "reliable author" see Booth, 1961, p.158.

22   Adams, Joyce Cary's Three Speakers, p.108

23   ibid., p.110

24   Barbara Hardy, "Form in Joyce Cary's Novels", Essays in Criticism,
      IV, April 1954, pp.180-90

25   ibid., p.183

26   ibid., pp.182-84

27   ibid., p.185

28   ibid., p.186

29   Barbara Hardy makes particular mention of Cary's use of visual
      contrast in the water-party scenes (TP, pp.136-38, 142-43, 146-47)
      and the threshing in the Adam room (TP, pp.326-28). It should,
      however, be pointed out that in these two cases the boldness of
      contrast is exceptional. Besides, in the speaker's divided vision
      such instances of juxtaposed action ultimately point to the sameness
      of man's choices. The very explicitness of Cary's use of contrast
      invariably suggests an inverted interpretation of facts.

30   Margie Averitt, And Three's A Crowd: A Study of Joyce Cary's First
      Trilogy, diss., 1964

31   ibid., p.75

32   Albert Cook, The Dark Descent and the Golden Mean: A Philosophy of
      Comedy, 1949

33   ibid., p.28

34   ibid., pp.3-28

35   ibid., p.28

36   ibid.

37   ibid., p.12

38   ibid., p.3

39   ibid., pp.3-4

40   ibid., p.45

41   ibid., p.11

42   Cook writes, "those who do seek [the nonprobable], even the most
      childish escapists, are more sensitive than those who do not - and
      more intelligent. Terman, in Genetic Studies of Genius, cites the
      case of a boy whose I.Q. was among the highest he studied, who burne
      himself out on the seas. In a sociological study of tramps, the
      University of Chicago found that I.Q.'s of 130 and above in their
      group are more than twice as frequent as in the general population."
      (Cook, 1949, p.8)

43   Cook, 1949, p.43

44   Averitt, 1964, pp.82-83

45   Foster, 1968, pp.413, 519

46   Kraus, p.139

47   See pp.120-22.

48   See pp.84-85, 104-05.

49   See chapter 5, pp.84-127.

50   See pp.18-20.

51   Golden L. Larsen, 1965, p.145

52   Averitt, 1964, p.92

53   This is, in my view, due to the fact that the virtual speaker cannot be identified with the objectified narrator-protagonist.

54   Averitt, 1964, p.84

55   ibid.

56   ibid.

57   ibid.

58   Frye, 1969, p.45

59   Schorer, 1946, pp.9-11; Baugh, 1967, p.1135; Raine, 1969, pp.30-31

60   Poetry and Prose of William Blake, ed. G. Keynes, 1948, pp.651-52

61   Bloom, 1962, p.91

62   ibid., p.95

63   ibid., p.96

64   AR, p.133

65   Kraus, 1966, pp.188-92

66   Langbaum, 1957, p.78

67   ibid., pp.137-38

68   ibid., p.137

69   ibid., p.85

70   ibid., p.137

71   ibid., p.83

72   ibid., p.109

73   ibid., pp.109-13

74   Kraus, 1966, p.204

75   Langbaum, 1957, p.112

PART TWO

CHAPTER 2:

1   Chapter 4, pp.57-83, gives a detailed account of the speaker's varying consciousness of his narrating role.

CHAPTER 4:

1   For a definition of "implied author" see Booth, 1961, pp.70-71.

2   In Gladys's view Wilcher's legs look like friction matches but, of course, the name of "Lucifer" ultimately refers to his character.

3   See HS, pp.171-72.

4   TP, p.117

5   See pp.52-56.

6   See p.45.

7   See pp.65, 50.

8   Cf. Cary's view of the impermanence of the symbol in Art and Reality, 1958, p.71.

9   Also the printer's typescript has no quotation mark after courage. (MS Cary 274 in the Bodleian Library, Oxford)

10   In the printer's typescript there is no quotation mark after Bill's. (MS Cary 274)

11   See TP, pp.44-45 (Lucy's attempted suicide) and pp.103-04 (Bill's proposal).

12   Romberg, 1962, p.29

13   At the outbreak of World War II Cary was in a similar situation. Foster writes, "The army was not interested in 50-year-old former lieutenants with bad sight. (Foster, 1968, p.335)

14   Tolbrook has two Adam rooms and a ceiling painted by Angelica Kauffman. The fact that the great Scottish architect's cooperation with the celebrated Swiss artist in the 1770's is a famous chapter in the history of British interior design adds to its symbolic status.

15   See p.47.

CHAPTER 5:

1   TP, p.93

2   TP, p.20

3   HS, pp.10, 125

4   Cary had a somewhat aquiline nose. Mrs. Davin described to me its bridge as a well developed "bump".

5   TP, pp.20, 95

6   TP, p.107

7   TP, pp.104, 105

8   HS, p.10

9   TP, p.338; HS, p.204

10   HS, p.141

11   HS, p.11; TP, p.264

12   TP, pp.137, 326

13   See p.84.

14   TP, p.77

15   Genesis, 18. 12-15; HS, p.88

16   TP, pp.93, 165

17   See p.86.

18   TP, p.293

19   TP, p.20

20   See pp.84-85.

21   No. 676 in the Church of England hymn-book.
      According to Mrs. Davin this hymn was sung at Cary's funeral.

22   Cf. Robert White's drawing of Bunyan in the British Museum (repro-
      duced in Talon, 1964). A painting of Bunyan by T. Sadler in the
      National Portrait Gallery, London, justifies Robert's view of his
      father as a "butcher" (TP, p.19).

23   See, for example, TP, pp.86, 99.

24   TP, pp.88, 97

25   TP, p.268

26   TP, p.264, cf. ibid., p.137 and HS, p.11.

27   TP, p.284

28   See p.60.

29   See pp.134-37.

30   TP, p.56

31   TP, pp.124, 159

32   Cf. TP, pp.13, 120, 149, 218.

33   TP, pp.45, 120, 144, 243

34   TP, pp.144, 243; cf. HS, p.15.

35   TP, pp.30-32, 191, 277

36   TP, p.29. "Bowyer" may be meant to suggest "Bow ye!"

37   See p.103.

38   TP, pp.271-72, 120, 267

39   TP, p.31

40   TP, pp.201, 229; cf. (about Edward) pp.269-70, 274.

41   TP, p.215; cf. ibid., p.229.

42   Cf. TP, p.148.

43   Encyclopaedia Britannica, 1965, vol. 7, p.786 (Duse) and p.58
      (D'Annunzio)
      Possibly Cary created the name of "Julie Eeles" to suggest some
      affinity with the great Italian actress. (I take it to be a per-
      version of "La Duse" or, rather, "El. Duse".)

44   See p.108.

45   See TP, pp.104-05.

46   For a discussion of Wilcher's mental health see p.146.

47   TP, p.304

48   TP, p.148; cf. Baugh, 1967, pp.1483-84 (Dowson), 1544-45 (Davidson).

49   TP, p.208

50   TP, p.75

51   Cf. TP, p.205.

52   TP, pp.13, 289

53   See TP, pp.119, 333, 342.

54 TP, pp.205, 271, 75

55 See TP, pp.109, 106, 214.

56 See pp.52-56.

57 See p.110.

58 Cf. the deluge scene discussed on pp.62-63.

59 See p.83.

60 Foster, 1968, pp.42-43, 66-68

61 ibid., pp.68-70

62 Mrs. Davin told me that Cary was very particular about his dress
    ("quite a dandy"). According to her he was also particular about
    having meals in style. Cf. the description of Edward in TP, p.269
    and Wilcher in HS, pp.161-62.

    For Cary's education at Clifton see Foster, 1968, p.29. Cf. TP, p.
    180.

63 Again a characteristic "perhaps" testifies to the author's presence

64 See p.108.

65 TP, pp.138-41

66 See p.109.

67 See TP, pp.334, 178. For other "softness" images see Edward's speech
    on the dynamics of revolutions (TP, pp.275-76), the deluge scene
    (ibid., pp.277-78), the description of Julie's increasing plumpness
    (ibid., pp.155, 179, 284).

68 See pp.118-19. Cary's choice of street is certainly not accidental.

CHAPTER 6:

1 As a poet Cary had little success. See Foster, 1968, pp.43-44.

2 For instances of "nose-pulling" etc. see TP, pp.311, 211, 322.

3 See, in particular, pp.108, 122.

4 TP, p.180

5 TP, p.20, 273

6 According to Walter Allen "the Senior Partner" was the great Nonconformist W.T. Stead's appellation of his Lord. (Allen, 1963, p.24

7 Cf. HS, p.13

8 See pp.79-83.

9 TP, p.76

10 See pp.117-21.

11 See pp.68, 122.

12 Encyclopaedia Britannica, 1965, vol. 13, p.1021 ("Liberalism Theo-
    logical"); ibid., vol. 4, p.673 ("Calvin")

13 Allen, 1963, pp.24-25

14 For information on English Nonconformity I am indebted to H. Davies
    The English Free Churches, 1952.

15   See pp.69-70.

16   Cf. Wilcher's comment on Sara's "confusion of grammar" (TP, p.319).

17   Allen, 1963, p.25

18   TP, p.88

19   Milton, Paradise Lost, book IV, l. 247

20   Cary's landscapes may testify to his familiarity with Blake's work,
     particularly in the visual arts, but in European literature the
     "fountain" or "fliessendes Licht" motif is both common and old. See
     E. Curtius, 1954, pp.130, 334, 365.

21   Wilcher spends his last days in a room that, in his childhood,
     served as his "nursery". (TP, pp.12, 15, 76, 79, 111)

22   Apparently gardening meant a great deal to Cary himself. See Foster,
     1968, pp.176 f., 189 f., 199, 236, 249, 297. In answer to my question
     about the Carys' financial status in the 20's and 30's Mrs. Davin
     significantly told me that they could afford a gardener.

23   See TP, pp.16-17, 49, 132, 329 (service); 221 (bad morals).

24   Milton, Paradise Lost, book IV, l. 247

25   Apparently the word "Jacobean" refers to both King James's Bible and
     James II's support of the Roman Catholic Church.

26   T. S. Eliot, Burnt Norton, I; cf. TP, pp.44, 100, 300. The "rose-
     garden" may also refer to Beardsley's "The Mysterious Rose-Garden"
     published in The Yellow Book. In his book on the artist Arthur Symons
     describes this drawing as "that terrible annunciation of evil."
     (Aubrey Beardsley, 1966, p.25) Discussing Beardsley's art with Julie
     and Edward Wilcher says, "They say he is decadent and amoral. . . .
     Can you be a great artist and have no morals? I mean in your art."
     To this Julie answers, "Of course not. But his art is moral. It's a
     criticism of life. . . ." (p.148) In Beardsley's drawings Cary
     probably found a paradox agreeing with his life philosophy. Symons
     says, "Here, then, we have a sort of abstract spiritual corruption,
     revealed in beautiful form; sin transfigured by beauty. And here,
     even if we go no further, is an art intensely spiritual, an art in
     which evil purifies itself by its own intensity, and by the beauty
     which transfigures it." (Symons, 1966, p.23)

27   T. S. Eliot, Burnt Norton, II, l. 89

28   T. S. Eliot, East Coker, II, ll. 84-87

29   ibid., III, ll. 202-09

30   TP, pp.32, 133-34

31   TP, pp.97 (Lucy-Brown); 173 (Ann-Robert); 32, 316 (Wilcher-Jaffery)

32   TP, p.309

33   TP, p.104

34   Cf. Wilcher's self-description in TP, p.129.

35   TP, pp. (about Wilcher) 23, 180, 212; (about Ann) 38, 254; (Ann about
     her father) 283

36   TP, pp.92-93

37   See p.126.

38   See also TP, pp.20, 52, 264, 265, 332.

39   Cf. TP, p.275.

40   See TP, p.131.

41   Encyclopaedia Britannica, 1965, vol. 2, p.73 ("Antinomianism")

42   See pp.37, 9.

43   See D. Saurat, 1946, p.184; cf. Baugh, 1967, p.690.

44   TP, p.99. See Foster, 1968, pp. (height) 29; (nose) 270, 169-70;
     (sight) 19; (insomnia) 299; (asthma, pleurisy, colds) 19, 109, 170,
     312, 399; (temper) 109, 151, 173-74; (Clifton College) 29-32;
     (Oxford) 48-57, 68; (Red Cross service) 70-81; (failure to enlist)
     335.

45   Foster, pp.169-70

46   Cf. E. Partridge, 1953 (hat and hatter).

CONCLUSION:

1   The printer's typescript of To be a Pilgrim, chapter 1. (MS Cary 74)

BIBLIOGRAPHY

A)   Joyce Cary's published novels

Note: Apart from Except the Lord and the unfinished Cock Jarvis the
      novels have been published by Michael Joseph Ltd., London, in
      the uniform Carfax Edition for which the author provided each
      book with a prefatory essay. All references are to this edition.
      The novels are listed in order of first publication. The year of
      appearance in the Carfax Edition is within brackets.

Aissa Saved, 1932 (1952).

An American Visitor, 1933 (1952).

The African Witch, 1936 (1951).

Castle Corner, 1938 (1952).

Mister Johnson, 1939 (1952).

Charlie Is My Darling, 1940 (1951).

A House of Children, 1941 (1951).

Herself Surprised, 1941 (1951).

To be a Pilgrim, 1942 (1951).

The Horse's Mouth, 1944 (1951).

The Moonlight, 1946 (1952).

A Fearful Joy, 1949 (1952).

Prisoner of Grace, 1952 (1954).

Except the Lord, London: Michael Joseph Ltd., 1953.

Not Honour More, 1955 (1966).

The Captive and the Free, 1959 (1963).

Cock Jarvis, edited by A. G. Bishop, London: Michael Joseph Ltd., 1974.

B)   Unpublished material

(The following items belong to the James Osborne Collection at the
Bodleian Library, Oxford.)

Typescript of To be a Pilgrim. It is the copy sent to the printer. It
contains some cancellations and interlineations in Cary's hand. (MS Cary
74: chapters 1-74; MS Cary 75: chapters 75-155)

Notebook with blue-green cover and red binding. it contains notes on the
characters, chronological tables, a sketch and plan of Tolbrook, etc.
(MS Cary 274/N 87)

Notebook with blue cover. It contains a wealth of notes and three pencil
drawings of Wilcher climbing Snowdon. (MS Cary 274/P 34)

Notebook with red cover and printed calendar for 1941 and 1942 inside.
It has, inter alia, some notes on form and a statement of Cary's epistemology. (MS Cary 274/P 36)

C)   Non-fiction by Joyce Cary

Power in Men. London: Nicholson and Watson, 1939; Seattle: University
of Washington Press, 1963.

Art and Reality. (The Clark Lectures 1956) Cambridge: Cambridge
University Press, 1958.

"My first Novel." Listener, April 16, 1953, pp.637, 738.

"A Novel is a Novel is a Novel." New York Times Book Review, April 30,
1950, pp.1, 34.

"The Way a Novel Gets Written." Harper's Magazine, February 1950,
pp.87-93.

D)   Other Works

Adams, Hazard.   "Joyce Cary's Three Speakers." Modern Fiction Studie
                         V (Summer 1959), pp.108-20

————————.   "Joyce Cary's Swimming Swan." American Scholar, XXI
                         (Spring 1960), pp.235-39

————————.   Introduction to Cary's Power in Men, see Cary, Power
                         in Men (above).

Allen, Walter.   Joyce Cary. Bibliographical Series of Supplements
                         to "British Book News" on Writers and their Work, No
                         41. London: Longmans, Green & Co., revised edition,
                         1963.

Averitt, Margie   And Three's a Crowd: A Study of Joyce Cary's First
Nell Thomas.   Trilogy. Diss., Austin, Texas, 1963.

Baugh, Albert, ed.,   A Literary History of England. London: Routledge &
                         Kegan Paul Ltd., second edition, 1967.

Barnet S., Berman   A Dictionary of Literary Terms. Boston and Toronto:
M., Burto W.   Little, Brown & Co., 1960.

Björck, Staffan.   Romanens Formvärld. Stockholm: Natur och Kultur, fi
                         edition, 1963.

Bloom, Robert.   The Indeterminate World: A Study of the Novels of
                         Joyce Cary. Philadelphia: University of Pennsylvani
                         Press, 1963.

Booth, Wayne C.   The Rhetoric of Fiction. Chicago and London: The
                         University of Chicago Press, 1961.

Cook, Albert.   The Dark Voyage and the Golden Mean: A Philosophy of
                         Comedy. Cambridge (Mass.): Harvard University Press
                         1949.

Curtius, Ernst   Europäische Literatur und Lateinisches Mittel-Alter.
Robert.   Bern: Francke Verlag, 2nd edition, 1954.

Davies, Horton.   The English Free Churches. London: Oxford University
                         Press, 1952.

Echeruo, Michael   Joyce Cary and the Novel of Africa. London: Longman
J. C.   Group Ltd., 1973.

Eliot, T. S.   Four Quartets. London: Faber and Faber, 1944.

The Encyclopaedia Britannica. Chicago, London, etc.: Encyclopaedia
                         Britannica, Inc., 1965.

Foster, Malcolm.   *Joyce Cary: A Biography*. Boston: Houghton Mifflin
                     Company, 1968.

Frye, Northrop.   *Fearful Symmetry: A Study of William Blake*. Princeton
                     University Press, Princeton, 1969.

Galligan, Edward L. "Intuition and Concept: Joyce Cary and the Critics."
                     Texas Studies in Literature and Language, VIII, pp.
                     581-87.

Hardy, Barbara.   "Form in Joyce Cary's Novels." *Essays in Criticism*,
                     IV (1954), pp.180-90.

——————.   *The Appropriate Form*. London: The Athlone Press,
                     first paperback edition, 1971.

Hoffman, Charles G. "Joyce Cary and the Comic Mask". *Western Humanities
                     Review*, XIII, Spring 1959, pp.135-42.

——————.   *Joyce Cary: The Comedy of Freedom*. Pittsburgh: The
                     University of Pittsburgh Press, 1964.

Jacobi, Jolan.   *The Psychology of Jung: An Introduction*. New Haven:
                     Yale University Press, 1943.

James, Henry.   *The Art of the Novel: Critical Prefaces*. New York:
                     Charles Scribner's Sons, 1934.

Keynes, Geoffrey,   *Poetry and Prose of William Blake*. London: The
ed.   Nonesuch Press, 1948.

Kraus, Richard.   *Archetypes and the Trilogy Structure: A Study of Joyce
                     Cary's Fiction*. Diss., Stanford, 1966.

Langbaum, Robert.   *The Poetry of Experience: The Dramatic Monologue in
                     Modern Literary Tradition*. London: Chatto & Windus,
                     1957.

Larsen, Golden L.   *The Dark Descent: Social Change and Moral Responsi-
                     bility in the Novels of Joyce Cary*. London: Michael
                     Joseph, 1965.

Lewis, C. S.   *The Allegory of Love: A Study in Medieval Tradition*.
                     London: Oxford University Press, 1953.

Lyons, Richard S.   "Narrative method in Cary's 'To be a Pilgrim'."
                     Texas Studies in Literature and Language, VII pp.269-
                     79.

Mahood, M. M.   *Joyce Cary's Africa*. London: Methuen & Co. Ltd, 1964.

Mitchell, Giles.   *The Art Theme in Joyce Cary's First Trilogy*. The Hague:
                     Mouton, 1971.

Noble, R. W.   *Joyce Cary*. Edinburgh: Oliver and Boyd, 1973.

Partridge, Eric.   *A Dictionary of Slang and Unconventional English*.
                     London: Routledge and Kegan Paul Ltd., 1951.

Raine, Kathleen.   *William Blake*. Bibliographical Series of Supplements to
                     'British Book News' on Writers and their Work, No.12.
                     London: Longmans, Green & Co., revised ed. 1969.

Reed, Peter John.   *Trial by Discard: Joyce Cary's First Trilogy*. Diss.,
                     Washington, 1965.

BIBLIOGRAPHY

Romberg, Bertil.   Studies in the Narrative Technique of the First-
                    Person Novel. Diss., Lund: Håkan Ohlssons Boktrycker
                    1962.

Ryan, Marjorie.   "An Interpretation of 'The Horse's Mouth'." Critique
                   II, Spring-Summer 1958, pp.29-38.

Saurat, Denis.   Milton: Man and Thinker. London: J. M. Dent & Sons
                  Ltd., 1946.

Schorer, Mark.   William Blake. New York: Henry Holt and Co., 1946.

Shapiro, Stephen A. "Joyce Cary's 'To be a Pilgrim': Mr. Facing-Both-Ways
                    Texas Studies in Literature and Language, VIII, Sprir
                    1966, pp.81-91.

Symons, Arthur.   Aubrey Beardsley. London: John Baker Publishers Ltd.
                   1966.

Talon, Henri A.   John Bunyan. Bibliographical Series of Supplements
                   to 'British Book News' on Writers and their Work, No.
                   73. London: Longmans, Green & Co., 1964.

Wellek, René.   Concepts of Criticism. New Haven and London: Yale
                 University Press, 1963.

Wolkenfeld, Jack.   Joyce Cary: The Developing Style. New York: New York
                     University Press, 1968.

Wright, Andrew.   Joyce Cary: A Preface to his Novels. London: Chatto
                   & Windus, 1958.